Additional Praise for *Designated Drivers*

"Refreshingly unbound by conventional assumptions about weak corporate governance in a state-dominated economy, and unconstrained by ponderous academic jargon, Greg Anderson uses his personal experience as a former financial executive to inform his analysis of the world's fastest-growing automobile industry. In the course of his investigation, he discovers that the apparent success of China's SOEs is not about corporate governance, as he first suspected; rather, it's about industry structure. It's about how central and local governments, in uneasy partnership with industry players both state-owned and private, have acted to create the complex, dynamic, rapidly expanding industry we see today. This is a first-rate book on an important subject."

—Richard Baum, Distinguished Professor Emeritus of
Political Science, UCLA

"With *Designated Drivers*, G. E. Anderson provides an indispensable roadmap to the world's most important automotive market. Anderson gives a dramatic account of the growth of China's auto industry and clearly lays out the key policies, institutions, and firms that have shaped this trajectory. In doing so, he gives important insight not only into the automotive sector, but also China's development path more generally."

—Eric Thun, Saïd Business School, University of Oxford,
author of *Changing Lanes in China*

"A problem with many books about China's auto industry is that by the time they hit the shelves they are outdated in many respects. Greg Anderson's book avoids this trap by explaining the framework in which China makes decisions regarding its auto industry. This book will be required reading for years to come for anyone trying to understand why China's government and its automakers behave as they do, and the development course the industry takes.

And while his subtitle is *How China Plans to Dominate the Global Auto Industry*, I think this book provides evidence of why China may not, in fact, achieve the world dominance many seem to believe is a *fait accompli*."

—Alysha Webb, former China Bureau Chief, *Automotive News*,
consultant and publisher of China-EV.org

Designated Drivers

Designated Drivers

How China Plans to Dominate the Global Auto Industry

G. E. Anderson

WILEY

John Wiley & Sons Singapore Pte. Ltd.

Other Wiley Editorial Offices

John Wiley & Sons, 111 River Street, Hoboken, NJ 07030, USA

John Wiley & Sons, The Atrium, Southern Gate, Chichester, West Sussex, P019 8SQ, United Kingdom

John Wiley & Sons (Canada) Ltd., 5353 Dundas Street West, Suite 400, Toronto, Ontario, M9B 6HB, Canada

John Wiley & Sons Australia Ltd., 42 McDougall Street, Milton, Queensland 4064, Australia

Wiley-VCH, Boschstrasse 12, D-69469 Weinheim, Germany

ISBN 978-1-118-32885-9 (cloth)
ISBN 978-1-118-32886-6 (ePDF)
ISBN 978-1-118-32887-3 (Mobi)
ISBN 978-1-118-32888-0 (ePub)

Typeset in 11.5/14 point Bembo by MPS Limited, Chennai, India.
Printed in Singapore by Markono Print Media Pte Ltd.

10 9 8 7 6 5 4 3 2 1

Dedicated to the memory of
Richard E. Anderson

Contents

Map of Chinese Provinces and Cities Mentioned in the Book

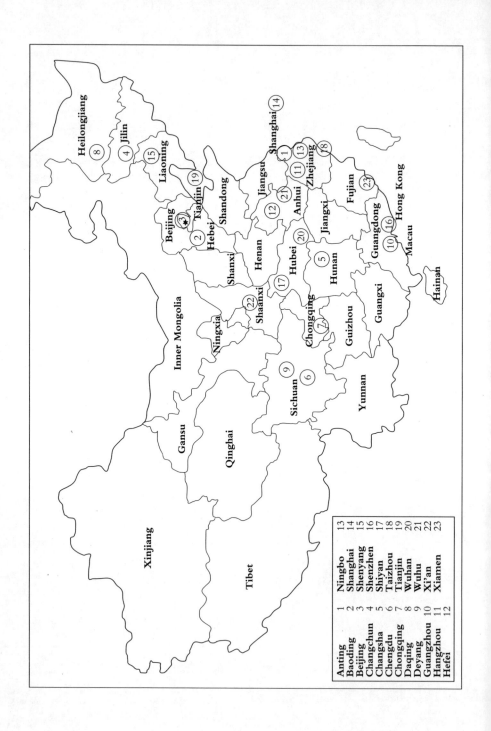

Anting	1	Ningbo	13
Baoding	2	Shanghai	14
Beijing	3	Shenyang	15
Changchun	4	Shenzhen	16
Changsha	5	Shiyan	17
Chengdu	6	Taizhou	18
Chongqing	7	Tianjin	19
Daqing	8	Wuhan	20
Deyang	9	Wuhu	21
Guangzhou	10	Xi'an	22
Hangzhou	11	Xiamen	23
Hefei	12		

List of Terms
and Acronyms

Words Used to Describe Types of Automobiles
and Their Chinese Equivalents

automobiles = passenger vehicles + commercial vehicles

汽车 = 乘用车 + 商用车

commercial vehicle = trucks, buses, delivery vans

商用车 = 卡车，客车，送货车

passenger vehicle = passenger cars, MPVs, SUVs, crossovers

乘用车 = 轿车, MPV, SUV, 交叉型乘用车

car/passenger/sedan = 轿车

MPV = multipurpose vehicle (commonly known as a *minivan* in the United States)

SUV = sport-utility vehicle

crossover = 交叉型乘用车

Other Terms and Acronyms

AMC: American Motors Corporation, owner of the Jeep brand at the time the Beijing-Jeep joint venture was formed.

BAW: Beijing Auto Works, the local automaker that formed the Beijing-Jeep joint venture with AMC.

CAIY: *China Automotive Industry Yearbook* (中国汽车工业年鉴), an annual compendium of facts, figures, policy recap, and documentation of significant events produced currently by the state-owned China Automotive Technology and Research Center. Published sporadically in the 1980s and annually since 1991.

CATARC: China Automotive Technology and Research Center.

CCP: Chinese Communist Party.

CKD: complete knock-down, a vehicle shipped in kit form to be assembled elsewhere. (See SKD.)

CNAIC: China National Automotive Industry Corporation. First formed by the central government in 1964 to oversee China's automobile industry. Disbanded during the Cultural Revolution. Reestablished in 1982 for a similar purpose, but reduced in authority from a corporation to an association in 1987.

CNG: compressed natural gas, a cleaner alternative fuel to gasoline.

CSOE: central state-owned enterprise, a term I introduce to distinguish enterprises owned by the central government and those owned by local governments. (See LSOE.)

DTI: Department of Trade and Industry, an organization of the British state that attempted to aid MG Rover Group and subsequently investigated its sale to new Chinese owners. Replaced by the Department for Business, Enterprise and Regulatory Reform and the Department for Innovation, Universities and Skills in 2007.

EV: electric vehicle.

FAW: First Auto Works, a central state-owned automaker.

foreigners/foreign – non-Chinese.

GAC: Guangzhou Automobile Group Company Ltd., a subsidiary of GAIG.

GAIG: Guangzhou Automobile Industry Group, parent company of GAC.

GM: General Motors.

ICE: internal combustion engine, describes the engine in a traditional gasoline-burning car.

JV: joint venture.

LPG: liquefied petroleum gas, a cleaner alternative fuel to gasoline.

LSOE: local state-owned enterprise, a term I introduce to distinguish enterprises owned by local governments and those owned by a central government. (See CSOE.)

MES: minimum efficiency scale, a "rule-of-thumb" term used to describe the minimum output at which an auto factory could conceivably break even on an accrual basis. In the auto industry, the general MES is approximately 250,000 vehicles per year.

MGRG: MG Rover Group, British auto group including the brands, MG, Rover, and Austin Healy, sold by BMW to a British consortium in 2000.

MIIT: Ministry of Industry and Information Technology, regulatory body charged with oversight and planning for China's automobile industry since 2008.

MITI: Ministry of International Trade and Industry, Japan's industrial planning agency during the formative years of its auto industry.

MMI: Ministry of Machinery Industry, organization responsible for regulatory oversight and planning for China's auto industry prior to MIIT.

MOST: Ministry of Science and Technology, organization responsible for China's technology policy. Has a major role in evaluating new automobile technologies and recommending strategic direction.

MTI: Ministry of Trade and Industry, South Korea's industrial planning organization during the formative years of its auto industry.

NDRC: National Development and Reform Commission, China's economic planning organization, which was named the successor to the State Development and Planning Commission in 2003.

NEV: new energy vehicles. An English translation of the Chinese term "新能源汽车"; describes vehicles powered by fuels other than gasoline and diesel. Can include vehicles powered by electricity (via on-board battery), hybrid gasoline-electric vehicles, plug-in hybrid vehicles, hydrogen fuel-cell vehicles, and vehicles powered by CNG or LPG.

NPC: National People's Congress, China's legislature.

PATAC: Pan-Asia Technical Automotive Center. A joint venture design and engineering firm established by General Motors and Shanghai Auto.

PHEV: plug-in hybrid electric vehicle. A gasoline-electric hybrid vehicle with a drive battery that may be charged by plugging into the mains.

Private company: a Chinese company in which the state does not hold a controlling ownership. Not to be confused with the American definition of a company whose shares are not listed on a stock exchange. In China, a "private" company may (or may not) be listed on a stock exchange.

Public company: a Chinese company in which the state holds a controlling ownership. Not to be confused with the American definition of a company whose shares are listed on a stock exchange. In China, a "public" company may (or may not) be listed on a stock exchange.

Renminbi: the currency of the People's Republic of China. Interchangeable with the term *yuan*.

SAIC: Shanghai Automotive Industry Corporation. An LSOE automaker headquartered in Shanghai. Not to be confused with the central government organization, State Administration for Industry and Commerce.

SASAC: State-owned Assets Supervision and Administration Commission. Formed in 2003 as a the unified shareholder of all of

China's CSOEs. Local governments were also ordered to form their own similar organizations at the same time.

SAW: Second Auto Works, a central state-owned automaker. Its name was changed to Dongfeng in the early 1990s.

SGM: Shanghai-General Motors, a joint venture between SAIC and GM.

SGMW: Shanghai-General Motors-Wuling, a joint venture among SAIC, GM, and Wuling Auto.

SKD: semi-knock-down, a vehicle shipped in partially assembled kit form for assembly elsewhere. (See CKD.)

SOE: state-owned enterprise. Includes both CSOEs and LSOEs.

Yuan: the currency of the People's Republic of China. Interchangeable with the term *renminbi*.

Foreword

China's economic growth model is notoriously difficult to describe. One confronts a series of contradictions: between a Leninist single-party state and a vibrant market economy; between a central government that sometimes seems all-powerful and local governments that often defy the center's mandates with impunity; between state-owned national champion enterprises awash with subsidies and scrappy private firms that sometimes manage to mobilize state backing. How much of China's spectacular economic growth and industrial development results from state-led planning, and how much from the unleashing of market forces, is endlessly debated.

In many respects, China since the beginning of economic reforms in 1979, and more particularly in the past decade, seems the latest example of the "East Asian developmental state," a term coined to describe the political economy of postwar Japan and South Korea. The goal of the developmental state is to achieve rapid economic growth and technological autonomy, via the development of broad-based industrial capacity and a relentless focus on exports. The principal mechanisms include industrial policy, financial repression through low administered interest rates, and a tightly regulated financial sector whose function is to channel household savings into investments in infrastructure and sunrise industries. Finally, export requirements are used to ensure that the industries benefiting from infusions of low-cost credit actually achieve technological progress, rather than simply growing fat on cheap funding and protected local markets.

Over the past three decades, China has clearly emulated both the goals and many of the mechanisms of the classic developmental state. In the 1980s paramount leader Deng Xiaoping sponsored the slogan *"fazhan cai shi ying daoli"* ("development is the only hard truth"), and successive generations of leaders since have consistently kept front and center the goals of rapid economic growth, a vibrant export economy, and aggressive technology acquisition. Today China is easily the world's largest producer of steel, cement, ships, motor vehicles, textiles, power generation equipment, telecoms network switches, textiles and consumer electronics, in volume if not in value terms. It is also the world's largest exporter, accounting for around 11 percent of global export value in 2011, a market share that has tripled in the past 15 years.

Yet beneath the surface China's economy differs dramatically from that of its East Asian predecessors. One crucial difference is the mechanism of technological upgrading. Japan and South Korea protected their national champion companies from competition at home but compelled them to upgrade their technology by imposing stringent export requirements, which could not be met without keeping pace with changes in global technology. China, by contrast, welcomed vast amounts of foreign direct investment and tried to induce technology transfer via joint ventures between multinational corporations and domestic state-owned enterprises (SOEs). One consequence is that while Japan's exports were generated exclusively by domestic private firms, over half of China's exports, and nearly 90 percent of its high-tech exports, are generated by foreign-invested firms. Most of the remaining exports are generated by small-scale domestic private firms that benefit from an undervalued exchange rate but have little access to subsidized credit. The principal beneficiaries of subsidized credit are SOEs, whose main job is to build national infrastructure, and who in aggregate are net importers.

The differences between China's development path and those of its East Asian predecessors arose from fundamental differences in starting points. China was less able to protect its domestic market in the 1980s than Japan and South Korea were in the 1960s, because its desperation for foreign exchange and foreign technology were greater, because evolving world trade rules made it harder, and perhaps most important because China was not a military ally of the United States and so could not gain preferential trade treatment in exchange for permitting U.S. military bases. On the other hand, China's domestic market potential was so enormous that it proved a powerful lure to entice investments from multinational companies on terms that they would have accepted in no other market.

A second key difference in conditions is that in addition to being a developing country, China is also a post-communist society, governed by a Leninist single party. In the 1980s and 1990s the task of catch-up development was paired with the task of dismantling an inappropriate and highly inefficient socialist industrial structure, while at the same time ensuring the continuity of Communist Party rule. Much of that structure has been demolished, but substantial vestiges remain and continue to exercise a powerful influence on policy and on the way markets function. In particular, reformed SOEs, shed of their costly social welfare obligations, continue to dominate many major industries and have increased their influence in the policy process. An enduring policy dilemma is finding the right balance between SOEs, which are effective agents of state directives, and private companies, which are far more efficient users of capital and generate far more employment.

Finally, China's late entry into the development game has several interesting consequences. One is that it has compressed in a relatively short period of time development phases that unfolded sequentially and over a much longer period in other countries. In some respects China today resembles Japan in the 1920s, when economic growth was very rapid but indigenous innovation and technological development capacity were still very weak and international influence was minimal. In others it seems more like Japan circa 1970: an export powerhouse with a disruptive influence on global trade and capital flows. Another is that by the time China started developing key industries, such as passenger cars and consumer electronics, global control of these industries was firmly in the hands of U.S., European, and Asian multinationals, and technological barriers to entry were far higher than when Japanese and Korean companies began their entry into these industries. Despite decades of effort, China has failed to produce a single globally competitive carmaker or consumer electronics firm (with the ambiguous exception of personal computer maker Lenovo, the vast majority of whose sales are in its home market).

G. E. Anderson's study of the Chinese automotive industry is an excellent introduction to the complexities and conflicting forces of China's unique development process. The passenger car business is a particularly telling exemplar of the strengths and weaknesses of the joint-venture model, under which foreign multinationals enter into joint ventures with domestic SOEs. This system enabled China to ramp up passenger car production very rapidly once household incomes got high enough to support large-scale car purchases. But the SOE partners have been largely captives of their joint ventures, and have so far failed to generate their own technology, designs and brands, as was the original intention of state planners. Meanwhile, China's huge size and high degree of economic decentralization meant that local governments could back smaller, independent carmakers—some privately owned and some controlled by local governments. Even though these firms emerged outside the central government's industry plan—and sometimes directly contravened Beijing's directives—they flourished because they satisfied two crucial state objectives that the SOE automakers could not. They generated substantial new employment, and they succeeded in developing their own designs and brands, although the designs are still heavily dependent on foreign models and the brands have yet to achieve traction outside of China. And it is a small independent firm (Geely), not a national-champion SOE, that engineered China's only successful takeover of an internationally significant carmaker (Volvo).

More broadly, this work illustrates the complexities of China's current economic structure, and the uncertainties about where Chinese companies—and the economy as a whole—are headed. The ambitions of central government economic planners, the differing aspirations of the leaders of SOE, multinational and domestic private companies, and the imperatives of local government officials, have created an intricate economic ecosystem with a bewildering variety of domestic and foreign stakeholders. State policy and market forces both continue to play crucial roles. Technology provides both a source of conflict (as the state presses for ever more technology transfer as the price of increased market access) and a means of collaboration (as foreign and Chinese automakers combine forces to develop new-energy vehicles). The example of the auto industry, as vividly portrayed here, enables us to understand how a complex and seemingly chaotic cocktail of forces produced the most impressive sustained economic growth in history. And while it provides no definitive answers about where that growth will lead in future, it gives us a better basis for asking the right questions.

Arthur Kroeber

Arthur Kroeber is managing director of GK Dragonomics, an economic research firm based in Beijing, and editor of the China Economic Quarterly.

Preface

It is human nature to fear what we don't understand. It is also human nature to ask "why," to satisfy our curiosity, to improve our understanding. Why, I am often asked by curious Americans, do you keep going back to China? My answer is typically along the lines of, "I still haven't figured it all out." China first came to my attention as I watched events in Beijing unfold on television in 1989. At the time I had no inkling that five years later I would first set foot in China, thereby launching myself into a lifelong effort to understand China better, nor did I realize that my efforts to understand China better would also make me want to understand my home country, the United States, better.

While I had long been interested in how politics affects economic decision making, I began the empirical research for this book in 2008, a year in which the first major cracks began to appear in the edifice of Western political economy. (The cracks, in hindsight, had been there all along, but few of us wanted to see them.) Having worked for over 15 years in the field of finance and having completely bought into the neoclassical economic theory that underpinned the system, I was amazed at how quickly things seemed to unravel once Lehman Brothers declared bankruptcy in the fall of 2008. How, I began to ask, can China continue to break all the rules—industrial planning, heavy state ownership, fixed interest and foreign exchange rates, an authoritarian political system—yet continue to turn in double-digit economic growth year-in and year-out? If we in the West possessed all of the answers, why weren't we the ones enjoying all of that growth? And, given that China does appear to be enjoying success, is there anything they are doing that we in the West could adopt to pull ourselves out of our collective funk?

While I was motivated by these big questions, my goal with this book is somewhat more modest. I hope to illuminate a small corner of these much larger questions, to shed light on China's method of industrial planning and business-government relations. It is my firm belief that, before other countries can make decisions regarding how to treat China as a trade partner/adversary, before they can adapt their own economies to the reality of a rising China, and indeed, before they can make investment decisions, they are all better served by fully understanding the politics behind the Chinese economy.

My approach to this question was to choose a single industry into which I could dive deeply so as to understand the nature of ownership, business-government relations, central-local relations, China's innovative capacity and the perceived role of foreign players. And while I hope anyone interested specifically in the auto industry will find much of interest here, it is also my hope that the reader who is interested in China, or in economic development in general, will benefit from an illumination of the overall political principles that drive economic decision making at the top of the Chinese system. I chose the automobile assembly industry because it offered a variety of ownership forms: massive state-owned enterprises, scrappy private enterprises, and foreign multinational firms all clamoring for a share of China's market. At the time I made this choice, I honestly had no idea that the auto industry would in 2009 and 2010 become one of China's hottest sectors, but in hindsight this worked to my benefit: Everyone in China wanted to talk about cars.

In the process of gathering information, I made three separate trips to China in 2008, 2009, and 2010, and interviewed over 100 professionals, academics, and government researchers with connections to China's auto industry. I also conducted an examination of Chinese-language source material documenting the development and evolution of China's auto industrial policy over the past 30-plus years. In keeping with UCLA's Human Research Protection Program, I guaranteed my interviewees anonymity. This guarantee accomplished two purposes. First, and most importantly, it ensured that the Chinese citizens whom I interviewed would not later be punished or harassed for their willingness to speak with a foreign researcher. Secondly, it decreased the likelihood that interviewees would alter their answers to my questions out of fear of repercussions from employers or other authorities.

A Few Notes for the Reader

Any reader who is familiar with China's economic development efforts, and particularly those of China's auto industry, will inevitably note that certain events presented in this book may have since been overshadowed by subsequent events. Such is the nature of writing about China: At least some of what one writes may have already been invalidated by subsequent events even before the ink is dry. My goal with this book is not to say, "this is the way China works, and it will never change." My goal here is to describe the path that actors in China's political-economy have taken to reach a certain point and to project what that may mean going forward. Of course, changes can and will happen, and these changes can send China's development on any number of interesting trajectories.

For the past 60-plus years, everything in China has happened within the boundaries of the immutable goal of the continued rule of the Communist Party, and my assumption is that this will not change anytime soon. Then again, very few people expected the Soviet Union to disintegrate when it did; nor did they expect the subsequent reconsolidation of power under Russian President/Prime Minister/President, Vladimir Putin. The point here is that life is full of surprises. We can implement detailed planning to cover the highest probability outcomes, but, if the events of the Great Recession have taught us anything, it is that we need also to ask ourselves how we might handle the sudden appearance of a "black swan." In short, while we are probably wise to plan for the continued rule of the Communist Party in China, our scenarios should at least consider how we might approach a sudden change in leadership.

And a few notes for academic readers . . .

The necessity of a publisher's page limits, e-book versions, and other guidelines requires that some content be deleted and the footnotes be moved to the ends of the chapters. Please visit www.designated drivers.co for additional material including photos, a more extensive literature review, and a printable version of the footnotes, references, and source material for this book. Please also note that, while I make occasional use of Chinese characters in this book, knowledge of Chinese is not essential to understanding the story. The use of characters is merely an added benefit for Chinese speakers who may wonder how I chose to translate certain terms, or for those who want to more quickly locate a Chinese language source. In general I adhere to tradition of presenting Chinese names with surname first and given name second (e.g., Deng Xiaoping), except for when a Chinese person has published a work in English under the Western tradition of given name first, surname second (e.g., Yasheng Huang).

Acknowledgments

Of course, no competent researcher should be willing or able to conduct research in a vacuum, and I was fortunate to benefit from the advice, support and oversight of many individuals who gave of their time. At the top of the list are my PhD dissertation committee: Richard Baum, Mike Thies, James Tong, and Barry Naughton. Each took his time to help me formulate my research questions, put together a research design, and then worked with me to make sense of my findings once I had returned from the field. I am grateful for their support and advice, and especially for pushing back when I attempted to get away with unfounded assumptions. If this book proves coherent and useful to others, they will have my committee to thank. To the degree that mistakes remain, I alone am responsible.

I am also grateful to UCLA's Center for Chinese Studies and the Department of Political Science for providing partial funding that helped me to carry out my field research.

I would also like to thank a number of UCLA political science colleagues whose help and advice either directly or indirectly served to improve this work: Hiroki Takeuchi, Zhang Xin, Vivian Zhan, Eric Zusman, Zhang Yongle, James Paradise, Wooyeal Paik, Stan Wong,

Josh Eisenman, and James Lo. I should also thank a number of scholars, business people, journalists, friends, and commenters to my blog who took the time to discuss with me research ideas and field-work methods or to provide logistical help and contacts in China. Special thanks to Jamil Anderlini, Clint Baines, Aimee Barnes, Janet Carmosky, Amy Chang, Crystal Chang, Don Clarke, Jason Dean, Dominik Declercq, Paul Denlinger, Mike Dunne, Gady Epstein, Peter Fischer, John Garnaut, Nancy Gougarty, Andrew Grieve, Gerwin Ho, Scott Kennedy, Dune Lawrence, Jing Liu, Rose Liu, Andy Mok, Malcolm Moore, Patrick Murphy, Phil Murtaugh, Klaus Paur, Mike Pettis, Will Pirie, Bill Russo, Victor Shih, Norihiko Shirouzu, Dorothy Solinger, Ed Steinfeld, Edith Terry, Eric Thun, Patti Waldmeir, William Wang, Alysha Webb, Calla Weimer, Boss Wu, Shirley Yam, Yunxiang Yan, and John Zeng. I also want to thank my dear friends, the Reece family for their love and support. Extra special thanks to Arthur Kroeber for helping me to brainstorm and for writing the book's foreword.

An even larger number of Chinese friends and interviewees con-tributed to my understanding and to the success of this research project, and though they are deserving of individual thanks, a big, group "thank you" will have to suffice. For reasons mentioned in the Preface, I am unable to list each of these helpful people by name. Among those I can mention are Zhou Congjun and Fan Zheng, two friends (with no connection to my research) who helped me to acquire and hone the language skills necessary to carry out my research. I am thankful to them for their patience and dedication, and for not allowing me to get away with ignoring my tones. I would also like to thank Beijing friends, Bernardo, Charlie, Jiwei, and Winser, for their logistical help, moral support, and warm friendship.

Special thanks is also due to the good folks at Wiley who made the process of writing and publishing a book remarkably pain free for a first-time author, particularly Nick Melchior, who shepherded the entire project, also Emilie Herman and Stefan Skeen, who improved the book's readability, and Cindy Chu who helped with marketing.

I owe many thanks to my family who shaped me into the person I have become. The steadfast support of my mother and sister throughout all of my research and travel has been invaluable. Though my dad did not live to see me finish this project, I know he was proud of my efforts. He taught me from an early age to be open-minded, to challenge the status quo, and never to allow the opinions of others to keep me from pursuing my dreams. Were it not for the influence of my family, this book would not exist.

Finally, my deepest gratitude goes to my lovely wife Yan, who suffered through many months while I conducted research in China, and through many more lonely nights and weekends while I toiled at my desk. Thank you for your kindness, patience, and love during my frequent absence and absentmindedness. Your support has made all the difference in the world. You are God's greatest gift to me.

Chapter One

Building National Champions

Insofar as the international division of labor is a hierarchy, worrying about development means worrying about your place in the hierarchy.

> —Peter B. Evans, *Embedded Autonomy: States and Industrial Transformation*

China's passenger car industry has received very little share of the benefit in the international division of labor in processing and manufacturing.

> —Chen Xiaohong, ed., 中国企业国际化战略
> [China enterprise internationalization strategy]*
> (Beijing: Renmin Chubanshe, 146.
> Development Research Council,
> State Council of the PRC, 2006)

---

*All translations appearing in this book are by the author except where indicated otherwise.

1

Perhaps the first Chinese automaker that many business-minded people in the developed world ever heard of was Chery. The company's name surfaced in Western publications in early 2005 when Malcolm Bricklin, the auto entrepreneur known for having imported the Yugo to America in the 1980s, announced that cars made by Chery would be the first Chinese-made automobiles sold in the United States beginning in 2007. But the agreement between Bricklin and the Anhui Province–based Chery Automobile collapsed in 2006, and as of this writing, Chinese automakers have yet successfully to export a passenger car to the United States.[1]

The story of how Chery came to exist is not well known outside of China, yet it is an interesting tale illustrating the evolution of business-government relations in China during the reform era. The story is interesting because it contains many of the elements that describe not only how China's auto industry has developed, but how China's central and local governments have both cooperated and competed to develop the national champions of China's most important industries.

The typical large industrial Chinese company is, like Chery, a local state-owned enterprise (or LSOE, as distinguished from a *central* state-owned enterprise or CSOE). It is wholly or majority-owned by a local government which appoints senior management and provides free or low-cost land and utilities, tax breaks, and, where possible, guarantees that locally made products will be favored by local government, consumers, and other businesses. In return, the enterprise provides the local state with a source of jobs for local workers, tax revenue, and dividends. Very often, the LSOE is also a source of local prestige and, depending on the product the LSOE makes, a source of free or inexpensive goods for local officials and bureaucrats.

But as this brief story about Chery will illustrate, the local government is but one player among several that have shaped and influenced the growth and development of China's industrial giants. While China's economy has become increasingly subject to market forces over the past three decades, these forces have been, and continue to be, directed by the wishes of the state. Throughout the reform era, China's five-year plans, developed by the central government with input from various central ministries, industries, and local governments, have become increasingly sophisticated in terms of their demands on

China's most important industries. And despite the increasingly influential role of local governments over the past three decades, the central government still manages to get most of what it wants. At the same time, the central government has demonstrated a pragmatic flexibility in that it is willing to bend its own rules when it sees fit.

Chery: A State-Owned Startup

The idea for starting Chery was first promoted in 1992 by Zhan Xialai, an assistant to the mayor of Wuhu City in Anhui Province.[2] Zhan was among those state officials known as a *hongding shangren* (红顶商人, literally, a "red-hat businessman"), a term originating from the Qing dynasty and originally used to describe state officials who also engage in commerce. Contrary to commonly held beliefs, not only among some in the Western media, but also among many Chinese citizens, Chery is not, nor has it ever been, a private company. From its founding, Chery's controlling shareholder has been the city of Wuhu, and its second largest shareholder is the Anhui Provincial Government.[3] When asked why this point on Chery's ownership is so confusing to so many, the typically knowledgeable Chinese auto industry insider answers that "Chery is entrepreneurial. It acts like a private company."[4]

Zhan Xialai, who ultimately became the Communist Party secretary of Wuhu, was also Chery's first chairman, but he was ultimately forced to choose between running the company and running the city.[5] He chose to keep his Party title where, presumably, he could have an even greater influence over, not only the business, but the local environment in which it operates. Many of those interviewed for this project believe it was Zhan's role in the founding of Chery that has influenced the entrepreneurial behavior of the company. Granted, all local governments wish to see their local companies succeed, but in the case of Chery, in which the local Party Secretary is also the company's founder, there exists a personal connection between the business and the local state. In the opinion of one interviewee, "Zhan still thinks of Chery as his company."

The involvement of the local government, however, did not mean that Chery's founding went smoothly. At the time Chery was founded in the mid-1990s, the central government, concerned with an increasingly fragmented auto industry, had called for a moratorium on the establishment of new passenger car manufacturers. This meant that Chery had to get its start—with the help of local government—under the radar.

Zhan recruited Chery's first chief engineer, Yin Tongyao, away from Volkswagen's joint venture with a major state-owned enterprise (SOE), First Auto Works (FAW). Yin is now Chery's chairman. The venture started out with a very low profile, making only engines on a used assembly line purchased from Ford in the United Kingdom. Eventually Chery's engineers "designed" a complete car based on the Volkswagen Jetta from plans Yin Tongyao had obtained from a Spanish subsidiary of VW.[6] With the help of a Taiwan-based molding company, Chery's first car came off the line in 1999, but these cars could only be sold and driven locally as Chery had still not obtained permission from Beijing to manufacture cars.[7] Without this permission (which required being listed in an official government catalogue), Chery cars could not be issued license plates. Chery's cars could be given a pass by local authorities in Anhui, but without official plates, they could not be legally sold in other provinces.

Eventually, the central government became aware of what was going on in Wuhu and issued an order for Chery to stop manufacturing cars. But rather than punishing Chery's leaders and dismantling the factory, the State Economic and Trade Commission (SETC) advised Chery to negotiate with one of China's largest automakers, Shanghai Automotive Industry Corporation (SAIC). This connection between Chery and a reluctant SAIC was facilitated by Wu Bangguo, who was at the time a vice premier.[8] Wu, who is originally from Chery's home province of Anhui, had also previously served as Party secretary in Shanghai. His connections with both Anhui and Shanghai placed him in a position to bring Chery and SAIC together.

The two companies negotiated a 20 percent ownership stake in Chery by SAIC, which would eventually allow Chery to manufacture vehicles under the "Shanghai-Chery" brand name. Chery was able to resume assembly of autos, which, due to Chery's new affiliation with SAIC, were legitimately listed in the official catalogue. During its time as part of SAIC, Chery was never under the direct management of SAIC and never paid dividends to SAIC.[9] It only received the "investment" of

SAIC, which, according to a veteran Chinese auto industry journalist, amounted to Chery simply *giving* SAIC shares in itself valued at 300 million yuan.

Within a few years, Chery's arrangement with SAIC began to unravel after Chery was accused by General Motors (GM), a joint venture partner of SAIC, of having copied its Chevrolet Spark. The Spark had been based on the Matiz made by GM's South Korean partner Daewoo. It was due to be sold in China toward the end of 2003, but Chery beat GM to the punch, releasing its QQ earlier in the year. How closely had the QQ been based on the Chevrolet Spark? GM's general counsel in Shanghai revealed to author and journalist Peter Hessler photos demonstrating that the doors of the Chevy Spark and the Chery QQ were completely interchangeable.[10] According to China auto consultant Michael Dunne, when GM asked its partner SAIC for advice in addressing Chery's apparent violation of GM's intellectual property, GM had not even been aware that SAIC was a 20 percent owner of Chery.[11] GM attempted three times to sue Chery for its apparent violation, twice in China and once in Korea (from whence the plans for the Spark had originated), but in no case was it demonstrated that Chery had *illegally* obtained the plans for its QQ.[12]

Surprisingly (or probably not surprisingly to veteran China watchers), the episode ended up working in Chery's favor anyway. Though Chery's violation of intellectual property rights was never proved in court, there existed the suspicion that Chery had used its relationship with SAIC to access illegally the blueprints of SAIC's partner, GM. Following this episode, SAIC washed its hands of Chery, leaving it as an independent, stand-alone company. By this time, Chery, having become one of China's largest exporters of automobiles, had no difficulties getting its vehicles properly listed in the central government's catalogue. SAIC had (albeit reluctantly) helped Chery to become a legal automaker in China, giving it the time it needed to demonstrate its importance to the central government.

Not only was Chery attracting notice because of its exports, but the company had also begun to catch the eye of the central government for another important reason. Because Chery did not have a foreign partner, the company had demonstrated its commitment (intellectual property issues notwithstanding) to developing its own, domestically branded cars.[13]

After China's entry into the World Trade Organization (WTO) at the end of 2001, the development of domestic Chinese brands (or 自主品牌, *zizhu pinpai*) had become a top priority of the central government for the auto industry. China's independent automakers, with Chery at the forefront, were leagues ahead of China's lumbering SOEs in carrying out this directive.

By the end of the 2000s, China's central government, having in the 1990s and early 2000s been practically antagonistic toward the independent automakers, had changed its tune—somewhat. These companies, particularly Chery, Geely, BYD, and Great Wall (the latter three of which are nominally private), began to receive encouragement from the central government, not only in the form of state leader visits, but also through access to state-owned bank funding.[14] Without a foreign partner whose brands it could sell, Chery has no choice but to rely on development of its own brands—something the central government has been demanding of its automakers for years. But research and development (R&D) does not come cheaply: the development of a new car model can cost upward of a billion dollars.[15] And herein lies the attractiveness of partnering with a foreign automaker: the foreign partner does all of the R&D heavy lifting.

What Chery Reveals About Chinese Industry

The story of Chery presents the recent development of Chinese industry in microcosm. Through this case we can see the important role that local governments play in the startup phase of industry—particularly when an enterprise must be formed out of the view of the central government. However, we can also see a central government that, despite its desire to see an auto industry shaped in a certain way, was nevertheless flexible enough to find a way to allow a job-creating, tax-generating enterprise to continue to operate within the rules. Furthermore, we see a central government that was able to learn and adapt, a central government that began to see the value that a smaller, independent automaker brought to the industry.

In Chery, we see a company that, like many Chinese businesses, got its start by "borrowing" foreign designs, but that has thus far had difficulty moving beyond this stage into one of real innovation. This raises the important question of whether China's industrial giants will be able to move beyond cost competition to compete head-on with the foreign multinationals (MNCs) in advanced technology. And Chery's difficulties in coming to an agreement with Malcolm Bricklin and subsequent lawsuit with GM are also illustrative of a Chinese auto industry (and a central government) with an ambivalent attitude toward foreigners. On the one hand, we see an industry still heavily reliant on foreign know-how, yet on the other hand, Chinese sources continue to lament what they see as a foreign "monopoly" over China's auto industry.[16]

What this case, and this book as a whole, do not illustrate are the infallibility or invincibility of the Chinese government. Indeed, mistakes have been made, and most certainly will continue to be made. What this book does illustrate is a government that is still largely "crossing the river while groping for stepping stones"* as it tries to balance the competing priorities of economic growth, social stability, and the continued rule of the Communist Party. What it also illustrates is that China's central government has a firm intention of dominating, not only its domestic markets, but as many of the world's markets as it possibly can. The words and actions of China's central government demonstrate its commitment to this goal, and this study of China's automobile industry demonstrates just how determined China's central government is to win.

While I offer no prognostication of China's ultimate success in dominating the global auto industry, I do offer the reader a clear picture of how China has become the world's largest auto market, and how it will very likely continue to pursue the growth of, and eventual dominance by, Chinese businesses throughout the world. But China's dominance is still not a given; whether China ultimately wins also depends very much upon the innovative visions and strategic behavior of the world's other automakers. Even if China's automakers were never to develop the design capabilities of the foreign multinationals, the multinationals would in any case find staying ahead of China to be

---

*The phrase "crossing the river while groping for stepping stones" (摸着石头过河) was used to describe the experimental nature of Deng Xiaoping's reforms. See Richard Baum, *Burying Mao: Chinese Politics in the Age of Deng Xiaoping*, (Princeton, NJ: Princeton University Press, 1994), 17.

increasingly difficult: the Chinese are good at copying, and they're getting better.

This story is, however, much larger than that of a single industry. It is a story about politics, a story about nationalism, and a story that seeks to answer some very important questions about business–government relations—questions that many economists thought they had already addressed, but that the Great Recession of the late 2000s has once again brought to the forefront.

Why China?

Writing over a year after China surpassed Japan to become the world's second-largest economy, behind the United States, it may seem almost absurd to ask, "Why China?" This is a country that, since its opening in 1978, has turned in double-digit economic growth for over three decades while allowing only selective expansion of the personal freedoms of its citizens. China has opened up opportunities for its private sector to grow and develop while maintaining state control over the country's largest and most important industries. The opportunities made available to Chinese citizens have led to an unprecedented generation of wealth, yet, while the industrial economy has grown, the country as a whole is still relatively poor in terms of its gross domestic product (GDP) per capita. And while there have been opportunities for some, there have not been opportunities for all. As some Chinese grow wealthier, the gap between rich and poor has grown wider.

Throughout the latter half of the twentieth century, many economists and political scientists studied the phenomenon of late development, asking why some late developers have chosen their respective paths of development, why some have succeeded, and why some have failed.[17] As an even *later* developer, China poses another set of questions, not only about the paths it has chosen, but about what it may have learned from other late developers that came before it. And while China seems to exhibit traits similar to other late-developing countries, notably, China's East Asian neighbors Japan, Korea, and Taiwan, the sheer magnitude of what China has accomplished, and is trying to accomplish, seems to place the country in a category all by itself in many respects.

Some scholars have even proposed a term to describe the uniqueness of China's approach to development. *Beijing Consensus* describes a prescription for economic development that includes heavy state involvement in economic development through both allocation of resources and commitment to innovation and experimentation. It also includes authoritarian government and limited personal freedoms for citizens.[18] It is contrasted with the *Washington Consensus*, a set of solutions many Western economists have recommended to late developers, which includes fiscal discipline, interest rate liberalization, privatization, deregulation, and free trade—accompanied by a democratic form of government.[19]

There are, of course, problems with both consensuses, and not all China watchers agree on how China has been able to achieve its success. According to Yasheng Huang, China's best performance, in terms of raising the living standards of average Chinese, came during times of its more liberal, less state-centric period in the 1980s, not in the 1990s and 2000s as is commonly assumed.[20] Furthermore, John Williamson, credited with coining the term *Washington Consensus*, points out that *Beijing Consensus* is not even used by the Chinese to describe their own system.[21] And the Washington Consensus, as it turns out, was not actually followed in Washington as the United States developed prior to World War II. The U.S. development model looked, in some respects, similar to that of today's China: heavy trade protectionism, fixed exchange rates, and government-controlled interest rates.[22] Nevertheless, the so-called Beijing Consensus—or however one might label China's model of state-led capitalism—may have a certain appeal for the leaders of other developing countries who have grown weary of Western lecturing about democracy, human rights and minimal state intervention in the economy in exchange for economic assistance. Aside from recognition of China's interests with respect to its territorial integrity, China's assistance tends to come with fewer strings attached.

Regardless of whether the term *Beijing Consensus* is taken seriously by economists or political scientists, it seems to touch upon a feeling common among Westerners that China's approach of capitalism *without* democracy may somehow give that country an advantage.[23] It raises the question of whether America's formula of capitalism *plus* democracy, long thought to be the *sine qua non* of progress, is as durable—or as effective—as once believed.

Ian Bremmer, president of the Eurasia Group, uses a broader term, *state capitalism*, to describe the political economy of China and other countries with similar systems.[24] State capitalism describes a "strategic long-term policy choice" that embraces markets as a tool of ruling elites to serve a country's national interest.[25] The rulers of a country that follows a form of state capitalism are typically motivated by a "fear of chaos" and, therefore, approach governance as an exercise in risk management. This engenders a type of micro-management in which the state attempts to use all of the tools at its disposal to minimize the inherent risks to power that arise from openness to market forces. Among the tools state capitalist countries use are state-owned corporations, sovereign wealth funds that invest abroad, "resource nationalism" (attempts to control stockpiles of, and access to, commodities and national resources), and development of state-backed "national champion" enterprises that can compete globally and that are not limited by concerns for democracy or human rights.

Bremmer quotes Chinese Premier Wen Jiabao, who gave a definition of China's brand of state capitalism in an interview on CNN television in 2008:

> The complete formulation of our economic policy is to give full play to the basic role of market forces in allocating resources under the macroeconomic guidance and regulation of the government. We have one important piece of experience of the past thirty years, that is to ensure that both the visible hand and invisible hand are given full play in regulating the market forces.[26]

What Wen Jiabao's definition fails to capture, however, is the fact that, through its five-year economic plans, China's government, not the markets, decides which industries will grow, which will receive resources, and which will be promoted. The market does have a role in state capitalism, but its role is limited primarily to acting on resources that have been allocated largely according to the state's wishes.

Bremmer makes the case that the financial crisis of the late 2000s cemented in the minds of many of China's leaders the determination to maintain a firm state hand in management of the economy. While they understand the vital role China's private sector has played in growth, they have made a conscious decision to concentrate resources in state hands so as to protect China from the "natural excesses of free-market capitalism" that they believe to have caused the Great Recession among the developed economies.[27]

A Challenge to the West

In the West—particularly among countries following the more traditionally *laissez-faire* Anglo-American model—it is accepted, almost as a matter of faith, that government involvement in business is not a good thing. Americans need look no further than Amtrak and the U.S. Postal Service as examples of perpetually money-losing, state-owned enterprises that constantly return to Congress with their hands out for subsidies. When GM faced bankruptcy and possible liquidation in early 2009, many Americans were astounded that part of the solution included the U.S. government taking an initial 61 percent ownership stake in the ailing automaker. A Gallup poll indicated that 55 percent of Americans disapproved of the government takeover.[28] Many Americans believed GM had failed for years to produce cars comparable in quality to those produced by their Japanese and German counterparts. If GM were unable to stand on its own, it should have been allowed to die. This is, in the minds of many Americans, how capitalism is supposed to work: those who cannot compete exit the market.

Regardless of how a majority of Americans may have arrived at their conclusions that state involvement in business is a bad thing, there also exists a body of economic literature that supports this position, both theoretically and empirically.[29] Over the two decades prior to the Great Recession that began to surface in 2008, a consensus had developed among economists that private ownership of firms is, in general, superior to that of public ownership. In theory, the managers of state-owned enterprises (SOEs) are not subject to many of the disciplinary measures that lead to the superior efficiency, productivity, and profitability achieved by private enterprises. Hard budget constraints (i.e., the threat of bankruptcy), oversight by creditors, greater exposure to competition, the threat of hostile takeover, and pressures from owners whose interests are not conflicted by political and social objectives are but a few of the disciplinary measures to which private sector managers are subject. On these and other points, economic theory is supported by dozens of empirical studies and (until recently) challenged by very few (non-Marxist) dissenting voices.

As long as governments around the world continued during the 1990s to move toward privatization of their economies, and as long as those governments that did not privatize were punished with poor economic outcomes, then countries that adhered to these beliefs of minimal government involvement were comfortable in their chosen paths. But there were two major changes in the latter 2000s that challenged this logic and set Western minds to worrying. The first change was a gradual trend throughout the course of the 2000s toward increased state involvement in China's economy—or, to be more precise, an apparent *reversal* of China's late-1990s trend toward *increased* private sector involvement. The second change was the onset of the Great Recession during 2008, which called into question the viability of the Western economic model.

The first change was highlighted by increased usage of the term *guo jin min tui* (国进民退; "the state advances, the private sector retreats") during the late 2000s. This was a clever reversal of a term with the exact opposite meaning, *guo tui min jin* (国退民进; "the state retreats, the private sector advances"), that emerged in the early 2000s to describe the trend of increased private sector involvement in the economy begun during the Premiership of Zhu Rongji. The reversal of private sector advancement began with the rollback of reforms in China's financial sector in 2005 chronicled by Walter and Howie in *Red Capitalism* (2011).[30] It became apparent in China's industrial sector during 2008 and into 2009 as Chinese newspapers began reporting on an increased pace of nationalization and favoritism toward SOEs. One of the most commonly reported stories was of the forced nationalization of dozens of privately owned coal mines in Shanxi Province.[31] There was also a vigorous debate about this phenomenon in the Chinese press among academics, economists, and government officials.[32] Many observers credited the strengthening of the state-owned sector at the private sector's expense with largesse heaped upon SOEs in the form of loans from local government financing vehicles as a result of the central government's stimulus program in late 2008.[33]

The second change was that the developed world, the United States in particular, fell into a major economic recession largely of its own making. Though the recession had temporary repercussions for emerging markets as well, by the middle of 2009, it was clear that the extent of the damage had been limited primarily to the developed markets. Developing countries such as China took steps to stimulate their economies, but otherwise continued their trends of world-beating economic growth. As a result, economic observers the world over began to question the viability of the Western model—particularly the notion that governments should generally remain aloof from business, allowing the market and the private sector to make all of the decisions. Former U.S. trade representative Charlene Barshefsky put the change in thinking into perspective: "Our competition has gotten tougher during a period for the United States of profound economic weakness that magnifies any perceived threat . . . There is a significant and pro-found—almost theological—question about the rules as they exist."[34]

Among the questions observers are asking are, what if a government not only refuses to relinquish control over important sectors of its economy, but also manages to achieve impressive economic outcomes? And what if those outcomes are superior to those achieved by any developed country in nearly half a century? Would that country's processes, institutions, and outcomes not be worthy of further scrutiny? More specifically, what are the trade-offs that China has accepted in order to maintain heavy state involvement in the country's most important businesses, and are any of these trade-offs possible, or even desirable, in free and democratic societies?

Why Autos?

In an attempt to answer some of these questions, I have chosen to conduct an in-depth analysis of China's automobile industry. The reason for this choice is that the automobile sector serves as a nice microcosm of China's industrial economy as a whole. Within this single industry, state-owned enterprises, private enterprises and Chinese-foreign joint ventures (JVs) compete for market share. The top three automakers, which together command nearly a 50 percent domestic market share, are all state-owned enterprises (SOEs) whose production comes primarily from joint ventures with foreign manufacturers. Among the top 12 automakers in China, three are privately held. The recent median five-year compound annual growth rate (CAGR) in unit sales among China's top 12 manufacturers was 30 percent.[35] The three private firms, BYD, Geely, and Great Wall, had five-year CAGRs of 116, 24, and 44 percent, respectively.[36] The point here is that, while China's auto industry is dominated by state-owned enterprises, there is room for private players to compete and grow—an empirical phenomenon that already calls into question economic theories that state-owned investment in an industry drives out private investment.[37]

It is not difficult for the impartial observer to view the recent success of China's auto industry with a measure of admiration. Within the space of 30 years, China has gone from having practically no passenger car production to building more cars than any other country in the world. But how does China's early growth stack up against that of other major players? Figure 1.1 charts the growth of auto production in four

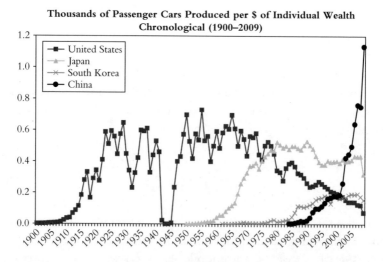

Figure 1.1 Relative Importance of Auto Industry in Selected Markets

Data Sources: Angus Maddison, *China Automotive Industry Yearbooks*, Japan Automobile Manufacturers Association, International Organization of Motor Vehicle Manufacturers.

countries from 1900 until 2009. The statistic measured, thousands of passenger cars produced per dollar of individual wealth, is simply the number of passenger cars produced in each given year in thousands (both for domestic consumption and export) divided by GDP per capita.[38] Using a common denominator, this measure describes how important each country's respective auto industry is as a part of its national economy.

The countries selected are the United States, Japan, South Korea, and China. As Figure 1.1 demonstrates, U.S. production, with the notable exceptions of some key interruptions such as the two world wars and the Great Depression, has experienced a clear rise and fall as the global leader, reaching its peak as Japan began production in the 1950s. Japan then also experienced a steep rise, which began to level off in the 1980s, around the time the United States forced it to accept "voluntary" export restraints of its cars. (The Japanese countered this resistance by building factories in the United States, but cars produced in these "transplant" factories show up in the U.S. figures.) Japan's auto production then began to stagnate as its real estate and investment bubbles burst in the early 1990s. Like Japan, Korea also experienced a fairly steep initial rise which also leveled off quickly as its smaller land mass and population quickly reached saturation with automobiles.

Though China began to produce passenger cars as early as 1958, for the purposes of comparison, I am using 1984 as the beginning date for the rise of China's auto industry. Until the late 1970s, China produced fewer than 3,000 passenger cars in any given year. Nineteen eighty-four was the first year that China began its focus on passenger cars in earnest as this was the year that negotiations with American Motors Corporation (AMC) and Volkswagen for China's first auto joint ventures were completed. As Figure 1.1 illustrates, China experienced growth somewhat comparable to that of the other three countries in its early years, only to level off slightly toward the end of the 1990s. Then, once China joined the WTO in 2001, production skyrocketed. The slight dip between 2007 and 2008 is the drop in China's growth rate due to a tightening of the money supply in 2007 and the global financial crisis that emerged in 2008. Subsequent to that time, China once again experienced outsized growth (48 percent growth in passenger car production in 2009 and 32 percent in 2010) due to stimulus measures enacted by the central government and a rebound in confidence as it became evident to Chinese consumers that their economy would be less affected by the global downturn than that of many other countries.

Each of the three countries that began production before China appears to have started strongly and then leveled off at some point. Though this point is not essential to this analysis, it seems plausible that the leveling-off point for each of these three represents a level of saturation of cars given each country's population and land mass. If that is the case, then the fact that China's line is still headed into the stratosphere should not come as a surprise: with a population approaching 1.4 billion and a burgeoning middle class, China's auto market still appears to hold potential.

A more important question that this picture raises is how well China has performed in its early years as compared to these other three markets. Is China's early growth rate any better or worse than that of the others? Figure 1.2 takes the first 30 years of each country from Figure 1.1 and starts them all in Year 1.

The first observation is that China's line is steeper than that of the others, which confirms that the growth of China's auto industry is

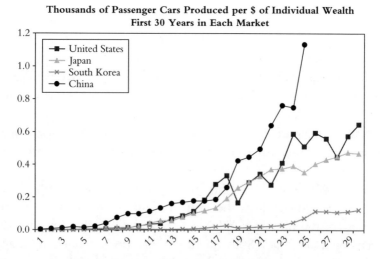

Figure 1.2   Relative Importance of Auto Industries—30-Year Comparison
Data Sources: China Automotive Industry Yearbooks.

indeed worthy of investigation. Second, this picture also highlights the fact that each successive entrant into the auto industry has experienced less volatility than the one before. Japan, Korea, and China have each benefited from a less volatile, U.S.-dominated world into which they could launch their auto industries.

While China also subjected imported autos to extremely high tariffs prior to 2006 (year 22 in Figure 1.2),[39] one major difference is that China invited foreign auto companies to build factories on its own soil, something Japan and Korea have never done.[40] Perhaps this is one of the primary reasons that China's curve turned initially steeper than those of the others. Another factor that may have also favored China is the "advantage of backwardness"—the fact that China was in a position, not only to copy what the United States and others had done, but to observe the successes and failures of two fellow latecomers, Japan and Korea.[41] China's authoritarian government may have been in a position to provide the country with the coordination it needed to launch a competitive auto industry where none had existed before.

Figure 1.2 shows that China is selling a lot of cars relative to individual wealth—more than the United States, Japan, or Korea ever did—but selling a lot of cars is not a sustainable activity if it cannot be done profitably. If China's automakers are losing money in the process, then we may conclude that the industry is on an unsustainable footing. However, that does not appear to be the case. Figure 1.3 shows combined industry profitability from 1993 through 2008. This represents only the profit on sale of vehicles, and does not include ancillary businesses.[42] With the exception of declines in 2004 and 2005, the trend is one of generally increasing profitability.[43]

Conclusion, and a Roadmap

My primary task in this book is to explain the figures shown in Figure 1.2—to explain how China was able to build a competitive industry from scratch while transitioning from a planned economy to one that is more market oriented; to explain how a formerly communist country (though still Communist in name) can both maintain an authoritarian political system and at the same time build a potentially globally

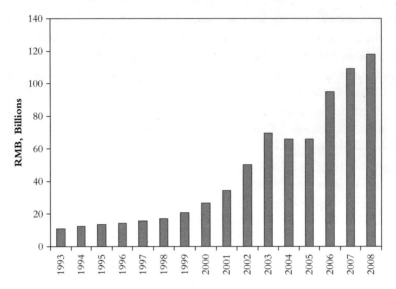

Figure 1.3   Auto Industry Profit, 1993 to 2008

Sources: Angus Maddison, *China Automotive Industry Yearbooks*, 1994–2009, Japan Automobile Manufacturers Association, International Organization of Motor Vehicle Manufacturers.

competitive industry—something that has, until now, proven elusive under authoritarian systems. This book aims to answer the questions: What is unique about China that has allowed it to succeed where many others have failed? Is China breaking the rules of capitalism or rewriting them? And finally, what are the weaknesses and limitations of China's model? Will the line on China's graph continue to shoot ever upward, or is China subject to the same laws of gravity as everyone else?

The arguments of this book are as follows:

- First, while China's state-led capitalism has achieved impressive results, China's one-party rule introduces contradictory objectives that have prevented the central government from achieving its economic objectives.
- Second, China's central government has nevertheless exhibited an ability to learn and adapt to achieve many of its desired outcomes.
- Third, while local governments have a certain amount of power to act outside the will of the center, the center will ultimately have its way.

- Fourth, China's insistence on state control over pillar industries is detrimental to innovation.
- This insistence on state control may not be as harmful to China's continued development prospects as we might think because, fifth, China has created an environment in which the unavoidable price of entry for foreign multinational firms is relinquishment of intellectual property. Innovation becomes less important when you can get your competitors voluntarily to hand over their technology.

This chapter began with the story of Chery, a story that illustrates many of the essential points describing the evolution of China's auto industry over the past several decades. Chapter Two contains the story that illustrates the main arguments of this book. Here we can see the major determinants of success and failure in China's industrial planning model. In this chapter I describe the auto industry's players and their objectives. From this description emerges a picture of how these elements result in an industry with clear strengths, but that is nevertheless beset by some key weaknesses.

Chapter Three contains the back-story, essentially, a moving picture that describes how China's auto industry developed over the past three decades. I cover three stages of auto development in the People's Republic of China (PRC)—state-centric (1949–1978), global partnering (1978–2001) and indigenous innovation (2001–present)—spending most of my time on the latter two. This chapter demonstrates how policy has developed and changed over time.

Chapters Four through Six contain the case studies that provide details to support the main arguments of this book. Chapter Four focuses on the backbone of China's auto industry, the Chinese-foreign joint ventures. This is the most unique aspect of China's auto industry, as no other country has relied so heavily on foreign partners to help build its domestic industry. To this day, the foreign brands continue to account for nearly 70 percent of all passenger cars (sedans) sold in China.[44] Chapter Five then looks at the case studies of the "independents," a group of Chinese automakers that lack foreign partners, and that must, by definition, rely on development of their own independent brands. The independents include one large local state-owned enterprise (Chery, a case study of which began this chapter), several prominent private enterprises, an SOE whose chief executive at one time believed the enterprise to be his own private company and one audacious automaker wannabe that captured attention briefly in 2009.

Chapter Six includes in-depth reviews of three of the most prominent mergers to have taken place in China's auto industry within the past decade. These stories are important because they illustrate two seemingly conflicting aspects of the role of China's central government in the auto industry. Depending on how evidence is presented, the central government can be made to look either impotent or all-powerful. These case studies show how the central government, despite its decades-long desire to see consolidation in the auto industry, has patiently waited for the market to encourage some of these mergers. Yet at the same time, when the timing was right, the central government was able to apply leverage in order to correct strategic mistakes or ensure policy adherence. Toward the end of this chapter, I also analyze data on the fragmentation of China's auto industry relative to that of the United States and highlight the interesting finding that China actually has *two* auto industries: one that the central government intends to be competitive, and another that serves as a sort of welfare system in local regions.

Chapter Seven then takes what we have learned about China's auto industry in Chapters Two through Six and compares this with the auto industries in Japan and Korea during their own start-up periods. For Japan, the time was roughly 1950 to 1980; for Korea it was roughly 1960 to 1990; and for China, we compare the reform era, from roughly 1980 until the present. The key aspects I compare are degree of state ownership versus private, the key institutions that each country appointed to manage development of its auto industry, each country's methods of technology acquisition, the degree of foreign involvement, the amount and types of industry support, and the structure of each auto industry. Many readers will not be surprised to learn that Japan and Korea experimented early with state ownership but quickly allowed the private sector to take over their auto industries. The state then "guided" the private sector during its early development. In China, most auto industry assets remain in state hands.

Chapter Eight, the conclusion, summarizes the evidence emerging from the policy analysis and case studies. This chapter then closes with a look forward and asks, among other questions, about the future promise of China's private sector, the ability of China to spur innovation, and whether foreign multinationals will always be welcomed.

Notes

1. Bricklin's negotiations with Chery were the subject of a documentary film released in 2009. Jonathan Bricklin, *The Entrepreneur*, Documentary, 2009, www.hulu.com/watch/85122/the-entrepreneur.
2. Gordon Fairclough, "In China, Chery Automobile Drives an Industry Shift," *wsj.com*, December 4, 2007, http://online.wsj.com/article/SB119671314593812115.html.
3. This fact was confirmed to me in no uncertain terms by a member of Chery's senior management team.
4. Surprisingly, even a few supposed auto industry experts whom I interviewed seemed confused as to whether Chery's status was public or private.
5. "8,000 Chinese officials quit business posts," *People's Daily Online*, December 29, 2004, http://english.people.com.cn/200412/29/eng20041229_168987.html.
6. Michael J. Dunne, *American Wheels, Chinese Roads: The Story of General Motors in China* (Hoboken, NJ: John Wiley & Sons, 2011), Ch. 14; Peter Hessler, *Country Driving: A Journey through China from Farm to Factory*, 1st ed. (New York: Harper, 2010), 65.
7. Lu Feng, "中国汽车工业的自主开发道路行得通吗?" [Is the Chinese auto industry's path toward self-development achievable?], *Unirule*, 2007, www.unirule.org.cn/symposium/c258.htm.
8. As of this writing, Wu serves as chairman of the National People's Congress (NPC).
9. Lu Feng, "中国汽车工业的自主开发道路行得通吗?" [Is the Chinese auto industry's path toward self-development achievable?].
10. Peter Hessler, "Letter from China: Car Town," The New Yorker, September 26, 2005, www.newyorker.com/archive/2005/09/26/050926fa_fact_hessler. The three-dimensional spaces into which the doors of a car fit are, according to automotive experts, as unique as fingerprints.
11. Dunne, *American Wheels, Chinese Roads*, 134.
12. Ibid., 135.
13. In addition to the failed negotiations with Malcolm Bricklin, Chery also negotiated separately with both Chrysler and Fiat in 2007, but failed to establish a venture with either company.
14. In 2008, Chery received 10 billion yuan in funding from China's (state-owned) Export-Import Bank, and in 2009 Chery received another 2 billion yuan from a private equity arm of the Bank of China. Then, in the spring of

2011, Chery was granted a 43 billion yuan (US$6.6 billion) credit line by the China Development Bank to use for research and development (R&D) over the course of the 12th Five-Year Plan (2011–2015).

15. Dunne, *American Wheels, Chinese Roads*, 131.

16. The following Chinese sources contain passages accusing foreign multi-nationals of "垄断" or monopoly over China's auto industry. The first source is an influential former bureaucrat in the auto industry, the second is from China's Ministry of Science and Technology, and the third is from the Development Research Council, a think tank attached to the State Council. Wu Facheng, 汽车强国之梦 [Dream of an automobile super-power], (Beijing: Xinhua Chubanshe, 2009), 151; Tang Jie, Yang Yanping, and Zhou Wenjie, 中国汽车产业自主创新战略 [China auto industry indigenous innovation strategy], (Beijing: Kexue Chubanshe, 2009), 84; Chen Xiaohong, 中国企业国际化战略 [China enterprise internationaliza-tion strategy], 149.

17. The following are but a portion of the literature that deals with this topic: Alice H. Amsden, Asia's Next Giant: *South Korea and Late Industrialization* (New York: Oxford University Press, 1989); Kent E. Calder, *Strategic Capitalism: Private Business and Public Purpose in Japanese Industrial Finance* (Princeton, N.J: Princeton University Press, 1993); The Political Economy of the New Asian Industrialism, Cornell Studies in Political Economy (Ithaca, N.Y: Cornell University Press, 1987); Richard F. Doner, "Limits of State Strength: Toward an Institutionalist View of Economic Development," *World Politics* 44, no. 3 (April 1992): 398–431; Evans, *Embedded Autonomy*; Alexander Gerschenkron, *Economic Backwardness in Historical Perspective: A Book of Essays* (Cambridge: Belknap Press of Harvard University Press, 1966); Chalmers Johnson, *MITI and the Japanese Miracle: The Growth of Industrial Policy, 1925–1975* (Stanford Calif.: Stanford University Press, 1982); Dani Rodrik, *One Economics, Many Recipes: Globalization, Institutions, and Economic Growth* (Princeton, NJ: Princeton University Press, 2007); Robert Wade, *Governing the Market: Economic Theory and the Role of Government in East Asian Industrialization* (Princeton, NJ: Princeton University Press, 1990); Meredith Woo-Cumings, *The Developmental State*, Cornell Studies in Political Economy (Ithaca, NY: Cornell University Press, 1999).

18. Joshua Cooper Ramo, *The Beijing Consensus: Notes on the New Physics* of *Chinese Power* (London: Foreign Policy Centre, 2004); Stefan A. Halper, *The Beijing Consensus: How China's Authoritarian Model Will Dominate the Twenty-First Century* (New York: Basic Books, 2010).

19. John Williamson, "Democracy and the 'Washington Consensus,'" *World Development* 21, no. 8 (1993): 1329–1336. The "Washington Consensus" is so named, not necessarily because its prescriptions have been promoted by the U.S. government, but because the group of economists who devised this "consensus" just happened to have been meeting in Washington, D.C.

20. Yasheng Huang, "Rethinking the Beijing Consensus," *Asia Policy* 11 (January 2011): 1–26.

21. John Williamson, "Beijing Consensus versus Washington Consensus?," November 2, 2010, www.piie.com/publications/interviews/pp20101102 williamson.pdf.

22. Wade, *Governing the Market*, xv, no. 5.; Barry J. Eichengreen, *Exorbitant Privilege: The Rise and Fall of the Dollar and the Future of the International Monetary System* (New York: Oxford University Press, 2011).

23. Kellee S. Tsai finds that entrepreneurs in China, far from agitating for democracy, seem to be content to work within the existing system. See *Capitalism without Democracy: The Private Sector in Contemporary China* (Ithaca, NY: Cornell University Press, 2007).

24. Ian Bremmer, *The End of the Free Market: Who Wins the War between States and Corporations?* (New York: Portfolio, 2010). Among countries that have adopted a form of state capitalism, Bremmer also lists Saudi Arabia, the United Arab Emirates, Egypt, Algeria, Ukraine, Russia, India, Mexico, Brazil, and Venezuela, among others.

25. Ibid., 51–52.

26. Ibid., 129.

27. Ibid., 144–145.

28. Gallup Poll results from: www.gallup.com/poll/120842/disapprove-majority-government-ownership.aspx.

29. William L Megginson, *The Financial Economics of Privatization* (New York: Oxford University Press, 2005); Armen Albert Alchian, *Economic Forces at Work* (Indianapolis: Liberty Press, 1977); Avinash Dixit, "Power of Incentives in Private versus Public Organizations," The American Economic Review 87, no. 2 (May 1997): 378–382; John Vickers and George Yarrow, "Economic Perspectives on Privatization," *The Journal of Economic Perspectives* 5, no. 2 (Spring 1991): 111–132; Eytan Sheshinski and Luis F. Lopez-Calva, "Privatization and Its Benefits: Theory and Evidence," *CESifo Economic Studies* 49, no. 3 (January 1, 2003): 429–459; Maxim Boycko, Andrei Shleifer, and Robert W. Vishny, "A Theory of Privatisation," *The Economic Journal* 106, no. 435 (March 1996): 309–319; Andrei Shleifer, "State versus Private Ownership," *The Journal of Economic Perspectives* 12, no. 4 (Autumn 1998): 133–150; János Kornai, *The Socialist System: The Political Economy of Communism* (Princeton, NJ: Princeton University Press, 1992).

30. Carl Walter and Fraser Howie, *Red capitalism: The fragile financial foundation of China's extraordinary rise* (Hoboken, NJ: Wiley, 2011), 14–21.

31. Yang Guang, "消失的利益链" [Disappearance of the chain of interests], *Economic Observer*, October 23, 2009, http://eeo.com.cn/eeo/jjgcb/2009/10/26/153709.shtml.

32. In a series of four posts on my blog, *ChinaBizGov*, in the spring of 2010, I analyzed this phenomenon along with several Chinese sources which are

linked in the accompanying posts. http://chinabizgov.blogspot.com/2010/03/is-china-really-re-nationalizing.html.

33. "China's state-owned enterprises: Nationalisation rides again," *The Economist*, November 12, 2009, www.economist.com/node/14859337; "Guojin mintui," *Caixin Online*, December 24, 2009, http://english.caing.com/2009–12–24/100102800.html.

34. Jason Dean, Andrew Browne, and Shai Oster, "China's 'State Capitalism' Sparks a Global Backlash," *Wall Street Journal*, November 16, 2010, http://online.wsj.com/article/SB10001424052748703514904575602731006315198.html.

35. Figures from *China Auto*, Tianjin, 2005, 2006, 2007. *China Auto Bluebooks*, 2008, 2009. China Association of Automobile Manufacturers.

36. The two highest growth rates among the top dozen were achieved by Great Wall and BYD.

37. Sheshinski and Lopez-Calva, "Privatization and Its Benefits."

38. GDP per capita figures are all expressed in 1990 Geary-Khamis dollars as compiled by Angus Maddison. Maddison's data are available at www.ggdc.net/MADDISON/oriindex.htm.

39. As a condition of WTO entry, China's auto import tariffs were gradually lowered from 80–100 percent in 2001 to 25 percent in 2006.

40. Though foreign automakers have subsequently invested in existing Japanese and Korean companies.

41. Gerschenkron, *Economic Backwardness in Historical Perspective*.

42. As two different China representatives of the American "Big 4" auditing firms acknowledged to me, there exists the probability that the profitability of at least some state-owned automakers may be overstated due to losses being absorbed by state-owned parts manufacturers whose losses are in turn being absorbed by the state. (In accounting parlance, this is a "transfer pricing" issue.) The concept of the "complete listing" (整体上市), by which all subsidiaries of exchange-listed enterprises are supposed to be consolidated on the balance sheet of the listed entity, was intended to alleviate this problem, but thus far only a handful of automakers have done a "complete listing"—and this still does not address the probability that unrelated state-owned entities could be selling parts to the listed automakers at a loss. Of course, the private automakers, which are listed on overseas markets (primarily Hong Kong), are less likely to benefit from such state generosity, and are, therefore, more likely to be genuinely profitable.

43. Profitability in 2004 and 2005 was affected by an overall tightening of credit in China as well as selling price decreases that had got ahead of related cost reductions in response to increasingly lower import tariffs required under WTO membership.

44. Xinhua News Agency, China Economic Information Service, "Profile of China's Passenger Vehicle Industry in 2010," January 14, 2011. Accessed through ISI Emerging Markets.

Chapter Two

The System

The tragedy of the Chinese auto industry is that you have private players who have passion, but no money, and you have SOEs with money, but no passion.

—East Asia auto industry analyst
Hong Kong, December 2009

This chapter looks at the current state of China's auto industry: its players, their objectives, and the results they've produced. While this book's focus is a single industry, the political principles that have shaped China's auto industry and the players' objectives have also shaped China's approach to industrial planning in general. China's economy may have become more market-oriented since the end of the Mao era, but the overall ebb and flow of state control have similarly affected all of China's important industries.

The Players

China's automobile industry is a complex system consisting of five major players, or groups of players with varying, and often incompatible, objectives and incentives. Those players are the central government, local governments, state-owned automakers, private automakers, and foreign multinational automakers (MNCs). While some of these players appear more powerful than others, each has bargaining power, and each has had to make compromises to accomplish its objectives. Though it should not come as a surprise that the different players have opposing objectives, a close examination of the industry also reveals that some players have multiple objectives that can be mutually contradictory.

Central Government

The central government, for the purposes of this story, is represented primarily by two entities, the National Development and Reform Commission (NDRC) and the Ministry of Industry and Information Technology (MIIT). While the relevant state organs differ among various industries, the NDRC and MIIT are the key government organizations that oversee the auto industry. The NDRC is responsible for China's overall economic planning, and the MIIT is responsible for microeconomic planning and regulatory oversight of the auto industry (among others). There are, of course, other government organs that become involved in the process—for example, the Ministry for Environmental Protection is responsible for regulation of auto emissions and the Ministry of Commerce approves foreign investment in China and external investments by Chinese companies—but the industry as a whole is driven by NDRC and MIIT. Two associations which are nominally independent, but that operate on behalf of the central government are the China Association of Automobile Manufacturers (CAAM) and the China Automotive Technology and Research Center (CATARC). CAAM is a typical industry association that is owned by its members (the automakers), but as those members are primarily SOEs, and CAAM's management are appointed by the state, it may be considered a government organization as well. CATARC is a research center and auto industry think tank that is also responsible for safety and emissions testing. No vehicle may be sold in China without first passing through CATARC's certification process.

While the auto industry, like all industries, still seems to suffer from the problem of "too many mothers-in-law," or too many regulators, when it comes to policy making in the auto industry, the result of the hidden internal processes that take place is a policy that supports the country's overall economic plans.[1] I introduce these multiple organizations to point out the fact that auto policy has the potential to be influenced by several players that bring different concerns to the table, but the end result, as Chapter Three demonstrates, is a unified policy. While the central government is far from being a unified actor, with regard to industrial policy, it is helpful to think of it in this way. The NDRC is powerful, and its job is to ensure that the other ministries' micro-plans conform to the NDRC's macro-plans, also known as China's "Five-Year Plans."

Layered on top of the central government is the Chinese Communist Party (CCP). While the Party is nominally a separate body from the government of China, because the individuals comprising the government's senior leadership are the same individuals who comprise the Party's senior leadership, I consider the two to be effectively one and the same. It is not uncommon for China specialists to refer to the "party-state" when referring to the intertwining of the two and their common objective, which is the unchallenged rule of the CCP over China. Because the CCP is organized in parallel to the government, it also serves as the main unifying force between the central government and local governments.[2]

Local Government

By "local governments," I mean all governments below the central level—from the provincial level down to the municipal level—whose jurisdictions include one or more assemblers of *finished automobiles* (as distinguished from manufacturers of automobile *components*). In most cases these local governments are also controlling owners of their local auto enterprises, though in some cases they oversee auto assemblers that are nominally private (in that no state body holds a controlling ownership share). So in some cases a local government is both owner and local regulator of an automaker, and in a few cases, the local government is only the regulator.

The Automakers

The next three groups of players represent three types of automobile firms: state-owned Chinese firms, private Chinese firms, and foreign firms. The state-owned enterprises (SOEs) can be further divided into two subgroups: centrally owned SOEs (CSOEs) and locally owned SOEs (LSOEs). For the purposes of this book I generally refer to all SOEs as a group except for instances in which central state ownership versus local state ownership is a critical factor. I will also at times refer to a cross section of automakers called "the independents." This grouping consists of all automakers in China that do not have major vehicle assembly partnerships with foreign multinational automakers. As such, this group contains both the private automakers and some of the LSOEs. The distinction between "privates" and "independents" is significant as "privates" emphasizes the lack of a state-held controlling ownership and "independents" emphasizes the lack of a major foreign partner. Foreign automakers, or multinational corporations (MNCs), are forbidden by law to assemble cars in China except in joint venture (JV) partnership with a Chinese firm.

Their Objectives

This section discusses each player's objectives—in short, what these players want to achieve. These are not only objectives with respect to the auto industry, but also general goals (such as survival) that shape these players' behavior. It is important to distinguish between goals and objectives here. While both refer to desired outcomes, goals are less specific, less flexible, and longer-term; objectives are more specific, more malleable, and shorter-term in nature. Goals are difficult to change, but the objectives that are deployed to achieve those goals may change in response to circumstances.

Central Government

The central government has one overarching goal: regime survival.[3] In the government's view, one of the critical underlying factors supporting regime survival is social stability. Accordingly, the key goal of main-taining social stability is sacrosanct among state leaders. This means that all other objectives of the state are subordinated to this key goal, and any event or situation deemed to threaten social stability should be either avoided or quashed immediately. In practice this means that factors negatively affecting the livelihoods of China's nearly 1.4 billion people, such as, for example, unemployment and inflation, are to be avoided.

Looking specifically at the auto industry, the central government also has a key goal which has remained constant from the 1980s, and that is for China to have a globally competitive automobile industry that is dominant at home and competitive abroad.[4] This fits into China's goal of becoming a global industrial power. From as far back as 1986, when the auto industry had been designated a "pillar" industry, this has remained the case.[5]

Though the central government's primary *goal* for the auto industry has not changed in three decades, the *objectives* by which it intends to achieve that goal have changed in part. The earliest objectives included consolidation of a very fragmented industry, technology acquisition from foreign multinationals and generation of foreign exchange. Con-solidation remains a key objective for the industry, as does technology acquisition, though the strategies the central government has deployed to acquire technology have changed over time. Of course, with its over 3 trillion U.S. dollars worth of foreign reserves, the central government has long since ceased to focus on its earlier objective of generating foreign exchange.

Among the central government's more recent objectives (empha-sized since around the turn of the century) are for Chinese automakers to develop their own Chinese brands, and to conduct R&D into alternative fuels and propulsion systems in order to compete in the next generation of automotive technologies. In China these new types of vehicles and technology are generally referred to as "new energy vehicles" (NEVs).[6]

Because the central government has centered its industrial planning efforts around these four auto industry objectives—consolidation, technology acquisition, development of Chinese brands, and develop-ment of NEVs—these are the key objectives by which this book will measure the central government's success with this industry. The key question in this book is not whether China's auto industry has performed according to some criteria imposed on it from outside; the key question is whether and how the central government has been able to achieve its own objectives.

Local Governments

Local governments, though often thought of as part of "the government," should be viewed separately from central government because their objectives are very often different from those of the center. And in the context of industrial development, the objectives of local government are essentially the objectives of local party-state leaders.

While different local regions may have differing priorities based on local needs, the objectives of the individuals who lead local regions all across China tend to be similar and are linked to their promotion as political leaders.[7] Local leaders respond to incentives for performance, and, as Li and Zhou (2005) have demonstrated, the likelihood of promotion for provincial level leaders increases with economic performance.[8] This serves to focus the attention of local leaders on local economic growth and a heavy role for the state in nurturing local industry while protecting markets from outside competition.

Closely linked to this objective of local economic performance is support for the central objective of social stability. Promotion incentives rely not only upon growth in economic activity, but also on maintenance of social order in local regions, and in general, economic opportunities that create employment are seen as one of the most effective guarantors of social stability. In other words, economic growth and social stability are mutually supporting objectives. If local government is generating economic activity that creates adequate employment opportunity for local citizens, the likelihood of the people protesting, demonstrating, or petitioning higher authorities decreases.

State-Owned Enterprises

Similarly to those of local governments, the objectives of SOEs tend also to be the objectives of their leaders. It is widely acknowledged that the leaders of SOEs in China are essentially political leaders in that their performance incentives depend upon the support by the SOE for party-state objectives.[9] Many SOE leaders spend their careers moving back and forth between political positions and enterprise positions, and those whose SOEs perform according to expectations are rewarded with promotions to positions of increasing responsibility and authority.

Leadership roles in SOEs are inherently political positions, and SOEs are expected by local and central party-state leaders to support the objectives of the party-state. Upon leaving their SOE positions, the high performers among these SOE leaders become ministers or vice ministers in the central government; some take up local government positions, and still others are given positions in industrial associations. (For example, former CEO of Dongfeng Auto Miao Wei is now the minister of industry and information technology. And the former CEO of Beijing Auto, An Qingheng, is now chairman of the Beijing Auto Manufacturers Association.) While leading their SOEs, the CEOs focus on increasing production capacity, and not losing money (a goal decidedly different from *increasing* profitability). To this degree the same objectives of the local state leaders, economic growth and social stability, also apply to SOEs. However, whereas local state leaders are concerned with economic development of an entire region, SOE leaders are concerned only with the performance of a single enterprise. This can lead to conflicts between an SOE and the local state. Furthermore, as the case studies in later chapters will demonstrate, SOE leaders are also expected to increase the absolute size of their organizations. And in fact, *size* often seems to be even more important than profitability in terms of how an SOE's performance is judged.[10]

Unlike enterprise leaders in the private sector, SOE leaders tend to be more conservative in their leadership and to have a shorter-term investment horizon. As these leaders typically serve in their positions for a political cycle (typically about five years), SOE leaders also tend to invest only in areas in which they are certain to see tangible benefits during their terms in office. And like the leaders of any profit-seeking enterprise, private- or state-owned, the leaders of SOEs also tend to be motivated to pursue profit for profit's sake as it is one of the most commonly quantified measures of corporate achievement. Still their conservative nature often forces them to prioritize *not* losing money over increasing profitability.

Private Enterprises

While all automakers, regardless of ownership, may list profitability among their objectives, China's private automakers, or rather, the entrepreneurs who lead them, have several unique objectives. Starting a private company in an industry designated by China's central government as a "pillar" industry requires a special tolerance for risk.[11] By definition a pillar industry (支柱产业) is one in which the central government has announced its long-term commitment for support and involvement and which also typically includes a preponderance of state ownership; therefore, an entrepreneur electing to establish a private automobile firm is electing to compete against state-owned enterprises.

Lacking the kind of state support that SOEs enjoy, private firms have survival as their prime objective, and this, of course, requires achieving a level of scale and profitability such that bankruptcy may be avoided. This requires, among other things, a level of innovation that makes the private firm's products attractive to potential customers. It requires competent management of corporate resources including financial, physical, and intellectual. It also requires access to external sources of funding as the private firm cannot count on the state for easy access to bank lending.

Related to the objective of survival is the simple objective of maintaining control over the company's assets. In China this means that an entrepreneur needs to know that not only will he someday recoup his initial investment, but that the value added by the organization will accrue to him in proportion to his ownership. Whether the entrepreneur intends someday to sell his organization, or whether he intends to own it indefinitely, his objective is that the assets remain firmly in his control without the risk of their being confiscated. Another of the entrepreneur's objectives is to compete on a level playing field with the SOEs in the industry.[12] We can assume that no entrepreneurs entered the auto industry under the illusion that this would be achievable in the short term, yet the leaders of private firms continue to be vocal in their desires to compete on a level playing field.

Given the circumstances under which entrepreneurs must compete, one may wonder what would motivate an entrepreneur to enter an industry in which the state has already announced its intention to dominate for the long-term. While individual motivations are beyond the scope of this analysis, we may assume that, like entrepreneurs in any country, entrepreneurs in China are also extremely ambitious and drawn to activities requiring a high tolerance for risk. And in the case of the auto industry, at least some of the entrepreneurs also very likely have a great affinity for cars. As some of the cases will reveal, some entrepreneurs entered the auto industry in the 1990s and early 2000s—around the time that the central government was privatizing many SOEs and private business people were being welcomed to join the CCP under former Party secretary Jiang Zemin's theory of the "three represents."[13] As they joined the industry during a time in which private enterprise enjoyed a positive outlook in China, these entrepreneurs were confident that their own drive and managerial abilities would lead to a prominent role for private firms in China's auto industry. To put it mildly, the recent trend toward increased state control in pillar industries has introduced unexpected challenges for China's entrepreneurs.

Foreign Multinationals

The primary objective of foreign multinational automakers for being in China is the pursuit of profit and returns for shareholders. There are, of course, rules and limitations set out by China that circumscribe the extent of foreign activity in China and the extent to which the foreign multinationals can profit from that activity. The objectives of the foreign multinationals are both to maximize the space in which they are allowed to compete, and then to maximize the profit they can earn within that space.

Another objective of the foreign multinationals is to protect intangible assets such as their brands and other intellectual property. Corporate brands carry with them perceptions of quality, safety, and reliability for consumers, and while business in China does subject a foreign brand to risks, foreign multinationals attempt (some more successfully than others) to mitigate these risks in their pursuit of profit in the China market. The same may be said for intellectual property. Because corporations can invest billions of dollars in the design of a single vehicle, and hundreds of millions in the design of complex components, these firms all enter

China with the intention of protecting these assets from being stolen or copied by other companies.

The Outcomes

Now that we have a picture of the players and their objectives, let us take a look at the results generated by their interactions. Here I will view these outcomes in terms of each of the central government's four key objectives: consolidation, technology acquisition, development of Chinese brands, and development of NEVs.

Consolidation

Among the central government's most important policy priorities, consolidation is the most simple and straightforward to measure. And while the case studies will shed light on *how* consolidation has taken place—and, more importantly, how it has not—the question of *whether* consolidation has happened at all is a relatively easy question to answer, as I will do here.

Just looking at the raw numbers, many would agree that the central government's demand for consolidation has been completely justified. In 1978, the year that Deng Xiaoping launched the first experimental market reforms in China, there were 55 auto assemblers. The number peaked at 124 in the mid-1990s, and by 2008 there were still 117.[14] By any measure, there are simply too many automakers in China, and very little consolidation appears to have taken place since the 1980s. But how do the market shares of China's top automakers compare with those in the United States? Table 2.1 compares cumulative market shares of the Chinese and U.S. markets in 2010.

If China were to take the United States as its example, then it would seem to have already achieved a fair amount of consolidation at the top of its auto industry. China's largest auto group has a slightly larger share of its market than does the largest automaker in the United States, and the top five in both markets are practically even. Of course, the U.S. market is somewhat less concentrated than it used to be; in 1980 the Big Three held 76 percent of the U.S. market.[15] The point here is that,

Table 2.1   Cumulative Market Shares in U.S. and China
Markets, 2010 Auto Sales

	United States	China
Top company	19.1%	19.7%
Top 2 companies	35.6%	34.8%
Top 3 companies	50.9%	49.0%
Top 4 companies	61.5%	62.1%
Top 5 companies	70.8%	70.4%

Sources: United States: Ward's Auto; China: CAAM.

while the central government appears to have got its wish for consolidation at the top of its industry, it appears to have been losing the battle at the bottom of its industry which is still very heavily fragmented.

The primary strategy that the central government has adopted to encourage industry consolidation involves both market pressures and direct government intervention. On one hand, the central government has said that it wishes for the market to have the greatest role in encouraging the combinations of auto enterprises, yet, on the other hand, the central government has also taken an active role in pushing automakers together when it has felt pressure was warranted. These strategies have achieved outcomes for the central government that are, at best, mixed. On one hand, China's largest automakers have begun, albeit slowly, to conduct mergers, and these mergers, along with organic growth from the satisfaction of growing market demand, have resulted in about a dozen viable auto firms—including several with production capacity of over 2 million vehicles per year. On the other hand, there remain in operation approximately 70 to 80 small, inefficient auto assemblers that, for some reason, the market has not driven out of business. (I will address how I arrived at this number of "70 to 80" in Chapter Six)

Why do these small, inefficient firms continue to operate? Because they are being protected by local governments whose leaders have job performance incentives built around local economic growth and social stability. Why has the central government not simply stepped in to complete the job of consolidation where the market has not? Because these 70 to 80 small, inefficient automakers actually help local governments to support one of the central government's primary goals: social stability. This brings us full circle to see how the central government has two primary goals that are contradictory: social stability and a competitive auto industry. The central government can and does take action to get what it wants, but it must balance these competing goals, and when push comes to shove, social stability wins.

Similarly, the central government has established policies designed to prevent new auto firms from being established, yet new auto firms have been established anyway. This has happened, again, because local governments, operating under performance incentives to deliver both economic growth and social stability, have been willing to help local automakers, whether state-owned or private, to become established under the radar. Once the central government has become aware of the existence of these firms, it finds itself torn between its contradictory goals of building a competitive auto industry (with resources devoted not to establishment of small firms, but to strengthening of large firms) and maintaining social stability. Closing the small firms would send the message that resources should not be "wasted" starting new automakers, but keeping them open helps to avoid the risk of social unrest in the event a business is closed and hundreds of workers become unemployed. Here again, the central government has had to compromise on its objectives.

Technology Acquisition

In the 1980s the central government already believed acquisition of foreign technology was key to development of Chinese industry. With respect to its auto industry, however, the government did not clearly define what it meant by "technology transfer," and this lack of specificity resulted in very little useful transfer of technology from the MNCs to their Chinese partners. Over time, however, the specificity has increased, and the means by which these demands are made have become more creative.

While technology transfer and acquisition are difficult to measure with any precision, I would like to suggest three basic scales, or hierarchies of skills, that may be used as rough yardsticks to measure the success of China's auto industry in the acquisition of technology.[16]

Figure 2.1   Hierarchy of Vehicle Assembly

One scale measures the degree of sophistication in vehicle assembly, another measures sophistication in components manufacturing, and another measures the degree to which the benefits of these activities accrue to China. My use of these hierarchies is for illustrative purposes only; they are not intended to imply any measure of precision. While different auto assembly firms have different degrees of in-house component manufacturing versus outsourcing of parts, in this case we want to look at this from the point of view of the central government, which assesses the capabilities of China's auto industry as a whole.

In terms of auto assembly, a company starts with the most basic activity of assembling CKDs or "complete knock-down" kits. This requires only the bare minimum of assembly skills as no parts are made in-house. SKD's or "semi-knock-down" kits are often referred to as incomplete kits, meaning that the factory must either acquire or man-ufacture additional parts to complete the vehicle. This extra step requires a higher level of engineering skills than mere assembly of CKDs. The next step up is the ability to copy the designs of existing vehicles and to assemble them, and at the very top of the scale lies the ability to design complete, unique vehicles. The points on this hierarchy (Figure 2.1) are not discrete, but continuous, and as the case studies will reveal, indi-vidual Chinese automakers tend to be spread out along this hierarchy at many different points.

In terms of component manufacture (Figure 2.2), the lowest end of the scale is manufacture of the simplest of vehicle components includ-ing nuts, bolts, fittings, and wiring harnesses. The next step up would include more complex subassemblies, some electrical components, and

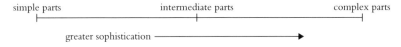

Figure 2.2   Hierarchy of Component Manufacturing

engineered components such as gears and some engine parts. Then, at the high end, are the more complex parts such as on-board computers, complete engines, transmissions, electronic fuel-injection systems, anti-lock brakes, body panels, and chassis.

The best way to determine where China's auto industry lies on these hierarchies is not to listen to what auto companies *say*, but rather to observe the results they achieve. For example, a company may claim that it has developed advanced lithium-ion battery technology or a continuously variable transmission, but the company must also be able to demonstrate the viability of its technologies by putting them in vehicles that consumers are willing to buy. And, for the purposes of this analysis, I remain agnostic as to whether a Chinese firm develops its own auto technology or buys it from another firm. *The key question is whether the Chinese industry possesses certain types of technologies and is able to deploy them without infringing on the legitimate intellectual property rights of others.*

From the central government's point of view, the larger question is whether the players in China's auto industry are able to derive the greatest benefit from deployment of advanced technologies. In this sense there exists yet another hierarchy, an intellectual property (IP) hierarchy (Figure 2.3). Paying royalties to a foreign company for every instance of usage of a particular technology would be the least preferable state of affairs. Purchasing technology (along with full IP rights) would be the next most desirable, and having the ability to develop one's own technology would be the most preferable state of affairs. "Preferable" here means that more benefits accrue to China.

There are a few caveats about this scale. First, purchase of foreign technology could be more cost-effective for a Chinese company than self-development of its own technology—especially if the purchasing firm simply does not have the in-house capability of self-development. Second—and foreign MNCs should already be aware of this—illicit copying of foreign technology is probably *the* most cost-effective

Figure 2.3   Hierarchy of Intellectual Property Benefit

strategy of all for a Chinese firm, at least in the short-term (assuming a firm has the capability of copying acquired components). However, China's membership in the WTO and increasing integration with the global economy have made this strategy increasingly difficult (though not impossible) to carry out over the long-term.

In terms of outcomes China's auto industry has, without question, achieved considerable progress. On the vehicle assembly hierarchy (Figure 2.1), the industry has moved from assembling CKDs in the 1980s to just the right side of "copy design." (The reader may feel free to disagree with the precise placement of this point. Again, the point here is not precision, but to illustrate that China's auto industry as a whole has moved the ball down the field.) While some Chinese manufacturers have become more creative in terms of overall vehicle design, the vast majority are still producing foreign models or domestic-branded cars that bear resemblance to foreign models.

On the components manufacturing hierarchy (Figure 2.2), the industry has moved from producing only simple parts in the 1980s to production of some complex parts now. Among the more complex parts being produced are transmissions and certain types of advanced internal combustion engines, the technology of which has, until now, been mostly purchased from abroad. There are still, however, many complex parts for which the industry relies on foreign suppliers.

On the intellectual property benefit hierarchy (Figure 2.3), the industry has moved from foreign licensing in the 1980s to somewhere between purchase and self-development of technology. While purchase of technology also involves acquisition of intellectual property, it still begins with an outflow of cash from China to a foreign supplier. While this may, for now, be more cost effective for the average Chinese company than self-development, it does not conform with the central government's objective that the benefits eventually accrue only to Chinese firms.

One broader measure of the advancement of China's technical capability is whether it has been able to export its cars to the developed world as Japan and Korea had been able to do within 20 years of the launch of their respective passenger car industries. The ability to export cars to developed markets is an indicator not only of the ability to pass safety and emissions inspections, but also of consumer acceptance of the industry's technology offerings. By the early 1980s, the Japanese had become so successful at exporting their cars to the United States that they became subject to "voluntary" export restraints forced upon them by the Reagan administration. Korean autos also later became subject to import tariffs in the United States. Not only was China unable to export to the developed markets within 20 years (which would have been around the early 2000s), but as of this writing almost all of China's exports are going primarily to other developing countries, with only a small number of Great Wall SUVs going to Italy and Australia.

The central government's technology acquisition strategies have shifted over the years in response to the counterstrategies of other industry players. In the 1980s the central government expected the formation of joint ventures naturally to result in transfer of foreign technology and know-how to Chinese SOEs, but this did not happen. It did not happen because, foreign automakers, whose objectives include protection of intellectual property were not eager to hand over corporate secrets that had cost them billions of dollars to develop. The central government's strategy then shifted to more specific and overt demands of technology transfer to which foreign automakers would have to agree if they wanted access to China's markets. But China also wanted to join the WTO, and as a member, it was forced in 2001 to give up the right to demand technology transfer as a condition for approval of foreign investment in China.

One might have predicted that WTO membership would have dampened China's enthusiasm for foreign partners, thereby causing China to halt approval of Chinese-foreign joint ventures. But in fact JVs have continued to be formed since 2001. There are two reasons why JVs continue to be important for China's auto industry. First, the central government gradually realized the foreigners were generating something equally as important as technology: cash. As a prominent East Asia auto industry analyst explained it to me, "the joint ventures are still an important part of the system. They help the SOEs generate cash which the SOEs can plow back into R&D." Rather than forbidding future JVs, restricting their operations or even throwing the foreigners out of China for not handing over their most advanced technologies, China's government has pragmatically recognized that the foreign multinationals are providing something else every bit as useful in China's pursuit of a competitive automotive industry.

The second reason why the foreign multinationals continue to be welcomed is that the central government still sees them as a source of technology—even if they have to bend WTO rules a little to get it. The central government's shift in strategy demonstrates a certain amount of creativity in how it has managed to balance its own objectives with its obligations to the WTO. This is where the central government's objectives of technology acquisition and development of Chinese brands begin to overlap.

Chinese Brand Development

Some observers may dismiss the importance of local brands, wondering why the central government would focus on development of local brands when Chinese automakers are selling massive numbers of foreign-branded cars. The importance here is, once again, linked to where the money flows. As (legitimate) use of foreign technology results in money flowing out of China, so does the manufacture and sale of foreign brands—hence the central government's increasingly insistent focus on development of Chinese brands. The deeper meaning here is that eventual Chinese dominance of this industry is, at this time, a higher priority for the central government than is affordable access to high quality automobiles for Chinese consumers. There is no judgment in this statement; it is a simple fact.

As with consolidation, the market share of Chinese versus foreign brands is relatively straightforward to measure. Table 2.2 presents passenger car sales from 2004 through 2010 and the market shares of Chinese brands. Though Chinese brands stagnated with approximately

Table 2.2 Market Share of Chinese Brand Passenger Cars, 2004 to 2010

Units = Thousands of Cars	2004	2005	2006	2007	2008	2009	2010
Total passenger cars	2,313	2,768	3,870	4,798	5,047	7,471	9,495
Chinese branded passenger cars	484	727	984	1,245	1,308	2,217	2,933
Chinese brand market share	20.9%	26.3%	25.4%	25.9%	25.9%	29.7%	30.9%

Sources: *China Auto Bluebook*, 2010, 252; Xinhua News Agency, January 14, 2011.

25 percent of the market in the mid-2000s, from 2008 to 2009, Chinese brands grew by nearly 4 percent of total. This was due primarily to the central government's stimulus measures that boosted sales of small, fuel-efficient cars, a segment in which, at the beginning of 2009, Chinese brands held an approximate market share of 85 percent.[17] In 2010, as more foreign manufacturers entered the small-car segment, and as the central government scaled back the stimulus, the market share of Chinese brands only grew by about 1 percent.

As China's market continues to grow, foreign automakers already doing business in China are applying to the central government for permission to expand, and in the process they are encountering new demands for technology transfer, but this time, the demands are only implicit—which may also explain why no foreign country has yet brought charges against China for violating the spirit of its WTO agreement in this regard. In order to gain permission to expand, the foreign multinationals are being urged to help their Chinese SOE partners to develop Chinese-branded cars, or, as I will refer to them throughout this book, "JV brands."[18] Faced with the choice to pour billions of dollars into development of cars that would compete with their own brands, most of the foreign automakers have chosen instead to contribute slightly out-of-date technology that will then be built and sold under a Chinese brand name. In this way the central government is helping to create more opportunities for Chinese automakers to learn and improve, and foreign automakers are gaining approval for expansion, but possibly at the cost of helping their future competitors to improve their abilities to build cars.

Table 2.3 illustrates the significance of this development. When China began its reforms in the late 1970s, it had essentially two options

Table 2.3 Types of Passenger Cars Sold in China

	(1) Imports	(2) Foreign Brands	(3) JV Brands [NEW]	(4) Chinese Brands
Technology	外	外	外	中
Brand	外	外	中	中
Where built	外	中	中	中

外 = foreign
中 = Chinese

to provide vehicles for the Chinese market. It could import cars, or it could make them itself. These options are represented by columns 1 and 4, respectively. At the time, Chinese automakers had very little to offer from column 4. Then, by inviting foreign automakers into China to build their own cars in Chinese factories beginning in the 1980s, China was able to offer its consumers reliable foreign technology and brands that were built in China. This is represented by column 2, and to this day, these are the cars that dominate China's market for passenger cars.

From the mid-1980s until the late 2000s, columns 1, 2, and 4 were really the only choices Chinese consumers had, but there was, and still is, a vast gap in perception of quality between columns 2 and 4. Column 3, JV brands, represents the compromise reached in the dueling technology transfer strategies between the central government and the foreign multinationals to which I referred above. After years of not getting the degree of technology transfer it wanted from the foreign multinationals in exchange for market access, the central government appears to have arrived at an ingenious compromise. Only time will tell whether this proves to have been a winning strategy.

The case studies will demonstrate that the SOEs have been less than enthusiastic in their support for this central government objective. While they *have* invested, the state-owned automakers have been reluctant to invest heavily in this area, and their reluctance stems from SOE leaders' job performance incentives which are built around profitability and getting bigger. The best route to these objectives for the SOEs is to continue producing mostly foreign-branded cars from which they can earn big profits, and not from plowing large sums into R&D that would only benefit future SOE leaders. In response, the central government has simply applied greater pressure to develop Chinese brands, and as a result, SOEs have belatedly, and reluctantly, begun to devote minimal resources toward this objective.

Fortunately for the central government, the private firms' objectives are more closely aligned with the central government on development of Chinese brands. But private firms are not driven to support central government policy as much as they are driven by the need to survive. Without foreign partners on whose technology they can rely, the private firms have, until now, had no choice other than to develop their own brands. But while this is good news for the central government, it also has a downside. Because the smaller private companies have greater difficulty raising funds than SOEs (they lack both government connections to the state-owned banks and foreign brands that they could sell), the quality, at least initially, of Chinese-branded cars has come to be viewed by Chinese consumers as inferior to that of foreign brands. Though the central government was initially antagonistic toward the private firms (as the central government was trying to combat fragmentation in the industry), in recent years it has begun to offer token support to some private firms for expansion and research. But this token support continues to pale in comparison to that enjoyed by the SOEs.

Subsequent chapters will explain in greater detail how and why Chinese brands became such an important focus and also why it has been difficult for the industry to produce more satisfying growth in this area.

New Energy Vehicle Development

Development of new energy vehicles (NEV) is still a relatively new policy focus for the central government, and also its most proactive. Whereas consolidation, technology acquisition and Chinese brand policies are presented as solutions to existing problems, the push for China's automakers to develop vehicle technologies of the future is an attempt to take advantage of a perceived level playing field and to get ahead of the foreign multinationals. Yet, because this is a nascent policy focus—not only for China, but also for the MNCs—progress is difficult to measure.

Arguably the Chinese automaker furthest along in NEV development is BYD, a private automaker which announced the impending availability of the world's first production plug-in hybrid vehicle, the F3DM, in December of 2008.[19] But as the case study on BYD will reveal, the company was much slower getting the F3DM to market than it had planned, not making it available to Chinese consumers until May of 2010. BYD's pure electric E6, which was originally to have been sold in the United States in 2009 has been postponed indefinitely, though it entered service on an experimental basis in the local taxi fleet of BYD's hometown, Shenzhen, in 2010. According to analysis by *China Car Times* only about 1,000 Chinese-branded NEVs were put into service in all of China in 2010, most of them by taxi or municipal fleets, but it is early yet to call China's efforts in this area a complete success or failure.[20] If the central government's initial target of production capacity of 500,000 NEVs by the end of 2011 is taken as the objective, then the lack of progress so far must be considered a failure—at least temporarily.[21]

As was also the case with Chinese brand development, SOEs have been less than enthusiastic in their pursuit of NEV development; however, despite the fact that none has thus far begun to market NEVs to consumers, all appear to be devoting money to R&D in this area. Unexpectedly, the private players, with BYD in the lead, seem to be slightly ahead of the SOEs in NEV development in that several private players do have NEVs on the market—even if consumers are not yet eager to buy them. For its part, the central government has introduced consumer subsidies to encourage purchase of these vehicles, but so far the subsidies are only available in six mainland cities. Several local governments have also demonstrated enthusiasm for this objective by partnering with automakers and electric utilities to build electric charging stands.

Conclusion

The case studies and policy analysis in the following chapters reveal many of the details that explain the outcomes we have seen in this industry. Of key importance here is that the factors that have influenced the development of this industry are macro-level factors. That is, they exist at a higher level than simply that of a single industry, and therefore, they affect China's industrial development at large. Among the most important observations that arise from the analysis is that China's central government holds tightly to the, at times, contradictory goals of social stability and development of competitive industry. The compromise, with respect to the auto industry, that the central government has chosen by default is essentially to have two auto industries: a handful of large, competitive enterprises at the top, and a mass of small, inefficient players at the bottom.

This contradiction may be more easily solved were it not for the contradictory incentives faced by local governments and SOEs. The pursuit of promotion by local state and SOE leaders sometimes leads to actions that are incompatible with the objectives of the central government. And the central government has, until now, not acted to remedy these incompatible incentives. To do so would risk its key overarching goal of regime survival.

Nevertheless, China's central government has managed to nurture robust industries out of the moribund state of its economy at the end of the Cultural Revolution. In terms of the auto industry, it has also helped to turn China into the world's largest market for passenger cars, a factor that has brought every major foreign automaker to China's doorstep, ready to negotiate for a piece of China's market. But the presence of these foreign MNCs has acted as a double-edged sword for China's automakers. On one hand they are an indispensable source of both cash generated from car sales and the world's best automotive technologies. On the other hand, the cash generated by sales of foreign brands has served as a disincentive for China's largest automakers, the SOEs, to devote significant sums to development of the Chinese brands that the central government demands.

China's private automakers, on yet another hand, while highly incentivized to build and sell Chinese-branded cars, lack the level of government support and funding that the SOEs enjoy. As a China auto industry analyst explained it to me, "the tragedy of the Chinese auto industry is that you have private players who have passion, but no money, and you have SOEs with money, but no passion."

For three decades the foreign multinationals and China's central government have played a cat-and-mouse game over technology transfer, and it is easy to understand why: these two players *also* have conflicting objectives. The central government wants Chinese auto-makers to learn how to do everything the foreigners can do so that Chinese automakers will not only come to dominate their home mar-ket, but challenge the MNCs in overseas markets as well. The MNCs, on the other hand, simply want to grow their sales and profits to enrich their shareholders—preferably without giving away the shareholders' intellectual property in which they have invested billions of dollars in development.

China's central government has taken to heart Deng Xiaoping's maxim of "crossing the river while groping for stepping stones." Over the past three decades, mistakes have been made and contradictory objectives have been adopted, but the one constant that remains is a central government that is not afraid of changing course when a change is warranted—a central government that still aims to win.

Notes

1. On "too many mothers-in-law" (婆婆多) see Susan L. Shirk, *The Political Logic of Economic Reform in China* (Berkeley: University of California Press, 1993), 179; Edward S. Steinfeld, *Forging Reform in China: The Fate of State-Owned Industry* (Cambridge, UK: Cambridge University Press, 1998), 91.

2. David Shambaugh, *The Modern Chinese State* (Cambridge: Cambridge University Press, 2000), Ch. 5.

3. According to Shambaugh, "[The CCP's] principal goal is to strengthen its rule and remain in power as a single ruling party." David Shambaugh, *China's Communist Party: Atrophy and Adaptation* (University of California Press, 2008), 3; Richard McGregor, The Party: The Secret World of China's Communist Rulers (New York: Harper, 2010), 26–30.

4. The consensus around this goal for the auto industry may not have been as solid during the 1980s when the central government was still feeling its way through early reforms, but it has been an unquestioned goal since at least the time of Deng Xiaoping's 1992 *nanxun* or "southern tour" that firmly entrenched economic growth as a goal for the country. On Deng's southern tour, see: Richard Baum, *Burying Mao: Chinese Politics in the Age of Deng Xiaoping* (Princeton, NJ: Princeton University Press, 1994), 341–345.

5. According to Thun, the auto industry was first designated as a "pillar" industry in 1986. Eric Thun, *Changing Lanes in China: Foreign Direct Investment, Local Government, and Auto Sector Development* (New York: Cambridge University Press, 2006), 55.

6. The term "NEVs" or "new energy vehicles" will be used frequently throughout this book. It refers to vehicles that do not run primarily on traditional ICE (internal combustion engine) technologies (i.e., purely gasoline-driven engines). It is the translation of the Chinese term "新能源汽车" (*xin nengyuan qiche*). Examples include hybrids, plug-in hybrids, pure electric vehicles, hydrogen fuel-cell vehicles and vehicles that run on alternative fuels such as ethanol, compressed natural gas (CNG), and liquefied petroleum gas (LPG).

7. O'Brien and Li describe the "cadre responsibility system" through which higher levels of government measure the job performance of lower level officials. They contend that the most quantifiable of measures (such as economic growth) become the most important factors for promotion. Kevin J. O'Brien and Lianjiang Li, "Selective Policy Implementation in Rural China," *Comparative Politics* 31, no. 2 (January 1, 1999), 167–186.

8. Hongbin Li and Li-An Zhou, "Political Turnover and Economic Performance: the Incentive Role of Personnel Control in China," *Journal of Public Economics* 89, nos. 9–10 (September 2005): 1743–1762.

9. McGregor, *The Party*.

10. A 2009 report by GaveKalDragonomics noted the NDRC's "obsession with Fortune 500 rankings." Yuxin He, "Chinese auto makers: The search for a car of one's own," GaveKalDragonomics China Insight, July 9, 2009.

11. The list of key industries was updated by SASAC chairman Li Rongrong in December of 2006. He said the state should "solely own, or have a majority share in" power generation, oil, petrochemicals, natural gas, telecommunications and armaments. The state must have a "controlling stake" in coal, aviation and shipping, and "become heavyweights" in machinery, automobiles, IT, construction, iron and steel, and nonferrous metals. See: Zhao Huanxin, "China names key industries for absolute state control," *China Daily*, December 19, 2006, www.chinadaily.com.cn/china/2006-12/19/content_762056.htm.

12. Among the advantages that SOEs enjoy over private firms is access to bank lending. For example, Ferri and Liu find that private Chinese firms pay interest rates that are, on average, more than 700 basis points greater than that charged to SOEs. Giovanni Ferri and Li-Gang Liu, *Honor Thy Creditors Beforan Thy Shareholders: Are the Profits of Chinese State-Owned Enterprises Real?* (Hong Kong Institute for Monetary Research, April 2009), http://ideas.repec.org/p/hkm/wpaper/162009.html.

13. The theory of "three represents" (三个代表) explained: Richard Baum, *China Watcher: Confessions of a Peking Tom* (Seattle: University of Washington Press, 2010), 262.

14. *CAIY*, 2009, 447.

15. Bernard Simon, Shannon Bond, and Emma Saunders, "In depth—Interactive graphic: The decline of US autos," *Financial Times*, FT.com, May 29, 2009, www.ft.com/cms/s/0/655892fa-4c83-11de-a6c5-00144feabdc0.html. The "Big Three," General Motors, Ford, and Chrysler, were formerly the three largest American automakers in terms of U.S. market share. Now that this is no longer the case (Japan's Toyota and Honda both outsold Chrysler in the United States in 2010), the former "Big Three" are now known as the "Detroit Three."

16. I would like to thank Barry Naughton for his suggestions on measuring technology transfer.

17. According to internal analysis shown to me by the China head of a foreign auto parts manufacturer.

18. Michael Dunne, "Launch a new brand in China—Whether you like it or not," *Automotive News China*, April 12, 2011, www.autonewschina.com/en/article.asp?id=6807; John Reed and Patti Waldmeir, "Foreign groups told to make Chinese cars," *Financial Times*, FT.com, March 20, 2011, www.ft.com/cms/s/0/4a5c8d82-5328-11e0-86e6-00144feab49a.html.

19. Toyota's Prius and Honda's Insight, both hybrids, had been available in Japan since the late 1990s and in the United States since the early 2000s, but neither was of the plug-in variety. Toyota's third generation Prius is a plug-in hybrid, but it would not be released for nearly two years following BYD's announcement about the F3DM.

20. "2010 Green Car Round Sales Round Up," *China Car Times*, January 13, 2011, www.chinacartimes.com/2011/01/13/2010-green-car-round-sales-round-up/.

21. This target, set by policy in 2009, will be discussed in Chapter Three.

Chapter Three

The Policy

Large-scale development of the auto industry is inevitable, and will probably become an important component of [China's] future economic growth.

—Premier Zhao Ziyang, 1984, *China Automotive Industry Yearbook* (1986).

There are a number of possible ways to break the story of China's automobile industry into manageable pieces. To better describe the evolving relationship between the industry and the Chinese party-state, I divide the evolution of the PRC's automobile industry policy into three distinct stages based on the broad policy vision of the central government. The first stage is the *state-centric* stage, which lasted roughly 30 years, from the founding of the PRC in 1949 until 1978, the year that Deng Xiaoping launched China's economic reforms. The second stage, *global partnering*, lasted from 1978 until China's WTO entry at the end of 2001. And the third stage, the *indigenous innovation* stage, has existed from 2002 to the present. Much of the analysis here is focused on the final two stages.

Even though these three stages are named based on the policy environment that existed at the time, my research does not find that Beijing's policy was faithfully implemented from the beginning to the end of each stage. As the case studies in later chapters will reveal, the story involves push and pull between central and local governments, between the state and industry, and between China and foreign multinationals (MNCs). This chapter will focus on what China's central government wanted to see in China's auto industry, what it did to make that happen, and the effects of policy. The story also looks at how local governments and automakers implemented, ignored, or thwarted policy, the results that ensued, and the policy adjustments that occurred in reaction to those results. The well-known Chinese saying that "the authorities have their measures, and the people have their countermeasures" (上有政策, 下有对策) appropriately describes both central-local and government-business interactions.

The purpose of this chapter is to lay out a timeline of policy development from the relaunch of China's auto industry in the late 1970s until the present. This chapter will highlight, among other things, the central government's key objectives of consolidation, technology transfer, Chinese brand development, and new energy vehicle (NEV) development. Policy analysis is important because it allows us to see at each step along the way what was most important to China's central government. Readers eager to get to the stories in later chapters may find this detailed policy analysis somewhat tedious; however, I would encourage the reader to at least skim this chapter as the analysis in this chapter places those stories in context.

In this particular chapter I rely primarily on a massive set of yearbooks produced by China's auto industry, and only secondarily on interviews, media and books by scholars and Chinese auto industry insiders. These *China Automotive Industry Yearbooks* (CAIYs) were produced sporadically beginning in the early 1980s and then annually after 1992. The government organization primarily responsible for these yearbooks has always been whichever organization functioned as the industry association or think tank at the time of publication. The value of printed resources (as opposed to electronic resources) is that, because libraries have physical possession of each yearbook, the contents of these yearbooks cannot be rewritten once they are printed. Though certain industry players may have fallen out of favor in subsequent years, or official assessment of them may have changed, the written record remains unaltered.

Stage One: State-Centric

The first stage of modern China's auto industry depended, as the name implies, solely on state planning. As there were no legal private businesses during the decades prior to the start of Deng Xiaoping's reforms in 1978, auto production was controlled by the state. And as there was essentially no consumer market aside from the basic necessities of life such as food and clothing (most of which were also controlled and allocated by the state) there existed no market for passenger cars aside from taxi services in the major cities and personal cars for China's leaders. Because the early focus of the People's Republic was on industrialization, central planners in Beijing aimed to ensure a steady supply of commercial vehicles—trucks and buses—that were needed to help a country beset by years of occupation and civil war get back on its feet.

Japan's occupation of China began in 1931 when the Imperial Army entered Manchuria (the northeast corner of modern China), and ended after the close of World War II in 1945. Though the occupation was in many ways devastating to Chinese society, the Japanese left behind an industrial base in Manchuria. And while China was fortunate enough to have gained from Japan some of the hardware necessary to support a commercial vehicle industry, it lacked much of the software or human expertise. In 1950 China reached out to the Soviet Union for help, and the USSR sent experts to help their communist brothers get their plans for an automobile industry off the ground, transferring designs for commercial trucks and a Jeep-like all-terrain vehicle.[1] Even at this early stage, China's leaders were already stressing "adoption of foreign methods and experiences."[2]

The first site for an auto factory chosen by the Chinese government was Changchun, capital of Jilin Province in northeast China. Here they located the First Auto Works (FAW), where they began producing trucks from Soviet designs in 1953. By 1958, FAW also began to produce the *Hongqi* limousine for state leaders, and that same year an auto factory in Shanghai began to produce a Phoenix model sedan. Unfortunately, political events and the disastrous economic policies of the Great Leap Forward (1958–1961) ensured that production of passenger cars never reached significant scale.[3] Also, the Sino-Soviet split, which had begun during the 1950s, became public in the early 1960s, leading to the exit of the Soviet experts, including those who were teaching the Chinese how to manufacture automobiles.

Not long after the Great Leap, Mao Zedong's Third Front campaign, begun in 1964, led to the dismantling of entire factories on China's east coast and their reconstruction far inland to protect China's industries against military attack.[4] While the factories may have been better protected, their scattered inland locations (along with China's undeveloped transport infrastructure) ensured that the supply chains of China's auto factories became even more inefficient. As of today, as many as one half of the original Third Front factories are still in place, including auto factories located in Hubei, Sichuan, and Shanxi Provinces.[5]

Prior to 1964, the auto industry had been overseen primarily by the First Ministry of Machine Building (FMMB), a powerful ministry that would continue to oversee the auto industry until 1982. Then, in a very brief period of devolution in the mid-1960s, China's President, Liu Shaoqi suggested the establishment of an "experimental automotive trust" named the China National Automotive Industry Corporation (CNAIC).[6] CNAIC was given authority over some 75 industrial plants including China's main auto factories in Changchun, Beijing, Nanjing, Chongqing and Wuhan.[7] Under CNAIC, China's auto industry prospered with automotive output increasing 64 percent (over an admittedly small base) from 1964 to 1965. CNAIC also approved the establishment of the Second Auto Works (SAW, a company that would later change its name to Dongfeng) in Shiyan, Hubei.

The success achieved under CNAIC was, unfortunately, short-lived, as it was interrupted by the Cultural Revolution (1966–1976). Annual vehicle production decreased by 64 percent during this time, and CNAIC, accused of being a "revisionist roader organization," was disbanded.[8] Though construction of the SAW factory began in

1967, Cultural Revolution chaos ensured production did not begin until 1975.[9]

During the Mao Zedong era, passenger cars were merely an after-thought. The communist paradise envisioned by Mao had little room for consumerism, much less convenience for the average citizen. From 1958, the year the first passenger car was assembled in the People's Republic, until 1978, China's entire auto industry barely managed to produce more than 600 cars in an average year.[10] The handful of cars that were manufactured went either to China's leaders or to taxi fleets in the larger cities. Richard Baum noted in his first trip to the PRC in 1975 that all of the taxis in Guangzhou appeared to be 1946 DeSoto-Plymouths. These had been imported when they were much newer and were being held together with "baling wire and electrical tape."[11] Such was the state of automobiles in China by the mid-1970s.

Following the death of Mao Zedong in 1976, there was a brief period of political upheaval until Deng Xiaoping was able to consolidate power and gain support for major economic reforms in 1978.[12] This was the year that supporters of the auto industry in China once again began to look beyond their borders for help. Only this time, they looked to the West.

Stage Two: Global Partnering

Following President Richard Nixon's trip to China in 1972, C. B. Sung, a Shanghai-born, American-educated businessman and former vice president of the Bendix Corporation, began traveling to China on occasion to give lectures in management to state officials. Following one of his lectures in 1978, he was approached by several cadres from the local Beijing Auto Works (BAW), the factory that had been producing "jeeps" from the same designs the Soviets had given them in the 1950s. The cadres asked Sung if he would help them find an American partner who could help them with the jeep factory. Sung then initiated contact with American Motors Corporation (AMC), owner of the Jeep brand, that ultimately led to the establishment of the Beijing-Jeep joint venture in 1984.[13]

Shanghai-Volkswagen also had its beginnings in 1978. According to Martin Posth, who would later lead Volkswagen's first joint venture in

China, the initial Chinese contact with Volkswagen occurred in November 1978 when a Chinese delegation arrived, unannounced and on foot, at the security gate of the Volkswagen plant in Wolfsburg, West Germany. One of the men, Zhou Zijian, announced to the guard through his interpreter, "I am the Chinese Machine Building Minister, and I would like to speak to somebody in charge at Volkswagen."[14] Casual observers may be surprised to learn that both AMC and Volkswagen were first approached by China, and not the other way around. While China made the first move, however, this did not mean that AMC and Volkswagen would get a free pass in the negotiations. The common Chinese negotiating tactic of playing the barbarians against each other was applied in both cases, as I will discuss in the case studies of these two joint ventures in Chapter Four.

Nineteen seventy-eight was perhaps the first year following the Cultural Revolution in which China enjoyed enough political stability that officials could begin to think seriously about industry. The fact that these contacts were initiated by the Chinese attests to the importance that at least some of China's leaders attached to having a viable auto industry. And unlike the Japanese and Koreans, whose respective auto industries were running strong by this time, the Chinese moved immediately to involve foreigners, the same foreigners whose brands had essentially been shut out of the Japanese and Korean auto markets. The Chinese did not yet understand how a viable auto industry should operate, so their first impulse was to reach out to those who did. The learning would come in time, but first priority was start building the vehicles that would support China's economic opening.

In the meantime, China was flooded with Japanese imports during the late 1970s and early 1980s. This followed from the call of Mao's successor, Hua Guofeng, for China to increase its technological imports from the West. Hua's rule did not last long, and his call for imports was tempered by Deng Xiaoping's stress on *learning* from the West.[15] It was under Deng's overall leadership that the auto industry's focus shifted from imports toward partnership with the foreign automakers. The hope was that Chinese workers would not only learn from the foreigners how to assemble cars, but also learn how to design them from the ground up. During the 1980s joint ventures were formed between Chinese companies and AMC of the United States, Volkswagen of Germany, and

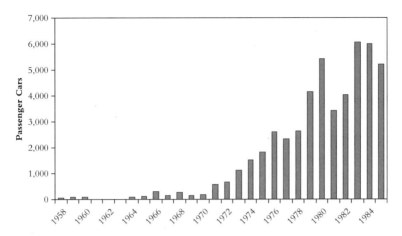

Figure 3.1   Passenger Car Production in China, 1958 to 1985
Source: China Automotive Industry Yearbook, 1986, p. 138.

PSA Peugeot-Citroën of France. Chinese automakers also licensed designs from Japanese automakers Daihatsu and Suzuki.

In the early days of economic reform, there were, of course, competing priorities. Not all of China's senior leaders agreed on the importance of an automobile industry, particularly one that produced passenger cars.[16] Personal ownership of vehicles would remain technically illegal until 1984, and even if ownership had not been illegal, few Chinese could afford to buy a car. Nevertheless, the Ministry of Machine Building Industry, along with local government officials in Beijing and Shanghai, continued to pursue their respective joint ventures with AMC and Volkswagen.

Meanwhile automotive assemblers and parts factories that had slowed production during the Cultural Revolution had begun to ramp up production once again. By 1980 annual vehicle production in China was 78 percent higher than it had been in 1977 (Figure 3.1). Nineteen eighty-one then saw a 20 percent pullback in production as China entered a period of political and economic backlash from conservatives on the Politburo.[17] This "retrenchment" led to an unintended financial decentralization as local regions sought to contend with a dramatic decrease in investment directed by Chen Yun at the central level.[18] In an effort to cope with apparent violent swings that were blamed on China's nascent quasi-market economy, China embarked on a bout of institutional reform including enterprise reforms, banking reforms, and even a new state constitution. It was out of this effort that the CNAIC, that former "revisionist roader organization," was reestablished to oversee China's automobile industry.

The new version of CNAIC that emerged in 1982 was, on paper, a powerful organization. It was headed by Rao Bin, a former Deputy Minister of Machine Building who was, according to Martin Posth of Volkswagen, "for all intents and purposes... China's automobile minister."[19] CNAIC also oversaw the major auto enterprises, FAW and SAW, as well as factories in Beijing, Tianjin, Shanghai, Jinan, Chongqing, and elsewhere. However, according to Harwit, CNAIC's powers were limited by its apparent lack of access to funds: the incomes of the factories flowed mostly to local governments.[20] CNAIC was, however, able to negotiate for itself a 25 percent stake in the eventual joint venture (JV) between Shanghai Automotive Industry Corporation (SAIC) and Volkswagen.

"Produce without Limits"

Its funding difficulties notwithstanding, CNAIC did play a key role in escalating the importance of the auto industry to the highest levels of leadership in China's State Council and economic planning apparatus. Though China lacked any real domestic automobile expertise, CNAIC also served as a think tank for the auto industry, producing analysis and policy recommendations that were submitted for consideration by senior leadership. In its very first policy recommendation document, CNAIC received the following instruction back from China's leaders: "As long as there is a market, produce without limits."[21]

The document had recommended to the State Council that the auto industry be accorded a strategic focus and that current production limits that remained as part of the old planned economy be abandoned.[22] The basic agreement and approval to "produce without limits" was a "*pishi*" (批示), or a marginal comment, handwritten by a member of the State Council, before the document was returned to CNAIC. Through this handwritten instruction, the CNAIC, nominal owner of all of China's automotive parts and assembly factories, was essentially given permission to abandon the planned economy and produce vehicles according to market demand. But old habits are hard to break: to this day China maintains a powerful economic planning apparatus, the National Development and Reform Commission (NDRC).

As the power of reformers waxed and waned during the 1980s, so did the attention paid to the auto industry by the highest levels of the state. Only a few years after its reestablishment, the CNAIC was, in effect, demoted by the State Council in 1987. The China National Automobile Industry *Corporation* was transformed into the China National Automobile Industry *Association*. (Though it continued to be known by the same English acronym, CNAIC.) As the new Association explained the change to its members, it was changing from

> a high-level, independent organization into one managed by its members, serving as a bridge between enterprises and the government...from directly managing enterprises through administrative means to guidance, service, indirect management and coordination...from decision-making as part of the government to providing advice and recommendations to the government.[23]

Upon its reestablishment in 1982, the CNAIC had been a very powerful government organ. Only five years later, in 1987, it was made into an association, a toothless support organization. In what sounds like a group reprimand, then Vice Premier Li Peng told gathered members of the organization upon announcing the change, "our auto industry is still relatively backward. It cannot meet the demands of other industries [for vehicles]. Variety and volume of products is lacking. We have to rely on imports for both heavy and light vehicles, causing us to spend the country's precious foreign exchange."[24]

Li's concerns about foreign exchange were not unfounded, and indeed, they highlight where priorities lay at the time. In addition to the need for auto industry expertise that led to the involvement of foreign multinationals, much government rhetoric at the time was infused with this almost obsessive focus on foreign exchange. And, in fact, this one point—how the Chinese-foreign JVs would generate foreign exchange—dominated the negotiations with China's prospective partners during the 1980s. The Chinese side wanted as much of the manufacturing process as possible to be localized as quickly as possible so that money need not flow out of China. On the other hand, the typical foreign point of view was that parts manufacture could only be localized to the extent that quality could be ensured.[25] Until that happened, the JVs would only be able to assemble CKDs (complete knock-down kits) shipped from overseas—and that required a lot of foreign exchange.

Early Five-Year Plans

Foreign exchange was also among the list of auto industry concerns as the industry began to insert itself into China's traditional five-year planning process. While the passenger car industry was not yet big enough to merit inclusion in the Seventh Five-Year Plan (1986–1990), CNAIC created its own adjunct plans intended to support the overall goals of China's economic planning apparatus through the Five-Year Plan. Though CNAIC was eventually dissolved, and its responsibilities handed to other organizations, this kind of planning has continued to the present day.

Among the top concerns of the industry in the Seventh Five-Year Plan were industry fragmentation, technology acquisition, and foreign exchange. At this early date, industry leaders had already become concerned that there were too many factories, and the stated goal for the industry was to "follow the lead of the backbone enterprises" (骨干企业) and "gradually form a number of enterprise groups" (集团).[26] No specifics were given as to which enterprises were considered to be "backbone enterprises," nor how enterprises were to form themselves into groups. At the time, all enterprises were still state-owned, and no stock market existed; therefore, China had (and still has) no market for corporate takeovers.

The planners already had in mind a system in which the industry would operate. Enterprises were to "make use of exports to get foreign exchange . . . make use of imports to get technology."[27] This explains why generation of foreign exchange was so important in negotiations with early JV partners. The joint ventures were counted upon to build cars and parts that could be exported (in addition to those to be built for the domestic market). Those exports would then generate foreign exchange needed to pay for imports of foreign made parts.

Figure 3.2 System Envisioned by Planners in the Mid-1980s

Those imports would bring Chinese automakers the technology they needed to advance their industry. With that technology in hand, the plan urges enterprises to "absorb equipment, technology and processes from overseas...[and] carry out improvements and innovation on imported car models."[28] (Figure 3.2 is a visual depiction of the intended system.) The most revealing aspect of this particular plan is in what it reveals about Chinese attitudes toward innovation—attitudes that persist to this day.[29] Innovation (创新) did not have to involve a complete reinvention of the wheel, merely an improvement on something China's foreign partners were already doing.

The system depicted in Figure 3.2 represents wishful thinking at the time that the mere presence of foreign auto assemblers would spontaneously generate a high-quality supply chain, but unfortunately, the cart (exports) came before the horse (technology). The volume of exports remained well below expectations in the early years because the expectations of the Chinese were unrealistic. China's planners had envisioned a fairly quick localization of parts production for cars assembled by the JVs, but the foreign partners resisted using locally made parts until the parts could be made according to their standards of quality and safety.[30] And the prospect of exporting locally assembled cars from imported parts was not feasible during the early years of the JVs due to the low productivity of inexperienced Chinese factory workers.

Without first mastering the technology, it would be impossible for China to sell exports, so the system never fully materialized. Shanghai-Volkswagen did manage to generate some foreign exchange by exporting engines made in Shanghai, and using those funds to buy CKDs from Volkswagen in Germany, but none of the early joint ventures ever successfully exported fully assembled cars.[31] The first year in which passenger cars were exported from China was 1989 when a total of six cars were exported. From 1989 to 2000, China only exported an average of 838 cars per year.[32]

If the JVs were not exporting cars, then where did the foreign exchange come from? Some of it came from export of parts that Chinese companies had already mastered, such as diesel engines and gears, to other developing countries.[33] The rest of it had to come from the joint venture partners. On the Chinese side of the partnerships, the only source for foreign exchange could have been the central government which has invested increasing amounts in the auto industry over the years, from 4 billion yuan under the Sixth Five-Year Plan (1981–1985) to 235 billion yuan under the Tenth Five-Year Plan (2001–2005).[34]

The Seventh Five-Year Plan envisioned that the industry would produce 600,000 vehicles by 1990. This target was reached two years early, in 1988, when China produced a total of 648,951 vehicles.[35] However, production dropped below the 600,000 mark in 1989 and 1990 during the upheaval following the unrest in Beijing in the spring of 1989 (after which Chinese companies had difficulty getting raw materials from overseas)[36] and subsequent backlash by conservative hardliners among Party leadership[37]—a clear demonstration of how China's macro-politics trickled down to affect the country's economic plans.

Big Three, Small Three

Though China's auto bureaucracy had been demonstrating its concern for the fragmented nature of China's auto industry since the early 1980s, 1988 seems to have been the first year in which the central government began to formulate policy aimed at solving this problem. The first such idea, discussed at the senior leaders' annual summer leadership conference at Bedaihe, was termed "big three, small three" (三大，三小). The instruction from senior leaders was for the industry to be consolidated around three "big" enterprises, First Auto, Second Auto (now Dongfeng), and Shanghai Auto, and three "small" joint venture enterprises, Beijing-Jeep, Guangzhou-Peugeot, and Tianjin Auto, that had a licensing agreement with Japan's Daihatsu. As with many political slogans in China, "big three, small three" suffered from a lack of details in terms of what the end goal was, how it would be reached, and who was responsible for its implementation, yet this same formulation would also appear in the auto industry's adjunct to the Eighth Five-Year Plan a few years later in 1991.[38] Despite the common use of this term at the time (the term was used innumerable times in auto industry documents and appeared 13 times in *People's Daily*, 1989–95), little if any effort was made by the central government to enforce this formulation.[39] China's *Automotive Industry Yearbooks* record no forced closures or mergers during the late 1980s.

In an effort to restrict market entry, the State Council passed a "notice" (通知) in late 1988 stating that, aside from the approved six enterprises (the big and small three), no other passenger car manufacturers could be established.[40] The wording of this notice would seem to have implied that, at the time, there existed no other enterprises in China aside from these six that had been approved to produce passenger cars; however, the auto industry's own statistics demonstrate that several manufacturers not listed among the six introduced new passenger car models in both 1991 and 1994. Among the local governments that approved production of these ostensibly illicit passenger car models were Guizhou Province, Guangxi Autonomous Region and the cities of Chongqing and Xi'an.[41] Though each of these upstarts entered production at a very small scale, knowledge of this may have been a signal to other local governments that Beijing was not serious in its attempts to limit market entry.

The Eighth Five-Year Plan

The Eighth Five-Year Plan (1991–1995) was introduced during the post-1989 period of conservative backlash, and contained mostly variations on a common theme. Whereas the previous plan had called for innovation through improvement of foreign technology, this plan simply wanted it done faster. It also built the "big three, small three" formulation into the plan, and once again, contained no concrete steps of how that target was to be achieved. The plan also sought to limit market entry by forbidding local areas from starting their own automakers outside of the plan.[42]

Continued concern on the part of the senior leadership was indeed warranted as the number of enterprises producing complete vehicles (including cars, trucks, and buses) had increased from 55 at the beginning of reforms in 1978 to 120 in 1991.[43] (These figures bear remarkable similarity to those of the U.S. auto industry at the turn of the twentieth century: in 1900 the United States had 57 automakers, and by 1905 there were 121.[44])

Where this plan differed from before was in taking a harder stance toward imports of foreign cars. By this time it had become abundantly clear that foreign brands dominated China's market for passenger cars, so the plan called for the industry to limit the number of imported cars.[45] And in a clear indication that China had yet to shake off the yoke of central planning, the industry's quantitative target was once again based on supply rather than demand. The industry set a production target of 900,000 vehicles by 1995 (from 509,000 in 1990), a target that it very easily surpassed with 1,452,737 vehicles produced in 1995.[46]

The 1994 Auto Policy

As CNAIC and economic planners prepared China's first auto industrial policy in 1994, the Communist Party's Finance Leading Small Group (LSG) sent instructions and warnings to the auto industry through CNAIC. This seems to be the earliest realization at the top that China was not going to get all of the advanced technology it wanted by simply forming joint ventures and hoping their foreign partners would share everything. The LSG's document said, "We cannot import the most advanced technology. The technology we get in this manner is only second-rate.[47] To improve your development capability, [the industry enterprises] cannot all act in isolation. You must find a suitable way to tackle this problem collectively... Consider whether you are *using* foreign capital or *being used by* foreign capital."[48] At this time, China's leaders had come to believe that the joint ventures were not yielding technology, yet they did not discontinue the policy of encouraging Chinese-foreign partnerships.

The 1994 Automotive Industry Policy, promulgated by the State Planning Commission in February of that year, was not only China's first official, comprehensive policy statement aimed at the auto industry, but it was also modern China's very first industrial policy for *any* industry.[49] Its first sentence acknowledges that, in China's auto industry at that time, "investment is scattered, production is still small-scale, and product technology is backward."[50] The aims of the policy were to "strengthen the development capability of the enterprises, lift product quality, rationalize industrial organization...to make China's auto industry a pillar industry of the people's economy by 2010."[51]

The 1994 policy was also the first in which the state began to offer specifics on which auto firms the state would support going forward. The criteria for receiving the state's support, however, still betrayed a command economy mentality as the focus continued to be on production capacity, not market demand. The state also, as can be seen in the first bullet point below, began to recognize the importance to the Chinese auto industry of being able to offer Chinese-designed vehicles—though, aside from some trucks and buses, at the time, practically none were on offer. Under the new policy, companies eligible for state support would have to demonstrate the following qualities:

- Produce independent products (独立产品).
- Demonstrate ability in technology development.
- Have a measurable market share.
- Have a minimum level of production.[52]

In addition, the policy published quantitative criteria that firms would have to meet in order to receive support. If companies met the following criteria by the end of 1995, they could receive state support, as shown in Table 3.1.

The support specified for companies meeting these criteria were:

- Zero percent tax rate on fixed asset investments.
- Priority for stock market listings or issuance of securities.

Table 3.1 1994 Auto Policy, Criteria for State Support

If a company (or group company) can demonstrate...			the state will...
Annual production capacity	Annual sales	R&D as a percentage of sales	Support increase in production capacity to
300K vehicles	200K vehicles	3.0%	600K vehicles
150K vehicles	100K vehicles	2.5%	300K vehicles
100K vehicles	80K vehicles	2.0%	200K vehicles

- "Active support" from banks.
- Priority use of foreign exchange.
- Policy loans for companies manufacturing economy passenger cars and key parts for passenger cars.
- Captive finance companies would be approved to expand their scope.[53]

And, in an attempt to discourage small players from entering the industry, the policy set a minimum production capacity of 150,000 cars for firms producing passenger cars with engine sizes 1.6 liters or smaller.[54] However, as China would learn from application of similar criteria to other industries, rather than discouraging the entry of smaller players, such requirements merely forced smaller players to plan their factories with unused excess capacity.[55]

The policy also included encouragement and support to establish research and development centers. And in a continuation of previous policy, auto firms were encouraged to "digest and absorb foreign technology [in order to] form independent product development capability."[56] Again, innovation, as envisioned by China's policy, did not require development of new, breakthrough technologies. It merely required Chinese firms to learn everything they could from their foreign partners, absorb the technology, then use it to create "independent" Chinese products.

This policy was also the first to place explicit limits on foreign investment in China's auto industry. Though no foreign multinationals held more than a 50 percent share of the joint ventures launched by 1994, this limit was enshrined in policy at this time.[57] Foreign multi-nationals were also forbidden from having more than two different joint venture partners for manufacturing passenger cars in China.[58] Perhaps the precedent had already been set by Volkswagen, which had already established JVs with both Shanghai Auto and First Auto Works.

The 1994 auto policy contained not only further limits on market entry, but also targets for consolidation. By this time the central government imposed a moratorium on new vehicle enterprises until the end of 1995, and this moratorium was apparently effective as the total number of auto assemblers remained steady at 122 from 1994 through 1996.[59] And, possibly taking its cue from the "Big Three" dominance of the U.S. market, the policy laid out a target for industry consolidation into "three or four large, globally competitive auto firms" by 2010.[60]

The 1994 policy also introduced a system of product certification (汽车产品型式认证制度) that, while ostensibly focused on ensuring safety, pollution control and energy conservation, was also, according to industry insiders, used as a tool for preventing market entry by small, local enterprises.[61] Automobile models that received certification would be listed in a catalogue (目录). Any automobile not listed in the official catalogue could not be issued a license by the local Public Security Bureau.[62] As some of the case studies will demonstrate, this certification process did not prevent market entry by startup firms, but it did require more creativity on the part of local governments and entrepreneurs who were compelled to skirt the rules.

The Ninth Five-Year Plan

For unexplained reasons, the *Auto Industry Yearbooks* contain little in the way of detail for the Ninth Five-Year Plan beyond a few statistical targets. Perhaps this is because the Ministry of Machinery Industry (MMI, the ministry charged with oversight of the auto industry at the time) focused much of its attention on a new quality standards campaign. Accordingly, the auto industry's discussion of the latest five-year plan also focused heavily on the quality campaign.

For starters, the industry set targets for both production capacity by 2000 and actual production, but still made no mention of anticipated demand. Capacity was to reach 3 million vehicles and actual production was to have reached 2.7 million vehicles.[63] This was an ambitious goal as the industry had only produced 1.45 million vehicles in 1995, and would only produce 2.07 million in 2000.[64]

A curiously *un*ambitious goal the industry set was for domestically produced passenger cars to "reach and maintain" a market share of 80 percent.[65] The goal refers to "domestically *produced*" (国产), not "domestically *branded*" (自主品牌) passenger cars (轿车), which are a subset of domestically produced passenger cars. The reason I believe this goal was unambitious is that, by my rough calculations, the market share of domestically produced vehicles surpassed the 80 percent mark during 1996 and never looked back, reaching 94 percent the following year.[66]

I also highlight this particular goal to point out that, at this time, the focus of the auto industry still seemed to be on import substitution, even though it had already achieved great success in that area. Furthermore, there was still no real focus on the *brands* of those domestically produced vehicles, a focus that would not become important until the next Five-Year Plan.

During the period of the Ninth Five-Year Plan, the auto industry chose to focus its planning on the MMI's quality standards campaign. Among the provisions highlighted in industry documents were a push to achieve international quality certifications and to reach levels of international standards in all vehicles. The industry set a goal for all automotive enterprises to obtain ISO9000 quality certifications by 2000.[67] The ISO9000 is a family of certification standards managed by the International Standards Organization that serves to assure customers, suppliers and other stakeholders that an organization has put in place certain standards and management systems to ensure quality. The industry also set the goal that all vehicles currently under production must meet at least late-1980s international standards, and any newly developed vehicles must meet mid-1990s international standards— though without explaining how such standards would be measured.[68] And also worthy of note, the industry ordered makers of passenger cars to adhere to minimum standards of guarantees for consumers. Depending on the size of the car, beginning in 2000, all cars were to carry a warranty of two to three years or 40,000 to 60,000 kilometers.[69]

The Late 1990s: Getting Serious about Policymaking

By 1997, the phenomenon of entrepreneurs skirting the rules to enter the auto industry began to draw the attention of China's senior leaders. The State Council, at the urging of a host of state organizations, released a notice to the auto industry recognizing violations of auto industry policy and rules surrounding management of the aforementioned auto "catalogue."[70] The notice pointed out that auto companies, with support of local governments, had been surreptitiously conducting negotiations with foreign automakers and starting their own joint ventures, only later presenting the central government with *faits accompli*.[71] Among other methods of rule breaking acknowledged by the

State Council was the purchase of certification for approved vehicles, then illegally transferring the certification to unapproved models or to modified vehicles.

But the 1994 policy, rather than providing for punishments and enforcement, had instead merely set up certification procedures and a national catalogue that were intended to prevent the very proliferation of automobile firms that was now happening in plain view of everyone. In a classic case of 上有政策，下有对策 ("the authorities have their measures, the people have their countermeasures"), local governments were making an end run around the policy, and apparently suffering no consequences from Beijing.

The State Council's notice instituted a list of new reporting requirements for auto firms; although, if there had been difficulty in getting accurate and timely reports under the previously minimal requirements, it is doubtful that local governments would have had much incentive to devote yet more time to yet more reports. There were, however, a few enforcement provisions that may have given local governments pause. Auto firms found to be in violation of reporting requirements for new project investment would be investigated by the State Administration of Industry and Commerce, and those found to be in serious violation could even have their existing (legally acquired) certifications revoked. However, it is possible local governments viewed this as a hollow threat, gambling that the central government would not wish to be responsible for closing a factory that employed hundreds or perhaps thousands of workers.[72]

Until the mid-1990s, China's leadership knew they wanted an automobile industry, and they knew that demand for passenger cars by private citizens would continue to increase, yet they also knew the quality of cars produced in China continued to trail that of cars made in Japan, Europe, and North America. And until this time, policies aimed at the automobile industry had remained very general in nature, offering high-level aspirations and highlighting the symptoms of problems within the industry, but offering very little in the way of specific directions for reaching desired goals.

This began to change in the latter half of the 1990s, which saw passage of a plethora of new policies related to the auto industry. During a period which coincided roughly with the early years of the Zhu

Rongji Premiership, China adopted policies on the following aspects of the auto industry:

1997[73]

- Market entry limitations.
- Used vehicle scrappage.
- Sales taxes on new vehicles.

1998[74]

- Auto rental market.
- Used car market.
- Inspection regime for imported vehicles and parts.
- Maintenance standards for transport vehicles.
- Initial limits on sale of leaded fuels and manufacture of vehicles burning leaded fuels.
- Inspection regime for vehicle pollution.

1999[75]

- Establishment of a VIN (vehicle identification number) system.
- A more comprehensive policy on vehicular pollution control along with more specific regulations on fuels and technology.
- Specifications for headlights, taillights, fog lights, turn signals, reflectors, back-up lights, and so on.
- A ban on use of CFCs (chlorofluorocarbons) in auto air conditioning.
- State Environmental Protection Agency added to list of organizations required to approve auto model changes.

With the exception of the reinforced market entry rules in 1997, each of these sounds like it may have been modeled after rules that had been enacted in the developed auto markets over prior decades.

Toward the end of 1999, the State Machinery Industry Bureau released a notice announcing that the state would continue to support the consolidation of the auto industry into three main players: FAW, SAIC, and Dongfeng (formerly Second Auto Works).[76] As of this time, these three SOEs had remained the top three assemblers in the industry since their founding. The bureau expressed its disappointment that the technology of China's "big three" still relied on foreign partners, and that their competitive position was still "relatively weak." Driving their concern was the knowledge that "in the new millennium, import tariffs on cars and parts would decrease, and market protection policies would be reduced [due to China's WTO entry agreements]. This would leave the industry to face a serious situation requiring [the state] to carry out a structural adjustment to the industry."[77] The Bureau made clear that its aim was to increase the competitive position of China's auto industry and to pursue consolidation in order to make that happen. The Bureau ended its notice with a veiled threat:

> with the "big three" as the core [of the industry], structural adjustment of the industry must give full play to the effect of market mechanisms ... The government will not give an executive order [to force consolidation], but, in its position as owner of state assets, the government will not rule out organizing and coordinating to reduce [domestic] competition in order to reduce losses on state assets.[78]

In other words, we (the central government) want to see the market play a role in consolidating the weaker players into the stronger, but if the market does not work, the central government will exercise its prerogative as owner to ensure consolidation happens. The irony here is that the market could not work its magic on SOEs that were coddled by both central and local governments. As case studies on the mergers in Chapter Six will demonstrate, the central government would indeed act to force mergers when it was deemed appropriate.

The Tenth Five-Year Plan: Focus on New Technologies, Anticipating WTO

The auto industry's adjunct to China's Tenth Five-Year Plan, adopted in 2001, echoed those same sentiments, that China's auto industry was not competitive with the foreign producers, and that a "structural adjustment" would be necessary. More importantly, however, this particular Five-Year Plan (not the auto industry's micro plans, but the actual Five-Year Plan adopted by the Party for *all* of China's industries) included specific directions for the auto industry. The plan's fourth chapter, entitled "Optimize Industrial Structure, Strengthen International Competitiveness," contained the following instructions:

> Develop . . . economy cars and improve manufacturing standards of both automobiles and critical components. *Actively develop engines and hybrid systems for energy efficient and low-emission vehicles.* Promote the integration of mechanical and electrical [components].[79]

What is most fascinating about this brief excerpt is that it came from the very top of China's Communist Party. Prior to this time, there had been little mention of electric or hybrid vehicles in policies affecting the automobile industry. Nor would this have been expected as even the most advanced auto markets had barely begun to experiment with alternative ways to power personal transportation. General Motors had developed the EV1 electric car during the 1990s, then unceremoniously killed the project in 1999.[80] The only production hybrid vehicles on the road at this time were Toyota's Prius and the Honda Insight, both still only items of curiosity outside of Japan at the time. In short, Japan's automakers were only beginning to test the market for alternative vehicles, Detroit appeared to have lost interest, and the leaders of China's Communist Party thought it an important enough trend to mention it in their economic plan *for the entire country.*[81]

The auto industry, for its part, elaborated on the role of "new energy vehicles" (NEVs) in its detailed plans to accompany the Tenth Five-Year Plan, discussing the need to invest in research and development for electric and hybrid vehicles. The plans cited another country's "Partnership for a New Generation of Vehicles" (PNGV) project as the example China should follow. Ironically, PNGV was a joint research project between the U.S. government and the Detroit Three automakers.[82] The PNGV, begun in 1993 was intended to conduct cooperative research with the goal of producing, by 2004, cars capable of holding five passengers that could achieve 80 miles per gallon. Though the project was canceled by the Bush administration in 2001 (at the request of the Detroit Three), all three Detroit automakers had produced diesel-powered concept cars capable of 70 to 80 miles per gallon by project's end.[83] Despite the demise of PNGV, this program, along with its successor, FreedomCAR, has continued to be cited by

Chinese sources as an example of business-government partnership for China's auto industry.[84]

The industry, now led by two associations, the CNAIC (which would soon be disbanded, again) and the Chinese Association of Automobile Manufacturers (CAAM), opened its micro plan with a summary of accomplishments followed by a typically Chinese self-criticism pointing out the industry's problems and shortcomings that the policy would aim to address:

- Lack of a policy to promote consumer purchases.
- Local protectionism that prevented vehicles made in one region from being sold—or in some cases driven—in other regions.
- A confusing array of taxes and fees that dampened consumer demand for autos.
- Manufacturers lacked the models consumers wanted.
- Prices were still out of reach of the vast majority of consumers.
- Manufacturers' managerial methods and after-sales service were lacking.
- Weak design capabilities.
- Low R&D expenditure (approximately 1 percent of sales in China compared to 3–5 percent in foreign countries).
- Chinese auto parts were uncompetitive in foreign markets.
- Various local governments and ministries continued to "blindly" launch new automobile-related projects despite the fragmented nature of the industry.[85]

Viewed as a whole, the auto industry's 2001 five-year plan adjunct reveals a sense of both entitlement and vulnerability: entitled, as an up-and-coming economic power, to have its own auto industry, yet vulnerable to an increasingly competitive global automotive environment. As an aspiring economic power, China had noted that all the other major economic powers (and some middling ones as well) had auto industries, and decided that this was an important status indicator. No fewer than five times does the document use the term "participate in the global division of labor" (参与国际分工). As this term had been less frequently used in prior policy documents, its increased usage beginning in 2001 seems to reveal a China keenly aware of its place in what it perceived to be a hierarchy in the global division of labor.

The document also observes that an increasing number of cross-border mergers, acquisitions, and alliances are only intensifying the challenge of competing in a global auto industry in which China has yet to conquer even its home market. The document runs down a list: the Daimler–Chrysler merger, the Renault–Nissan alliance, GM's controlling stake in Isuzu, and (ironically)[86] Ford's purchase of Volvo.[87]

With respect to passenger cars, the plan was to focus on developing economy cars with engine displacements of 1.3 liters or less. According to the plan, this focus on economy cars was driven by two important considerations. First, the plan expected consumer demand to be highest for small, efficient cars costing approximately 80,000 renminbi (US $10,256 at the time). And secondly, the plan set a goal of reaching emissions control at a Euro II or Euro III standard.[88] Part of the goal for reaching these standards included development of alternative fuels such as compressed natural gas (CNG) and liquefied petroleum gas (LPG) as well as hybrid power trains.

For the five years covered under this plan (through 2005), the policy plans included seven priorities.[89] First was the introduction of a unified national auto consumption policy that lowered taxes on economy cars, eliminated local protectionism, and established an orderly used car market. A second priority was to set standards for certification and inspection and establish a third party authority to universally implement and enforce the inspection regime. The third priority would be of little surprise to anyone: to guide and promote the formation of large group enterprises, centered around First Auto, Dongfeng, and Shanghai Auto. Fourth was to strengthen self-development capacity by importing technology, joint development with foreign firms, and a focus on education and training.

Fifth priority was to promote self-development within the parts industry and gain the indigenous ability to develop key critical components. Sixth was to strengthen foreign partnerships, expand export opportunities and avoid "disorderly competition" among Chinese firms in foreign markets. And the final priority was to improve ancillary activities such as emissions control, fuel standards, roads, parking lots, and the management thereof. Note that, until this time, many of these provisions had already been mentioned as priorities, indicating continued widespread noncompliance by the industry. Over the coming years, however, China would begin to issue specific policies to achieve many of these aims. Note also that, despite the realization in recent years that foreign partnerships had yielded little of the technology transfers China had wished for, this policy still listed "strengthening of foreign partnerships" as a priority.

Finally, the Tenth Five-Year Plan represented another milestone in thinking for China's auto industry. For the first time, the industry's quantitative target included forecasts for consumer demand.[90] Whereas previous plans had only contained targets of production or production capacity, from now on, consumer demand would become the most important driver of industry targets.

Stage Three: Indigenous Innovation

This final stage, Indigenous Innovation, began in approximately 2002 with China's accession to the World Trade Organization, an event that resulted in a rapid increase in auto sales among Chinese consumers. The massive sales increase, which occurred primarily among foreign-branded cars, served to highlight for China's leaders the fact that Chinese-branded cars were far less innovative and competitive than those of the foreign multinationals. Policy in this decade would begin to focus more on how Chinese automakers might begin to develop their own intellectual property so that Chinese brands might someday gain a competitive foothold in their home market. In addition, there was increasing acceptance that Chinese automakers may never catch up with the multinationals in terms of traditional internal combustion engine development. This led to a determined effort for Chinese automakers to gain a competitive position with respect to the multinationals in development of electric and hybrid vehicles—the presumed vehicle technologies of the future.

WTO Accession

China's entry into the World Trade Organization had arguably the greatest impact on the auto industry of any event since the beginning of economic reforms in 1978. China's negotiations to join the WTO's precursor, the General Agreement on Tariffs and Trade (GATT) began in 1986 and continued off and on during the 1990s. Throughout the 1990s as state president and CCP secretary-general Jiang Zemin pushed for China's eventual membership, he encountered resistance, both economic and political, to the idea of opening China's industries to the influence and competition of foreign business.[91] The political objections came typically from the more conservative members of the Communist Party leadership who did not favor increased opening of China's markets to foreign businesses. The economic objections, as one might expect, came from businesses, typically the larger state-owned enterprises, that feared the potential impacts of increased competition on Chinese jobs and profitability. Jiang, with the support of Premier Zhu Rongji who was China's point person in negotiating with the Americans, ultimately prevailed, and China formally joined the WTO on December 11, 2001.

According to Joseph Fewsmith, Premier Zhu, who had already put his reputation as an economic reformer on the line by pushing for closings and privatization of SOEs in the late 1990s, supported WTO membership because, in his view, further openness to competition would push intransigent SOEs to carry out restructuring and improve operational efficiency. Furthermore, by binding the government within WTO rules, bureaucrats would then be forced to drop protectionist measures that allowed the SOEs to be content in their inefficiency.[92]

The major provisions of China's WTO accession agreement that would affect the auto industry included a gradual reduction in tariffs on assembled cars from 80–100 percent to 25 percent by 2006, and a decrease in tariffs on auto parts to an average of 10 percent. China would also phase out quotas on automobile imports by 2005 and allow foreign companies to engage in previously prohibited business lines of domestic distribution of autos and nonbank auto financing. China also agreed that the United States could take action against China under America's unfair trade laws if China were seen to be providing subsidies that went primarily to SOEs or providing equity infusions or soft loans that were not made using "market-based" criteria.[93] And finally, foreign automakers would also no longer be subject to the local content provisions, technology transfer requirements or export offsets in order to establish business ventures in China. That last point bears repeating: *China would no longer be allowed to require technology transfer as a condition for establishing a business in China.*[94]

China auto specialist Eric Harwit conducted interviews with auto executives and officials, both Chinese and expatriate, during 2000 and encountered mixed expectations with regard to the impact of WTO membership. In general, officials and managers from the Chinese sides of joint ventures felt that China was not ready for open competition, and were hoping WTO accession could be delayed for at least a few more years. On the foreign sides of the joint ventures, however, Harwit encountered mostly optimism. Several, including Shanghai-Volkswagen, were planning cash infusions to upgrade plant and equipment.[95]

Before WTO accession even took place, however, some Chinese automakers started to lower prices in anticipation of the eventual decrease in import tariffs. This touched off a price war among many Chinese automakers that hurt the profits of some of the weaker players.

As it turned out, the SOEs' fears of import domination were misplaced. China's first full year under WTO rules, 2002, was by far its best yet for year-over-year growth in automobile output. Total vehicle production increased 39 percent from 2.3 million in 2001 to 3.3 million in 2002. Passenger cars saw an increase of 55 percent from 0.7 million to 1.1 million.[96] Contrary to expectations, automobile imports experienced only a modest absolute increase from 71,398 vehicles in 2001 to 127,513 in 2002.[97] Numerous Chinese auto industry analysts and insiders credit WTO membership for the impetus local manufacturers needed to improve quality and efficiency so as to compete with imported automobiles. The anticipation of lower import tariffs pushed China's manufacturers to compete on price, and the lower prices suddenly made passenger cars, long out of reach of the average Chinese, affordable for many urban dwellers.

2004 Auto Industry Development Policy

By 2004 it had been 10 years since the State Planning Commission (SPC) introduced China's first auto industry policy, and the SPC's successor, the National Development and Reform Commission (NDRC), introduced a new policy to take its place. The first difference to note between these two policies is their titles. The 1994 policy was entitled "Automotive Industrial Policy" (汽车工业产业政策), whereas the new 2004 policy was entitled "Automotive Industry *Development* Policy" (汽车产业发展政策). The insertion of the word "development" into the title indicated that, whether the NDRC truly saw any difference in its role from that of the SPC of 1994, the organization wanted, at a minimum, to *project* a difference. This reflected the change in China's planning apparatus that had taken place since the beginning of the reform era. The all-powerful State Planning Commission had given way in 1998 to the State Development and Planning Commission, which finally became the National Development and Reform Commission in 2003.[98] Note the gradual shift away from emphasis on planning to emphasis on development. China's 1994 auto policy was an "industrial policy," with all the state intervention that implied, but by 2004 it had become a "development policy." And this title change was indeed an accurate description of the policy's change in substance. Whereas the 1994 policy was built around an industrial output forecast, the 2004 policy was built around a demand forecast. Growth was no longer determined by state planners, but by consumer demand.

Still, the state would maintain a firm hand in "planning" for the industry, as the policy itself made clear:

> The State directs the formulation of the industry's development planning in accordance with the Automotive Industry Development Policy. The development planning includes medium- and long-term development planning for the industry and development planning for large automotive enterprise corporations. Medium- and long-term development planning for the industry are drawn up by the National Development and Reform Commission (NDRC) jointly with other relevant departments on the basis of widely solicited opinions, and submitted to the State Council for approval and implementation. Large automotive enterprise corporations are to formulate the corporation's proper development planning in conformity with the medium- and long-term development planning for the industry.[99]

The policy defined a "large automotive enterprise" as any group plus subsidiaries (including Chinese-foreign JVs) commanding a domestic market share of 15 percent or greater.[100] As of 2004, that would have included only two companies, First Auto Works (FAW) and Shanghai Automotive Industry Corporation (SAIC), which had market shares of 20 and 17 percent, respectively.[101]

The 2004 update to China's comprehensive auto policy reflected an expanded goal of growing and combining Chinese auto firms into several auto groups with global scale. Reflecting China's curious fascination with rankings compiled by foreigners, the 2004 policy also called for the industry to create several groups that would be large enough to be listed among the *Fortune* Global 500 by 2010.[102] But China would not need to wait until 2010 to get its wish in this regard: Shanghai Auto debuted on the Global 500 list at number 461 in that very same year, 2004.[103] However, only 2 percent of passenger cars produced by Shanghai Auto in 2004 had been developed in China; the remaining 98 percent were primarily Volkswagen- or GM-branded cars.[104]

The fact that auto production and sales increased so rapidly in the years following WTO accession was likely of cold comfort to planners in Beijing who undoubtedly noted that only about 10 percent of the passenger cars produced in China in 2002 were Chinese-branded.[105] In other words, 50 percent of the profit earned from 90 percent of the cars sold in China accrued to foreign joint venture partners.[106] The central government was seeing the sales of its SOEs increase, but up to half of the profit generated per vehicle flowed out of the country. This realization by planners in both the automotive bureaucracy and the NDRC, led to a sharpening of auto policy. This new direction pushed toward not merely an improvement in quality and efficiency, but a dedication of those efforts to the development of indigenous Chinese brands—brands to which the Chinese would hold "autonomous intellectual property rights." From this point forward the terms "indigenous brands" (自主品牌, *zizhu pinpai*) and "indigenous innovation" (自主创新, *zizhu chuangxin*) would become regular features of China's automobile policy.[107]

Many of the provisions in this policy regarding improvements in efficiency and lowering vehicle emissions were aspirational in that they did not include concrete rules for implementation. The overall aim announced in the policy was for China to achieve a 15 percent reduction in the average fuel consumption of passenger cars by 2010.

The state indicated its support for R&D activities in electric vehicles, hybrids, and alternative fuels by announcing its intention to make the facilities used for such R&D tax deductible. The policy also stated that the government planned to enact measures in the future that would encourage consumers to buy low-emission and low-energy-consuming vehicles. Auto enterprises were also "encouraged to actively participate in research projects organized by the state."[108] Though it would still be several years before the central government would begin to introduce concrete plans for implementation of these environmental- and efficiency-related provisions, these rules telegraphed to the industry that the central government planned to take the industry in this direction.

Another important measure taken under the 2004 policy was a new rule that bankrupt automakers would no longer be allowed to sell their certifications (their permission from the NDRC to produce autos) to other companies. The policy specifically stated that these certifications could not be sold to nonautomotive companies. Rather, bankrupt automakers were encouraged under the policy either to combine with, or transfer their assets to, another automaker.[109] Interestingly, two of China's private automakers, Geely and BYD, had both already entered the auto industry through this exact method. Geely had got its auto certification by buying a near-bankrupt factory run by a prison in Sichuan (yes, a prison) in 1997. BYD had got its certification by buying Qinchuan Auto, a bankrupt factory in Xi'an in 2003. By introducing this policy, the central government was, in effect, closing the barn door after a couple of horses had already escaped, but this was also an effective way to prevent the establishment of new private automakers without explicitly forbidding their establishment. The private players would eventually begin to prove their worth to the central government, but that was not to happen for several more years.

A final policy provision from 2004 worth noting involves the state's plans to encourage the development of credit and insurance products to support the auto industry. Until this time, Chinese consumers were unaccustomed to borrowing money for auto purchases, but the state introduced rules encouraging both bank and nonbank financial institutions to support the auto industry by introducing credit products, allowing consumers to mortgage their new vehicles.[110] The policy also encouraged the insurance industry to offer automotive insurance products.

While the 2004 policy did urge automakers to introduce their own branded cars with full intellectual property rights, 2005 seems to have been the year that China's leaders discovered the true importance of domestic brands. Prior to 2004, the term *zizhu pinpai* (自主品牌) was seldom used, and attempts by outside analysts to determine the market shares of China's domestic brands required a painstaking model-by-model analysis of sales and production figures. In an indication of the newfound importance of this term, the 2006 *Auto Industry Yearbook* (containing statistics from 2005), for the first time, included a chart breaking out sales and production of domestic versus foreign brands.[111]

The Eleventh Five-Year Plan: Innovation and Sustainable Development

At the beginning of a typical Five-Year Plan, the auto industry first assesses the industry's performance relative to the previous Five-Year Plan. The industry began its Eleventh Five-Year Plan (2006–2010), with the observation that China's approach to auto manufacture would need to become more strategic. The assessment noted that in the crossover and economy car segments, Chinese companies had staked out solid market shares using their own intellectual property. In the mid- to high-end sedan segments, however, they note that the intellectual property is owned by the foreign joint venture partners and that the Chinese sides of these partnerships "have little say."[112]

When viewing these industry plans over the years, the observer can begin to see an increasingly sophisticated approach to policy-making and a gradual evolution from a list of wants and production targets, to more detailed plans covering aspects of the industry that had not even rated a mention in years past. In the latter half of the 2000s, policies have tended to begin with a guiding direction and a few paragraphs intended to tie the provisions of the policy back to achievement of that guiding direction. The opening paragraphs of the auto industry's portion of the Eleventh Five-Year Plan contains words that had not previously appeared in industrial plans: independent development (自主发展), sustainable development (可持续发展), structural optimization (结构优化). Translated, this meant that Chinese automakers would continue to be urged to develop their own brands and vehicles, and that those vehicles needed to be more efficient, more environmentally friendly, and made from more recycled and recyclable materials. The industry also reinforced the current industry structure, including the mix of SOEs, private firms and joint ventures, indicating that there would continue to be a role for each type of firm.

The industry's contribution to the Eleventh Five-Year Plan, contained two key watchwords "indigenous brands" (自主品牌) and "new energy vehicles" (新能源汽车). Initiatives to develop domestic brands and new energy vehicles were also part of the impetus behind consolidation and market entry policies beginning with the Eleventh Five-Year Plan. Rather than vague demands that the industry have "two or three globally competitive auto groups" as before, this time the demands were somewhat more specific and measurable. The central government called for, by 2010, one or two enterprises with production capacity of at least 2 million vehicles, 50 percent of which would be indigenous brands and 10 percent of which would be exported.[113] The plan also called for several other auto groups with capacities of 1 million vehicles.

And while the plan reinforced roles for all three types of firms in the industry, the more specific plans still reflected the central government's continued ambivalence over private automakers. The plan called for SOEs to be "core of the industry and to strengthen their competitiveness," for the private firms to "join the SOEs in their reforms," and for the foreign joint venture partners to "support a win-win strategy and develop products with local partners."[114] The call for the private firms to join the SOEs in reforms seems especially ironic as most of the private firms were still relatively new, lacking many of the inefficiencies and encumbrances necessitating SOE reform. And even though China had, through its WTO accession agreement, ostensibly committed itself to no longer demanding technology transfer from foreign joint venture partners, the policy still indicated that China's planners expected of the foreigners some sort of *quid pro quo* for being allowed access to China's market.

The overall message of the Eleventh Five-Year Plan was that auto firms would no longer be judged simply by size or number of vehicles produced annually, but also by whether they truly contributed to the eventual dominance by Chinese automakers of their domestic market and to the industry's independence from reliance on foreign technology and intellectual property.[115] China's economic planners had finally begun to shake off the legacy of central planning. Competitiveness, they had finally begun to understand, requires more than simply getting big; it requires innovation.

The following year (2007) saw a number of events reinforcing the importance of indigenous brands, and in the process, enhancing the status of the private automakers. Despite continued concerns about industry fragmentation, the NDRC approved the applications of five different companies to begin building passenger cars, among the five were two LSOEs and three private automakers, each with plans to build Chinese-branded cars. These three private companies (Great Wall, Qingnian, and Zhongtai) would be the first non–state-owned firms to be allowed to make sedans since BYD entered the auto business through the backdoor in 2003.[116] As the *Auto Industry Yearbook* explained these decisions:

> These new firms will bring competition to the auto industry. This competition will raise the international competitiveness of domestic firms, ... force enterprises to focus more attention on building a system of independent innovation, accelerate improvement of R&D capabilities, accelerate the cultivation of indigenous brands.[117]

The industry also highlighted the progress a number of domestic automakers made in self-developed engines, long a weak point in China's auto industry. In 2007 nine different enterprises successfully introduced self-developed engines, and among these nine were four private enterprises: Geely, Lifan, BYD, and Great Wall. Once again, the *Auto Industry Yearbook* explained the importance of these accomplishments:

> The emergence of a large number of indigeneously developed engines has broken the control and monopoly of China's advanced engine market by the multinational corporations.[118]

This kind of propaganda is significant, if for no other reason than that it demonstrates to the industry as a whole what Beijing is looking for from its home-grown auto companies, and more importantly, it demonstrates that those companies do not necessarily have to be state-owned.

Also important was the use of the words "control" and "monopoly" to describe the role of the foreign multinationals in China. This was not

the first time such words have been used to describe the role of foreigners, nor would it be the last.[119] Of course the notion that any single
multinational company held a "monopoly," much less control, over
China's auto market was preposterous. The foreign automakers are all in
China at China's invitation, none is allowed to operate a wholly-owned
assembly venture, none is allowed to own a controlling stake in a joint
venture, and all compete viciously against each other. These words,
"control" and "monopoly" are the words of victimization to which
China's central government occasionally resorts in order to engender
solidarity with the Chinese people—particularly during times in which
China has perceived itself to be under attack from outside.[120] At this
time, the attack was even given a name by the Chinese: "crash-gate."

Contained in the same report that discussed China's achievements in
engine technology was a discussion of "crash-gate" (碰撞门), which used
the American "gate" suffix to describe an allegedly scandalous series of
crash tests of Chinese made vehicles by German and Russian test centers
from late 2005 through early 2008.[121] Each of these tests resulted in a
disastrous outcome in which a driver would not have survived, and videos
of each were, unfortunately for the Chinese manufacturers, posted on
YouTube (which had not yet been blocked in China).[122] The Chinese
were caught off-guard as the crash tests had not been coordinated with the
manufacturers, and the industry leveled allegations that the tests had been
somehow rigged so as to prevent the lower-cost Chinese cars from taking
market share away from European and Russian automakers. The auto
industry's report on "crash-gate," while alleging a conspiracy to keep
China down and "damage the reputation of Chinese brands" also recognized that China could not compete in developed markets on low cost
alone. Manufacturers would also have to take into account higher safety
standards of the United States and Europe. But the damage had already
been done, and Chinese consumers, who already preferred foreign
brands, became even less likely to choose a Chinese-branded car.

Recession and Stimulus

The year 2008 brought with it a new set of challenges for China's auto
industry. This was the first year in which the global financial crisis,

which had yet to become known as the Great Recession, began to be felt all over the world. A combination of financial scandals and housing price declines in the United States plus record high prices for crude oil resulted in a decline in the growth rates of auto sales in every market. But the decline meant something different in different markets. Whereas the United States had an 18 percent decline in total vehicle sales in 2008, China's total vehicle sales *grew* by 7 percent; however, in comparison to their respective average growth rates of the prior five years (U.S. = −1 percent, China = +22 percent), both countries had disastrous years in 2008. Figure 3.3 compares the growth rates of China and the United States from 2000 through 2008. (Note that the right-hand scales for China and the United States are different: the Chinese scale begins at 0 percent, but the U.S. scale is mostly negative.)

While China was distracted by the Beijing Olympics for much of 2008, in the final quarter of the year, Chinese consumers began to turn conservative in their spending habits causing a significant slide in sales growth for the year. The downturn also affected China's exports of cars and parts to the rest of the world. While assembled passenger car exports still grew by 20 percent in 2008, this represented a drop from growth rates of 195 percent and 130 percent in the previous two years.[123] And China's exports of automotive parts to the United States, China's largest parts export market, dropped by 10.2 percent.[124]

The central government took swift action to try to prop up not just the auto industry, but China's economy as a whole. The most obvious action taken by the central government was to announce in the fall of 2008 a 4 trillion yuan (approx. US$600 billion) stimulus package intended to boost spending on public infrastructure. Furthermore, without any public acknowledgment, the People's Bank of China, during the summer of 2008, repegged the renminbi to the U.S. dollar. The renminbi, which had been depegged from the dollar in the summer of 2005, had been gradually strengthening against the U.S. dollar since that time. The primary reason for the repegging (which was later to be acknowledged as a sort of managed float) was to mitigate the potential impact of decreasing consumer spending in the developed world on employment in China's export sector.

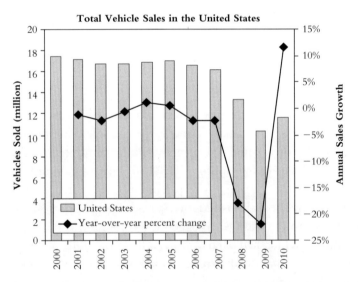

Figure 3.3   China and U.S. Vehicle Sales and Sales Growth, 2000 to 2010

The action China's central government would take specifically to stimulate its auto industry would come early in the following year.

The 2009 Auto Industry Adjustment and Stimulus Plan

By the time China's Auto Industry Adjustment and Stimulus Plan was released in full in March of 2009, many of its provisions had already been announced, and some had already been implemented.[125] Given its content and the timing of its release, stimulus of growth to counteract the effects of the global recession were the main impetus behind the policy. However, aside from the stimulus measures, much of the policy reads like it could have been an update to China's 2004 Auto Industry Policy. The policy introduced some important tax and subsidy measures to stimulate auto sales, funding for research and development in NEVs, new targets for industry growth, and a completely revamped formulation for industry consolidation.

The provision with the greatest immediate impact was a cut in sales tax on vehicles with engine displacement of 1.6 liters or less. Until January 2009 this 10 percent tax applied to sales of all vehicles, but following a severe slowdown in sales growth at the end of 2008, the tax was cut in half, to 5 percent, for smaller displacement vehicles as a means of stimulating sales. Another purpose was to encourage increased sales of more energy efficient vehicles. And, as a parts company executive shared with me, her company's analysis indicated that the 1.6 liter cutoff point for the 50 percent tax break was intended to most benefit manufacturers of domestic-branded cars; the foreign manufacturers had very little to offer in the sub-1.6 liter category. The tax cut was a tremendous success. Sales of passenger vehicles in the target category increased by 71 percent in 2009, compared to only 23 percent for all other passenger vehicles (with displacements greater than 1.6 liters).[126]

Another stimulus program introduced under this policy was called "vehicles to the countryside" (汽车下乡). This program provided government subsidies of 10 to 13 percent to people living in rural areas who purchased motorcycles or cars with displacements of 1.3 liters or less. This was modeled on a similar program introduced in 2008 called "home appliances to the countryside" (家电下乡) providing subsidies for purchases of refrigerators, washing machines, televisions, and the like.

In addition, the policy introduced a "cash-for-clunkers" program similar to those that would be implemented later in both the U.S. and Europe. The state set aside one billion yuan to provide subsidies for purchases of new vehicles that replaced old, inefficient vehicles.

China's push for the development of new energy vehicles (NEVs) also had a prominent role in this policy. The government pledged to fund research and development efforts in this area with 10 billion yuan (about US$1.5 billion), and also established targets for the industry. Within three years (by year-end 2011), the aim was to develop annual production capacity of 500,000 NEVs and to have at least 5 percent of all passenger vehicles fall into this category. These targets were over-ambitious. Though most Chinese automakers were engaged in development of NEVs by the end of 2010, only BYD had begun to sell them to the general public, and their sales were disappointing. In 2010 BYD had sold only 33 electric vehicles and 417 plug-in hybrids.[127]

The policy also set targets for domestic-branded vehicles. The aim was for domestic brands to surpass 40 percent of annual passenger vehicle sales and 30 percent of passenger car sales within three years. This target, however, was achieved in the very year that it was set. By the end of 2009, domestic brands had comprised 44 percent of passenger vehicle sales and 30 percent of passenger car sales.[128]

The final important target was for that most important of central government wishes: consolidation. The central government aimed, within three years, to have two or three companies with annual production capacity of at least 2 million vehicles and another four or five with capacities of at least 1 million. (By the end of 2010, the top four all produced in excess of 2 million.) An additional target was for the 14 largest auto groups, accounting for 90 percent of sales, to be reduced to 10 or fewer groups—and the government even had a good idea as to which companies should be left standing. In a formulation Chinese media dubbed "big four, small four" (similar to the "big three, small three" of the late 1980s), the policy lists four companies that are encouraged to conduct *nationwide* mergers and another four encouraged to conduct *regional* mergers. The "big four" are First Auto Works, Dongfeng, Shanghai Auto, and Chang'an. The "small four" are Beijing Auto, Guangzhou Auto, Chery, and China Heavy Duty Truck Group (Sinotruk). All eight are state-owned, and all but Sinotruk manufacture primarily passenger vehicles. Remaining among the top 14 largest companies (but not among the "big four, small four") are three private firms: BYD, Geely, and Great Wall. Also not listed were state-owned firms Brilliance, Jianghuai (JAC), Hafei, and Changhe. Hafei and Changhe, as will be noted in Chapter Six, were bought by the CSOE Chang'an in 2010.

The policy also stated that a new merger policy specifically for the auto industry would soon be introduced, and that part of that policy would require that any new auto ventures could only be established *after the enterprise first merges with a domestic rival*—a policy that would be enforced almost immediately, resulting in the Guangzhou-Changfeng merger (also detailed in Chapter Six). Eighteen months later, in September of 2010, an article appeared in *People's Daily* stating that China's Ministry of Industry and Information Technology (MIIT) was drawing up plans for the merger policy with the intention to introduce it by year's end; however, no policy had been released as of this writing (Fall 2011).[129]

Of key importance in the 2009 Adjustment and Stimulus Policy was the fact that the central government saw a need to inject some hope into this important "pillar" industry in order to prevent the negative effects of a depressed global economic environment. The industry was able very quickly to rush out the most important policies for stimulus and see their effects almost instantly. The central government also began to put its money where its mouth is with regard to NEVs. Beyond merely pushing for NEV development, the government demonstrated its seriousness by devoting a large sum expressly for that purpose. Also important is the fact that, despite the small number of mergers that have happened in China's auto industry thus far, and despite the fact that the central government has yet to begin forcing a lot of mergers, the central government has not let up in its determination to see the industry consolidated into fewer, larger firms. The end target is for China's automakers to eventually stand on their own without help from foreign partners. The continued push for Chinese brands, NEVs, and consolidation reflect the central government's strategy for domestic dominance and eventual global competitiveness.

In 2010, the central government announced a pilot project to stimulate the manufacture and sale of NEVs.[130] The pilot, to be run first in five cities (Shanghai, Changchun, Shenzhen, Hangzhou, and Hefei—and Beijing was later added as a sixth city) includes subsidies of up to 50,000 yuan for a plug-in hybrid (PHEV) and up to 60,000 yuan for a pure electric vehicle (EV). The pilot also includes subsidies of up to 3,000 yuan for small, fossil-fuel-burning, energy-efficient vehicles included on a preapproved list. In addition to the central government subsidies, the local governments involved in the pilot also announced their own subsidies to be added to those of the central government. For example, BYD's E6 electric car is expected to retail for about 300,000 yuan. With the combination of the central government's 60,000 yuan subsidy and the City of Shenzhen's 60,000 yuan subsidy, the price of the E6 could be as little as 170,000 yuan, a price reduction from about US $45,000 to $26,000.

The Twelfth Five-Year Plan: Focus on New Energy Vehicles

The auto industry received specific mention in China's Twelfth Five-Year Plan (2011–2015) in regards to the continued desire for industrial consolidation. This plan also included general objectives for the industry of improvement in safety and energy efficiency as well as toward self-reliance in R&D. The auto industry was also specifically mentioned in regard to a plan to revitalize China's former industrial heartland in the northeast of the country. However, NEVs figured most prominently, being listed among seven "new strategic industries" (战略性新兴产业) that would be targeted for development with the intention of reaching a collective 8 percent of GDP.[131]

Not long after China's Twelfth Five-Year Plan was adopted by the National People's Congress in March of 2011, officials from MIIT, announced that, for the first time, there would be no separate auto industry plan. Instead, the ministry would introduce, at a later date, a more comprehensive plan for energy efficient and alternative energy vehicles. A plan for the industry as a whole would be unnecessary.[132] Perhaps this is an indication that the central government is satisfied with the growth of China's auto industry as a whole and that the focus will now shift entirely toward new technologies in which China's central government believes the foreign multinationals do not yet have a significant advantage.

Conclusion

This historical analysis of the evolution of China's auto industry policy provides a moving picture of three decades of development, tracking the thinking of China's central government and the behavior of firms and local governments as they have evolved year by year. Early policy documents from the 1980s reflect a central government concerned primarily with three issues: a fragmented industry, a lack of access to technology, and an obsessive attention to foreign exchange. The earliest plans for consolidation involved a "big three, small three" formulation in which the central government attempted to pick the winners of an expected race to consolidate. Over time these plans have taken on various guises, and while China's largest automakers have become larger—the largest now producing more than three million vehicles in a year—the industry remains heavily fragmented, but the central government remains no less desirous of consolidation. The latest formulation, "big four, small four," appears more achievable than the original "big three, small three," yet it appears that the central government's formulations have done more to follow the industry than to shape it. Then again, maybe no one should be surprised that the "big four" consists of China's largest automaker (SAIC) and China's only three CSOEs (First Auto Works, Dongfeng, and Chang'an). In a "pillar" industry, this is as it should be.

The central government's earliest impulse was to bring in foreign automakers who could transfer technology and teach China's automakers how to design cars; however, China's central government came to believe fairly early that this tech transfer was not happening. This fact then leads us to wonder: why, if the central government believed by the mid-1990s that the foreign partners were not transferring technology, did they continue to approve formation of new joint ventures? Did the central government still hope that some technology transfer would happen by osmosis? Was the central government concerned that China continue to appear open to foreign investment? Or did the central government still view foreign partners as necessary to fill gaps in China's passenger vehicle market? The story in Chapter Two has already revealed that the central government now looks to the JVs to generate cash as well as technology.

The early obsession over foreign exchange, while based on a real need at the time, eventually dissipated. As China's export-oriented economy grew throughout the 1990s, China built up world's largest store of foreign reserves, and by the early 1990s, the topic of foreign exchange was no longer emphasized in China's policy documents. This still did not mean that China's government would ease the pressure for the joint ventures to generate exports, but by the mid-1990s, the focus was more on creating jobs for Chinese workers than on generating foreign exchange.

Interestingly, however, the joint ventures have yet to manufacture many cars for export. Though some JVs are beginning to generate exports, until now, China's biggest exporters have been the independent automakers—essentially, Chery plus the private firms. And this reality has contributed to a change in attitude by China's central government toward the independents. Whereas policy has, since the 1980s, attempted to thwart the formation of independent firms, during the 2000s the independent firms that had earlier managed to enter the industry under the radar had also begun to satisfy policy requirements that the big SOEs had not. The independent firms began to lead the industry in exports, indigenous brands and NEV technology, and by the end of the 2000s the central government, finally becoming aware of the value these independent firms brought to the industry, began to reward them with limited support.

Those latter two accomplishments of the independent automakers, Chinese brands and NEV technology, also happen to form the foundation of the central government's newest policy objectives. From the policy documents we see that, as early as the mid-1990s, the central government believed China's automakers suffered from a lack of innovative ability. From that point, policy began gradually to include provisions to encourage Chinese automakers to move beyond manufacture of foreign brands toward introduction of "indigenous brands." But these policies focused only on the desired end result, not on the processes necessary to get there.

And by the early 2000s, central policy also began to reflect a belief that China's automakers would be unable to catch up with the foreign multinationals in terms of traditional ICE technology. China needed to find a way to leapfrog the multinationals to the next wave of technology: new energy vehicles. But while copying a traditional ICE car and applying a Chinese badge would prove difficult enough for Chinese automakers, the question of whether Chinese automakers possessed the necessary skills and innovative spirit to make that technological leap into NEVs has remained an open question.

China's central government has demonstrated its ability to learn and adapt along with a willingness to overlook policy violations when it believed such violations worked for the overall good of society. Yet, as some of the case studies in later chapters will demonstrate, the central government also has the ability to get its way when it wants. It has been able to push through a few mergers that likely would not have otherwise happened and to bend the will of a few local governments—including that of Shanghai's—to its own.

The policy evolution story reveals the central government's policy concerns over the past three decades. Concerns about industry consolidation and mastery of technology have existed all along, but, whereas local governments and the automakers seem to have pushed back against consolidation policy, the central government has pushed forward with its technology policy and achieved some limited results. Over three decades, the push for consolidation has yet to subside, but government formulations for consolidation have largely been reactive to how the industry itself has developed. On the other hand, the government, in its desire to see China's automakers improve their ability to innovate has continually raised the bar in terms the innovation expected, and in the process, the independent automakers have demonstrated the greatest ability to rise to the occasion.

Still, the joint ventures remain critically important to this pillar industry, and the central government has revealed no signs that this fact will change anytime soon. The next chapter reviews how some of China's more prominent joint ventures came about and the roles they play in industry.

Notes

1. Eric Harwit, *China's Automobile Industry: Policies, Problems, and Prospects*, Studies on contemporary China (Armonk, NY: M.E. Sharpe, 1995), 17.
2. Ibid., 19.

3. Ibid., 17–18. China never produced more than 100 passenger cars in a single year prior to 1965.

4. Barry Naughton, "The Third Front: Defence Industrialization in the Chinese Interior," *The China Quarterly* 115 (1988): 351–386.

5. Kelly Sims Gallagher, *China Shifts Gears: Automakers, Oil, Pollution, and Development* (Cambridge, MA: MIT Press, 2006), 36.

6. Harwit, *China's Automobile Industry*, 50.

7. Ibid.

8. *CAIY*, 1986, 138. Harwit, *China's Automobile Industry*, 51.

9. Gallagher, *China Shifts Gears*, 36.

10. *CAIY*, 2009, 46.

11. Richard Baum, *China Watcher: Confessions of a Peking Tom* (Seattle: University of Washington Press, 2010), 68–69.

12. On Deng Xiaoping's consolidation, see Richard Baum, *Burying Mao: Chinese Politics in the Age of Deng Xiaoping* (Princeton, NJ: Princeton University Press, 1994), 27–47.

13. Jim Mann, *Beijing Jeep: The Short, Unhappy Romance of American Business in China* (New York: Simon and Schuster, 1989), 37–42. AMC would later be bought by Chrysler in 1987.

14. Martin Posth, *1,000 Days in Shanghai: The Story of Volkswagen: The First Chinese-German Car Factory* (Singapore: John Wiley & Sons [Asia], 2008), 4–5.

15. Baum, *Burying Mao*, 54–56.

16. Wu Facheng, 汽车强国之梦 [Dream of an automobile superpower] (Beijing: Xinhua Chubanshe, 2009), 5.

17. Baum, *Burying Mao*, 110–113. This was the beginning of one of the *shou*, or pullback, phases of the *fang/shou* cycles that Baum describes.

18. Barry Naughton, *Growing Out of the Plan: Chinese Economic Reform, 1978– 1993* (New York: Cambridge University Press, 1995), 119–125.

19. Posth, *1,000 Days in Shanghai*, 17.

20. Harwit, *China's Automobile Industry*, 52.

21. The full quote was: "只要市场有销路，当然允许生产，不要限制." Wu Facheng, 汽车强国之梦 = *Dream of an Automobile Superpower*, 9.

22. From digest of a speech delivered by Chairman of CNAIC, Rao Bin, to the CNAIC Board of Directors on November 8, 1985. *CAIY*, 1986, 13. The document, entitled《关于发展汽车工业几个问题的意见》had been forwarded to central authorities by CNAIC in November of 1982.

23. 中国汽车工业公司，"中国汽车工业公司关于组建中国汽车工业联合会的报告," paragraph 1. *CAIY*, 1988, 36.

24. "李鹏副总理在中国汽车工业联合会成立大会上的讲话，" *CAIY*, 1988, 38. Such concern for foreign exchange seems out of place now that China has become the world's largest holder of foreign exchange with over $3 trillion equivalent of foreign reserves.

25. Posth, *1,000 Days in Shanghai*, 156–158.
26. Annual Work Report of CNAIC General Manager, Chen Zutao, November 11, 1985, "团结奋斗，努力实现'七五'汽车工业发展目标," *CAIY*, 1986, 20.
27. Ibid., *CAIY*, 1986, 21.
28. Ibid., *CAIY*, 1986, 19.
29. A comprehensive 2010 report by James McGregor discusses China's policies of "co-innovation" and "re-innovation" of foreign technologies. James McGregor, "China's Drive for 'Indigenous Innovation': A Web of Industrial Policies" (Global Intellectual Property Center, U.S. Chamber of Commerce, APCO Worldwide, July 28, 2010), www.uschamber.com/reports/chinas-drive-indigenous-innovation-web-industrial-policies.
30. Posth, *1,000 Days in Shanghai*, 162.
31. As of this writing, only two major joint ventures, Guangzhou Honda and SAIC-GM, export cars. So far, China's major car exporters are the "independents" (automakers without joint venture partners)—yet another reason the central government would begin to appreciate the role of the private players in the future.
32. *CAIY*, 2009, 47. Guowuyuan fazhan yanjiu zhongxin, 中国汽车产业发展报告 [China automotive industry development report] (Beijing: Shehui kexue wenxian chubanshe, multiple years), 2010, 256. Of course, exports did increase significantly after WTO entry in 2001, peaking at 241,316 in 2008. Exports later fell by more than half in 2009 due to the global recession.
33. Annual Work Report of CNAIC General Manager, Cai Shiqing, February 11, 1990, Section 2.2.5. *CAIY*, 1991, 9.
34. *CAIY*, 2009, 45. Though records do not clarify this point, I assume at least part of those investments included working capital for purchases of foreign-made parts and components.
35. *CAIY*, 2009, 45.
36. Annual Work Report of CNAIC General Manager, Cai Shiqing, February 11, 1990, Section 1. *CAIY*, 1991, 6.
37. Baum, *Burying Mao*, Chapter 13.
38. Annual Work Report of CNAIC General Manager, Cai Shiqing, January 22, 1991, Section 2.2. *CAIY*, 1991, 13.
39. *People's Daily* online database, http://oriprobe.com/peoplesdaily.html.
40. The notice, entitled 《关于严格控制轿车生产点的通知》or "Notice regarding strict control of passenger car production sites," was summarized in "汽车工业大事记," *CAIY*, 1991, 32.
41. This is not necessarily an indication that these local governments directly disobeyed orders from the central government. There exists the possibility that these local authorities appealed to central authorities for an exception, though I was unable to find documentation to that effect. Among these possibly "illicit" manufacturers, only the enterprises located in Chongqing and

Xi'an produced more than 1,000 cars per year at the time. These were Chang'an, at the time a military-owned vehicle manufacturer located in Chongqing, and Qinchuan, a small car manufacturer owned by the city of Xi'an. Chang'an is now indirectly owned by central SASAC and is a joint venture partner with Suzuki, Ford, Mazda, and PSA Peugeot-Citroen. Qinchuan ultimately went bankrupt and was sold in 2003 to BYD, a private company located in Shenzhen that, at the time, had never before manufactured automobiles.

42. Annual Work Report of CNAIC General Manager, Cai Shiqing, January 22, 1991, Section 3.3.3. *CAIY*, 1991, 15.

43. *CAIY*, 1995, 73.

44. Harold Katz, *The Decline in Competition in the Automobile Industry, 1920–1940*, Dissertations in American Economic History (New York: Arno Press, 1977), 15.

45. 《汽车行业贯彻执行国家产业政策实施办法》 [Method of carrying out implementation of national automotive industry policy], Section 2.3.5.1. *CAIY*, 1991, 21.

46. Target mentioned in Annual Work Report of CNAIC General Manager, Cai Shiqing, January 21, 1992, Section 2: "关于'八五'发展的任务和目标," *CAIY*, 1993, 10. Production numbers from 1995: *CAIY*, 2009, 46.

47. This complaint about "second-rate" technology obtained from foreign multinationals has persisted to the present day. A similar complaint may also be seen in a book on auto industry innovation strategy published by China's Ministry of Science and Technology in 2009. Tang Jie, Yang Yanping, and Zhou Wenjie, 中国汽车产业自主创新战略 [China auto industry indigenous innovation strategy] (Beijing: Kexue Chubanshe, 2009), 88.

48. "中央财经领导小组对汽车工业发展的指标(要点) [Central finance leading small group instructions for development of the auto industry (main points)]," *CAIY*, 1995, 11. Emphasis added.

49. "1994年7月,《汽车工业产业政策》真是颁布实施 这是我国汽车工业的一部政策性法规,也是我国工业行业第一部出台的政策性法规." *CAIY*, 2000, 8.

50. Preamble, 《汽车工业产业政策》, "Automotive Industry Policy," *CAIY*, 1995, 12.

51. Ibid.

52. Chapter 3, Article 8, "Automotive Industry Policy," *CAIY*, 1995, 12.

53. Chapter 3, Article 10, "Automotive Industry Policy," *CAIY*, 1995, 12.

54. Chapter 3, Article 12, "Automotive Industry Policy," *CAIY*, 1995, 13.

55. An economist who had advised the NDRC on planning policy described to me how similar orders given to China's copper industry years earlier had merely led producers to add production capacity that they would never use.

56. Chapter 4, Article 14, "Automotive Industry Policy," *CAIY*, 1995, 13.

57. Chapter 6, Article 32, "Automotive Industry Policy," *CAIY*, 1995, 14.
58. Chapter 6, Article 29, "Automotive Industry Policy," *CAIY*, 1995, 14.
59. *CAIY*, 1998, 64.
60. Chapter 1, Article 2, "Automotive Industry Policy," *CAIY*, 1995, 12. China would still have 117 automakers by the end of 2008, *CAIY*, 2009, 447.
61. At the time, the Ministry of Machinery Industry (MMI or 机械工业部) was responsible for the certification process. As of this writing, this process is now managed by the Ministry of Industry and Information Technology (MIIT or 工业和信息化部), which has assumed most functions previously owned by MMI.
62. Chapter 2, Article 6, "Automotive Industry Policy," *CAIY*, 1995, 12. China's arrangement is similar to that of the United States. Each state's Department of Motor Vehicles issues license plates for new cars, but those cars must be approved for on-road use by federal agencies, including the Environmental Protection Agency and the National Highway Traffic and Safety Administration.
63. Summary of speech given by MMI Auto Office Director, Zhang Xiaoyu to the China Automobile Association, Section 2. *CAIY*, 1996, 5.
64. *CAIY*, 2009, 46.
65. Excerpt of speech by MMI Auto Office Director, Zhang Xiaoyu to the All-China industrial quality work meeting in October of 1996. *CAIY*, 1997, 7.
66. While the Auto Industry Yearbooks show sales figures for all vehicles by year, it has not done so for passenger cars only. As a proxy I began with passenger cars produced, added imports and subtracted exports to get an approximate figure for annual passenger car sales. I then divided passenger cars produced domestically (less exports) by annual passenger car sales to get an approximate market share figure. See calculation in Appendix B, Table B.1.
67. 《中国汽车工业与可持续发展战略（节选）》[China automotive industry and sustainable development strategy] (excerpt), Section 2(2), *CAIY*, 1997, 11.
68. Ibid., Section 2(3).
69. Ibid., Section 2(4).
70. 《关于进一步加强汽车工业项目管理的意见》[Opinions regarding further strengthening project management in the auto industry], *CAIY*, 1998, 8.
71. Or, as the document termed it "先斩后奏"—literally, "to behead first and report later."
72. A thorough search of both automobile industry documents and publicly available news sources has revealed neither a revocation of an auto company's certifications, nor news that any companies had been investigated for these types of violations.
73. *CAIY*, 1998, 6–14.
74. *CAIY*, 1999, 63–74.
75. *CAIY*, 2000, 13–40.

76. 《2000年国家重点扶持的汽车企业仍是3家》 [In 2000, the state reiterates its support for (the big) three auto firms], *CAIY*, 2000, 40.
77. Ibid.
78. Ibid.
79. "'十五'计划纲要全文 [Tenth Five-Year Plan, complete text]" March 15, 2001, www.chinaemb.or.kr/chn/zgzt/zgjj/t81068.htm. Emphasis added.
80. Iain Carson and Vijay V. Vaitheeswaran, *Zoom: The Global Race to Fuel the Car of the Future* (Penguin, 2008), 270–271.
81. On Detroit's resistance to hybrid technology, see Micheline Maynard, *The End of Detroit: How the Big Three Lost Their Grip on the American Car Market* (New York: Currency/Doubleday, 2003), 288.
82. Standing Committee to Review the Research Program of the Partnership for a New Generation of Vehicles, Board on Energy and Environmental Systems, Transportation Research Board, National Research Council, *Review of the Research Program of the Partnership for a New Generation of Vehicles: Seventh Report* (Washington, DC: The National Academies Press, 2001).
83. PNGV was replaced by the "FreedomCAR" project under the Bush administration, and is now part of the Department of Energy's Office of FreedomCAR and Vehicle technologies. See www1.eere.energy.gov/vehiclesandfuels/.
84. Tang Jie, Yang Yanping, and Zhou Wenjie, 中国汽车产业自主创新战略 [China auto industry indigenous innovation strategy], 198ff.
85. 《汽车工业'十五'规划》 [Auto industry Tenth Five-Year Plan, Section 1], *CAIY*, 2001, 23–24.
86. Because Volvo is now owned by a Chinese company. See Geely case in Chapter Five.
87. 《汽车工业'十五'规划》 [Auto industry Tenth Five-Year Plan, Section 2.1.1], *CAIY*, 2001, 25.
88. Euro II and III standards went into effect in the EU in 1992 and 1996, respectively. China eventually enforced Euro II and III standards for passenger cars in 2004 and 2007, respectively.
89. 《汽车工业'十五'规划》 [Auto industry Tenth Five-Year Plan, Sections 6.1–6.7], *CAIY*, 2001, 29–30.
90. Ibid., Section 3, 26.
91. Joseph Fewsmith, *China Since Tiananmen: The Politics of Transition* (Cambridge, UK: Cambridge University Press, 2001), 204–214.
92. Ibid., 208.
93. "China's Agreement with the United States on WTO accession," *Chinability*, 2001, www.chinability.com/WTO.htm#auto%20package.
94. Ibid.
95. Eric Harwit, "The Impact of WTO Membership on the Automobile Industry in China," *The China Quarterly* 167, no. 1 (2001): 655–670.
96. *CAIY*, 2009, 456.

97. *CAIY*, 2009, 326. And vehicle imports into China had previously reached as high as 310,099 in 1993, a figure that would not be reached again until 2007, a year in which China would manufacture 8.9 million vehicles. See Table B.2 in Appendix B.
98. Kenneth Lieberthal, *Governing China: From Revolution through Reform*, 2nd ed. (New York: W. W. Norton, 2004), 259–260.
99. 《汽车产业发展政策》 = Automotive Industry Development Policy, Chapter 2, Article 5. *CAIY*, 2005, 14. Dominik Declercq, Chief Representative of the European Auto Manufacturers Association in Beijing, helpfully provided a complete English translation of the 2004 Automotive Industry Development Policy (saving the author many hours of translation work).
100. 《汽车产业发展政策》 [Automotive industry development policy], Chapter 2, Article 6. *CAIY*, 2005, 14.
101. *CAIY*, 2005, 6.
102. 《汽车产业发展政策》 [Automotive industry development policy], Chapter 1, Article 4. *CAIY*, 2005, 14.
103. As of 2010, China's top three automakers, SAIC, FAW, and Dongfeng are all listed among the *Fortune* Global 500.
104. *CAIY*, 2005, 525–526.
105. *CAIY*, 2002, 451–452, and 2003, 449–450. The 10 percent figure is the author's estimate based on analysis of production and sales figures by car model as presented on the foregoing pages in the *Auto Industry Yearbooks*. The first report breaking out aggregate sales by domestic and foreign brands did not appear in an *Auto Yearbook* until 2006, and such reports have still not become a regular feature of the yearbooks, though they have been published in the China Auto Bluebooks which are published jointly by the Development Research Council of the State Council, the China Society of Automotive Engineers and Volkswagen Auto Group (China). Guowuyuan fazhan yanjiu zhongxin, 中国汽车产业发展报告 [China automotive industry development report], 2010, 252. See Tables B.3 and B.4 in Appendix B.
106. Since promulgation of the 1994 Auto Policy, by law, no foreign partner in an automotive joint venture could hold more than 50 percent of the equity, and most held the maximum 50 percent.
107. The Chinese term "自主" is commonly translated as "independent." In this context, it means "independent of foreign countries." There are a number of ways to express the above terms in English, and how I translate them at various points in this book often depends on what sounds better in the English context. The terms "indigenous brands," "Chinese brands," "own brands," and so on are all translations of 自主品牌.
108. 《汽车产业发展政策》 [Automotive industry development policy], Chapter 7, Article 29. *CAIY*, 2005, 16.
109. 《汽车产业发展政策》 [Automotive industry development policy], Chapter 4, Article 17. *CAIY*, 2005, 15.

110. By 2009 Chinese consumers had yet to take universal advantage of available credit facilities. The Finance Manager at a Beijing auto dealership revealed to me that, according to his company's statistics, in the southern part of China, about 40 percent of consumers financed their transactions, whereas only 5 percent of northerners did.

111. *CAIY*, 2006, 5. According to the figures presented, among passenger vehicles (including sedans, MPVs, and SUVs, but not crossover vehicles) Chinese brands held a 20 percent market share in 2004, increasing to 24 percent in 2005. This manner of reporting was repeated in the following year (*CAIY*, 2007, 4), but was discontinued thereafter. See Table B.3 in Appendix B.

112. 《2005年汽车工业发展概览》 [2005 Overview of auto industry development], Section 3.2. *CAIY*, 2006, 4. "中方较少有话语权."

113. 《中国汽车产业'十一五'发展规划纲要》 [China auto industry Eleventh Five-Year Development Plan outline], Part 1, Chapter 2. *CAIY*, 2006, 42.

114. 《中国汽车产业'十一五'发展规划纲要》 [China auto industry Eleventh Five-Year Development Plan outline], Part 3, Chapter 1. *CAIY*, 2006, 43.

115. Though evidence indicates that SOEs are still motivated primarily by size, as will be demonstrated in some of the cases in later chapters.

116. Great Wall had been building SUVs for a number of years, but this would be its first attempt to make cars.

117. *CAIY*, 2008, 47.

118. *CAIY*, 2008, 52.

119. The following Chinese sources contain passages accusing foreign multinationals of "垄断" or monopoly over China's auto industry. The first source is an influential former bureaucrat in the auto industry, the second is from China's Ministry of Science and Technology, and the third is from the Development Research Council, a think tank attached to the State Council. Wu Facheng, 汽车强国之梦 [Dream of an automobile superpower], 151; Tang Jie, Yang Yanping, and Zhou Wenjie, 中国汽车产业自主创新战略 [China auto industry indigenous innovation strategy], 84; Chen Xiaohong, ed., 中国企业国际化战略 [China enterprise internationalization strategy (Beijing: Renmin Chubanshe, 2006), 149.

120. Peter Hays Gries, "Narratives to Live By: The Century of Humiliation and Chinese National Identity Today," in *China's Transformations: The Stories Beyond the Headlines* (Lanham: Rowman & Littlefield, 2007), 117–118; David M. Lampton, *Same Bed, Different Dreams: Managing U.S.-China Relations, 1989–2000* (Berkeley: University of California Press, 2001), 255–257.

121. *CAIY*, 2008, 48–49.

122. Cars tested were all indigenous brands. A search for "Chinese crash test" on YouTube will yield many of these videos.

123. Guowuyuan fazhan yanjiu zhongxin, 中国汽车产业发展报告 [China automotive industry development report], 2010, 256.
124. *CAIY*, 2009, 56.
125. "汽车产业调整和振兴规划" [Auto industry adjustment and stimulus plan], *The Central People's Government of the PRC*, March 20, 2009, http://www.gov.cn/zwgk/2009–03/20/content_1264324.htm.
126. Guowuyuan fazhan yanjiu zhongxin, 中国汽车产业发展报告 [China automotive industry development report], 2010, 48.
127. "New energy vehicle sales in China disappoint automakers," *Global Times*, December 6, 2010, http://autos.globaltimes.cn/china/2010–12/599331.html. China Association of Automobile Manufacturers.
128. Guowuyuan fazhan yanjiu zhongxin, 中国汽车产业发展报告 [China automotive industry development report], 2010, 29.
129. "New guidelines for mergers in auto industry expected at year end," *People's Daily Online*, September 14, 2010, http://english.peopledaily.com.cn/90001/90778/90860/7139873.html.
130. "私人购买新能源汽车补贴试点工作正式启动" [Subsidy pilot for individual purchase of NEVs formally begins], *Ministry of Finance, PRC*, June 1, 2010, www.mof.gov.cn/zhengwuxinxi/caizhengxinwen/201006/t20100601_320713.html.
131. The seven "new strategic industries" include high-end equipment manufacturing, alternative energy, biotechnology, new generation information technology, energy-saving technology, environmentally friendly technology, and new energy vehicles.
132. Liang Dongmei, "China to Forgo Five-Year Plan for Auto Industry," *Caixin Online*, April 7, 2011, http://english.caing.com/2011–04–07/100245836.html.

Chapter Four

The Joint Ventures

China's auto industry is like an ecosystem. All of the players have an important function. Originally, the joint ventures were intended to bring technology. That didn't work, so instead they are bringing cash—and lots of it. The SOEs use that cash to fund development of their own brands.

—East Asia auto industry analyst
Hong Kong, December 2009

When China launched its economic reforms in the late 1970s, there was a sense among many senior government leaders that China had fallen behind much of the outside world in its industrialization. Accordingly, most of the major industries in China embarked on modernization programs with at least one eye on what had been done in other countries. The automobile industry was no exception, and the industry began reaching out early to foreign partners who could help bring China's auto industry up to speed. This chapter describes in particular how four Chinese-foreign automotive joint ventures were negotiated and launched, and how the partners handled the inevitable difficulties that arose in the course of business.

The case studies I have chosen are the three earliest joint ventures formed in the 1980s: Beijing-Jeep, Shanghai-Volkswagen (SVW) and Guangzhou-PSA. A fourth joint venture, Shanghai-General Motors (SGM), was formed later in the 1990s. While the Beijing and Guangzhou JVs no longer exist, the two Shanghai-based JVs are still going strong, and together they have helped to make the Shanghai Automotive Industry Corporation (SAIC), a local state-owned enterprise (LSOE), China's largest automotive group. There are, of course, many more joint ventures than these (see a complete list of Chinese-foreign JVs in Appendix A), but I have chosen these as they illustrate well the most important points surrounding the critical role of joint ventures in China's auto industry.

As I compare the startup phases of each of these joint ventures, the reader will see how the central government's understanding of the meaning of technology transfer has evolved over time. By the time the SGM joint venture was formed in the late 1990s, the central government had a much clearer idea of what it wanted in terms of tech transfer, and General Motors was eager to provide it in exchange for a piece of the market. Also, toward the end of each case study, I will review how each partner has also learned and adapted since the early days of joint ventures in China. Even the failed joint ventures have led to later successes for most of the original partners.

This chapter also shows how the central government's expectations of the joint ventures have changed, not only in light of the central government's improved understanding of technology transfer, but also in light of the important external factor of WTO membership. Since WTO membership forbid China from demanding technology transfer as a condition for approval of foreign investment, the central government had to become more creative in how it attempted to gain technology from the industry's foreign partners. Of key importance here is the relatively new phenomenon, first mentioned above in Chapter Two, that I call "JV brands," which are essentially Chinese-built, Chinese-branded cars whose technology originates with the foreign multinationals (MNCs). But long before JV brands became the latest attempt to acquire technology, the SOEs all began eagerly to seek out foreign partners because they discovered building foreign-branded cars to be far more profitable—at least in the short-term—than investing in their own brands. This fact set up a conflict between the central government and the SOEs: while the central government was focused more on building an auto industry that would eventually become independent of the foreign MNCs, the SOEs focused on the most expedient route to short-term profits.

Beijing-Jeep

James Mann's *Beijing-Jeep* is a detailed and remarkably entertaining case study of this first Chinese-foreign auto joint venture, and it goes far beyond the few pages I devote to it in this chapter.[1] My purpose here is to highlight elements of the story that demonstrate unrealistic expectations on the part of the Chinese in terms of technology transfer and the difficulties faced by both sides of this early joint venture. At the end of this section I discuss how the two partners of this ill-fated joint venture have changed their respective approaches to the China auto market.

Recall from Chapter Three that the leaders of Beijing Auto dispatched C. B. Sung to establish relations with an American partner who could assist them in revitalizing the jeep factory in Beijing. Though Beijing Auto first reached out in 1978 to American Motors (AMC), owner of the Jeep brand, about cooperating to build Jeeps in Beijing, the final agreement would not be signed until several years later. At first, success seemed to come easy. In early 1979, after only a couple of weeks in Beijing, AMC representatives were able to hammer out an agreement with Chinese officials covering the basic points of their future cooperation. James Mann reports that AMC officials thought at the time their final agreement "was going to be a pushover."[2] Further paving the way in the interim was the passage of China's first law permitting joint ventures.

Despite the apparent early success, negotiations stagnated, and it would be another two years before serious discussions between the Chinese and AMC would begin again. At the time, the Americans thought the Chinese had simply lost interest. What they did not know was that Chinese officials had been courting other global automakers, among them Toyota, who were not interested in manufacturing in

China or in technology transfer, but were insistent that they could serve China's needs by exporting cars made in Japan. This sticking point ended the discussions with Toyota for the time being. The Chinese government was not looking for cars to be *sold* in China; they were looking for cars to be *built* in China.

When the Chinese eventually showed interest in a deal with AMC again, discussions did not go smoothly. More than 10 different Chinese government organizations became involved in the negotiations, and none wanted to risk taking responsibility for such a potentially large venture, so they passed it around like a hot potato.[3] Among the major issues was Chinese insistence on the ability to export Chinese-made Jeeps to earn foreign exchange. The Americans were hesitant to make such a commitment due to doubts about the initial quality of vehicles made in China. During the course of negotiations, AMC flew Chinese officials to Detroit at least twice, and also, toward the end of negotiations, flew Chinese officials to Cairo, Egypt, so they could see AMC operations there and hear the views of AMC's Egyptian partners.

The contract was finally signed in May of 1983. This would be the first Chinese-foreign manufacturing joint venture formed since China's reopening to the world.[4] AMC would own 31 percent of the JV with Beijing Auto Works (BAW) holding the balance. The duration of the contract was to be 20 years. The Chinese agreed initially to parts imports, but they expected a gradual shift toward local production. The Americans were in agreement as localization would lower their costs, though their quality concerns persisted. The initial method of manufacturing was to import "complete knock-down" kits (CKDs) of Jeep Cherokees that would be assembled in the BAW factory. The factory would also continue production of the old BJ212 jeep model it had inherited from the Soviets as a way to continue generating cash during the early years of the JV. (This model was later upgraded to the BJ2020, which is still being made in Beijing.) The contract also required technology transfer, and fully one half of AMC's contribution to the JV consisted of intellectual property; the rest was in cash.

There was also a requirement that the JV would develop an all-new, canvas-top, all-terrain vehicle for use by the People's Liberation Army (PLA). It is unclear whether AMC ever intended to comply with this provision as the cost for developing such a model would have been in excess of US$1 billion, and AMC had no expectations that the JV would be capable of generating that amount of excess cash flow in the near term.[5] It is also unclear whether the Chinese did not understand the cost of developing a new vehicle, or whether they simply expected AMC to just *give* the new design to the JV, but they eventually accepted, reluctantly, that developing a new model was not financially feasible. This was, however, a major disappointment for the Chinese side, and this "wishful thinking," as Harwit characterizes it, would continue to contribute to difficulties early in the life of the joint venture.[6]

In 1986 the joint venture essentially ran out of foreign exchange, and AMC refused to extend any more credit to the JV for the purchase of more CKDs. Production ground to a halt as the Americans and Chinese attempted to work out a solution. The local Beijing government was either unable or unwilling to help, so AMC's representative in Beijing, Don St. Pierre, escalated the issue to Premier Zhao Ziyang who delegated resolution to Zhu Rongji, then Vice Minister of the State Economic Commission. The solution worked out by Zhu involved payment of debts to the JV by BAW and permission for the JV to convert some of its Chinese yuan to U.S. dollars.[7] AMC then agreed to limit the number of Cherokees to 12,500 annually, a move that would place a ceiling on CKDs and, therefore, the need for foreign exchange. This was when the two sides also agreed to drop the requirement for the JV to develop a new Jeep vehicle for the PLA.

In 1987 AMC was purchased by Chrysler Corporation, and in 1988 Chrysler's iconic Chairman Lee Iacocca paid the JV a visit. Under Chrysler, Beijing-Jeep continued to increase the localization of parts, reaching nearly 61 percent by 1993, but Chrysler Corp, which had very little global presence, seemed to lose interest in the venture in the late 1990s. In 1999 Chrysler was purchased by Daimler Corporation of Germany. A former Daimler official who had been in China since the 1980s says that the venture was "loss-making" and plagued with "various kinds of fraud," including purchases by the JV of counterfeit parts, and that Chrysler had basically stopped investing in the Jeep venture around 1994, hoping to simply ride out the remainder of the 20-year contract. The former Daimler official says, "this was a big mistake. It damaged Chrysler's reputation with the government... The Chinese remember these things."

Once Daimler took over, the Germans took steps to reverse the damage caused by Chrysler's mismanagement of its relationship with Beijing Auto. The new DaimlerChrysler introduced the larger and more luxurious Grand Cherokee in 2001, and by 2002 had reached a 90 percent localization of all Cherokee parts.[8] In 2001, DaimlerChrysler signed a new 30-year contract with the parent of Beijing Auto, BAIC (Beijing Automotive Industry Corp.), and the new venture also began to assemble Mercedes-Benz sedans and, eventually, the Chrysler 300C sedan.[9]

By 2007, however, it had long been apparent that the Daimler and Chrysler cultures were not meshing well, and Daimler sold Chrysler to private equity firm Cerberus. Following this change the Cherokee ceased to be made in China, but in early 2011 BAIC introduced a new SUV named the Qishi that is essentially a rebadged Jeep Cherokee.[10] BAIC also continues to build a few variants of the old BJ2020 SUV (fewer than 10,000 in 2008).[11]

BAIC introduced its first-ever own-brand sedan in late 2010. The awkwardly named BC301Z bears a striking resemblance to BAIC partner Daimler's Mercedes-Benz B-Class, though slightly smaller.[12] And after attempting to buy the Sweden-based Saab Auto from a desperate General Motors for much of 2009, BAIC ultimately came away with only portions of the company. BAIC now owns the intellectual property for Saab's 9–3 and 9–5 models along with their engines and associated manufacturing equipment. As of this writing, BAIC-branded cars based on Saab technology are expected in 2012.

The most significant and successful move thus far for BAIC, however, has been its joint venture with Hyundai Motors of South Korea. The Hyundai brand now occupies more than 6 percent of China's market for passenger vehicles, and even the casual visitor to Beijing cannot help but notice the nearly ubiquitous Hyundai Elantra taxis.[13] According to a senior Beijing-Hyundai executive, BAIC sought out Hyundai for talks in 2001 and concluded their agreement the following year. The Beijing city government was helpful to the venture, granting it tax-free status for its first two years and allowing it a 50 percent tax exemption in year three.

The executive admits that conflicts are inevitable in any JV as the two sides have different interests, but says that relations have generally been amicable and any disagreements are resolved within the JV without having to bring in the BAIC parent company or the Beijing city government. The JV has achieved an 85 percent localization, but the Beijing Hyundai executive admits there is no Chinese technology in the cars produced by the venture. I asked him whether Hyundai and BAIC had cooperated in any technology transfer that could help BAIC produce its own cars (at the time, BAIC had yet to introduce a passenger car under its own brand), and he said there had been no transfer of technology from Hyundai.

Though China's original auto joint venture, Beijing-Jeep, no longer exists, it continues to be cited in China's auto industry official documentation as an example of successful technology transfer. Technology acquired through the Beijing-Jeep JV, and later modified by BAIC, is today considered to be "self-developed" (自主开发).[14] And though BAIC owns China's largest commercial vehicle manufacturer, Beiqi Foton, BAIC continues to play catch-up with the larger Chinese manufacturers of passenger cars.[15]

As a typical SOE, BAIC has, until very recently, relied completely on its partnerships with Hyundai and Daimler in the passenger car market. However, under its current CEO, Wang Dazhong, a U.S.-educated, former General Motors engineer, Beijing Auto has demonstrated a new level of aggressiveness in its efforts to acquire foreign technology for its own use, its purchase of Saab assets being but one example. Beijing Auto has also, as part of a local government investment group, benefited from a recent purchase of General Motor's Michigan-based Nexteer division, which makes advanced power steering systems. Beijing Auto has also been listed among several Chinese firms bidding to purchase the famous Italian auto design firm, Pininfarina.

BAIC's former partner, Chrysler, took another run at the China market even before it became independent of Daimler in 2007. In that year Chrysler announced an impending partnership with Chery and plans to export Chinese-made, Dodge-branded cars to the United States, but within 18 months the alliance was ended without having produced a single car. Since that time, neither Chrysler nor Chery has managed to form a significant joint venture in China, though Chrysler, under its new owner, Fiat, is expected to make an eventual return to

China as part of Fiat's joint venture with Guangzhou Auto. Even though Chrysler was once part of China's very first automotive joint venture, aside from a relative handful of imports and licensed production, Chrysler continues to lack a significant presence in China.

Shanghai-Volkswagen

Similarly to the experience of AMC, Volkswagen's representatives also perceived a loss of interest on the part of the Chinese following their initial contact in 1978.[16] The following year, Rao Bin, the new machine-building minister, invited a delegation from Volkswagen to visit China to resume discussions. While AMC was discussing the Jeep JV in Beijing, officials from the Machine Building Ministry suggested to the Germans that they consider Shanghai. (Unknown to the Germans, China's delays in talking to Volkswagen also occurred because of simultaneous discussions with other global automakers, including Toyota, which once again, balked at the insistence on technology transfer.) Unlike the AMC negotiations, which took place primarily between AMC and central government representatives, the Volkswagen negotiations were dominated by local Shanghai officials.[17]

The Volkswagen delegation was given a tour of the Shanghai Auto factory in Anting, a small city in the Shanghai region, but outside the metropolitan area. Workers in this factory were building the "Shanghai brand" sedan that was the successor to the old Phoenix sedan of the 1960s. The Germans were horrified by the outdated conditions of the Anting factory; much improvement would be needed before they could produce cars there. To emphasize their sincerity however, the Germans offered to run a trial experiment to determine whether Chinese workers could assemble Volkswagen CKDs shipped from Germany. This experiment went on for at least two years, assembling nearly 900 Volkswagen Santanas and training Chinese engineers in vehicle assembly. Eight Chinese workers were also sent to Germany for advanced training.

As with Beijing-Jeep, the Chinese also expected their counterparts to develop a new model of sedan for the Shanghai factory, but the Germans, like the Americans, were concerned about the quality of a fully Chinese-made sedan. They had demonstrated the feasibility of assembling Santana CKDs for the Chinese market, and insisted on following this model with the understanding that parts production would be localized as quickly as possible. Perhaps foreseeing potential difficulties with this model of localizing parts, the Germans worded the contract so that the Chinese side of the JV would be solely responsible for producing local parts in line with Volkswagen's quality standards. Until that could happen, the JV would continue to assemble CKDs imported from Germany.

There still remained the issue of how the JV would earn foreign exchange—a requirement of all joint ventures that China would be forced to drop as a condition of WTO membership nearly two decades later. This issue was solved by establishing an engine plant with a capacity of 100,000 units a year to export engines to Volkswagen in other countries.

The final agreement establishing Shanghai-Volkswagen (SVW) was signed in October of 1984. Unlike the Beijing-Jeep JV in which AMC held a minority share, Volkswagen insisted on having an equal share with its Chinese partners. Volkswagen would own 50 percent, and the Chinese share would be split among three partners that had been designated by Beijing. The Shanghai Tractor Automobile Corporation (STAC, predecessor to Shanghai Automotive Industry Corporation or SAIC) would hold 25 percent; the Bank of China would hold 15 percent, and the remaining 10 percent would be held by CNAIC. The contract, which would have an initial duration of 25 years, also included a provision for technology transfer.[18]

In the late 1980s, Volkswagen representatives became aware of an impending "big project" to be announced by Beijing for mass production of sedans. According to Volkswagen's chief representative in Shanghai, Martin Posth, the competition appeared to be among Beijing, Guangzhou, Shanghai, Changchun, and Shiyan (in Hubei Province). The first three cities had already established joint ventures between their respective LSOEs and foreign automakers. Changchun and Shiyan, home to two CSOEs, FAW, and SAW, respectively, also hoped to win the project.[19] While Volkswagen had hoped early on that Shanghai Auto would win the "big project," German expatriates understood that competition among multinationals was keen as most of the other major global automakers, including Ford, GM, Chrysler, and Toyota, were also angling for a position in China.

Not wanting to miss out on the opportunity, Volkswagen officials determined to pursue any possible lead, including direct talks with some of the other factories in China. During this time they paid visits to both SAW and FAW, the latter of which was already deep into negotiations with Chrysler. During their visit to Changchun, Carl Hahn, CEO of Volkswagen AG, managed to persuade FAW not to expand cooperation with Chrysler beyond production of an engine and instead to build the Audi 100 in partnership with Volkswagen. These talks ultimately led to the formation of another joint venture, FAW-Volkswagen that would go on to produce the Audi 100 (with, of all things, a Chrysler engine), beginning in 1988, and the VW Jetta, beginning in 1990. It is interesting that, despite there being as many as a dozen foreign automakers interested in investing in China at the time, FAW chose to limit its most serious discussions to the two foreign companies that were already in China, Chrysler and VW. Perhaps this highlights the conservative nature of this CSOE: rather than consider bringing in a new-to-China foreign auto brand, FAW chose the partner with which its owner, the central government was already most familiar.

As Volkswagen later discovered, Beijing, particularly the State Economic Commission and its vice chairman, Zhu Rongji, had been vigorously pushing for Chrysler to get the FAW joint venture so that there would be more competition among foreign automakers in China.[20] But Zhu did not get his way. What Zhu probably knew at the time that Volkswagen did not was that he would soon become Party secretary in the city of Shanghai, and eventually, its mayor as well. Posth speculates that Zhu probably regretted that the Audi 100 would be built in Changchun and not Shanghai.[21] As I discovered in discussions with a SAIC official, Volkswagen's divided loyalties between SAIC and FAW may have recently worked against it. I will discuss this possibility in the following case on Shanghai-GM.

From these two early joint ventures, Beijing-Jeep and Shanghai-Volkswagen, we can see what was important to the Chinese. Early in the negotiations, we can also see a real ambivalence toward the foreign automakers. While the Chinese wanted foreign technology, they also had a very valuable bargaining chip: access to China's market. In both cases, the initial Chinese approaches to these two foreign automakers turned into lengthy, on-again, off-again negotiations in which the Chinese attempted to extract the best deals by talking with several automakers simultaneously.

At this early stage, however, the Chinese did not know what they did not know. They wanted technology, and they knew foreigners possessed it, so early negotiations simply demanded an undefined "technology transfer." What the Chinese did not understand was that getting one's hands on blueprints did not confer the ability to design vehicles. What they also did not understand was that foreign automakers, who had at the time been investing upward of $1 billion to develop each new vehicle model, were not simply going to hand over the designs of their latest creations. This would all become clear to the Chinese soon enough, but they would not be able to shortcut the learning process necessary to build a world-class auto industry.

Where the Beijing and Shanghai JVs differ, of course, is that, despite the early difficulties both experienced, only one is still in existence. Whereas AMC's, and then Chrysler's, early difficulties seem to have stemmed from a lack of global sensibility, Volkswagen had long been accustomed to operating in markets outside its home in Germany. And according to political scientist and China auto specialist Eric Thun, the Chinese sides of these two joint ventures differed in their respective local governments' demands for localization—not merely for production in China, but for production in the *local region*. Whereas Beijing's local government took a hands-off, *laissez-faire* attitude toward localization— meaning that the JV was free to source parts from anywhere in China—the Shanghai government insisted on maximizing parts production in the Shanghai area. Thun attributes the superior performance of Shanghai Auto to this localization strategy, and this attitude has been at least partially responsible for the success of SAIC's other major joint venture, Shanghai-GM.[22]

Shanghai–GM

Despite the difficulties faced by General Motors in 2009 and 2010— including bankruptcy, a U.S. government bailout and a rapid-fire succession of CEOs—the story of GM in China has been one of success and relative harmony.[23] GM was not one of the earliest foreign automakers to invest in post-Mao China; Jeep and VW had already been operating in China for eight years by the time GM established a representative office in Beijing in 1992. By 1994 Shanghai Auto, which already had a JV with Volkswagen, began looking for another foreign partner to produce a domestically made luxury sedan for state leaders. The central government had been concerned that, until this time, senior leaders were being driven around in imported Mercedes-Benz sedans.

Early competitors to become SAIC's new partner were GM, Ford, Toyota, and Chrysler, the latter two dropping out of the competition fairly early in the process. SAIC had been looking for a partner that could offer both a luxury sedan and an MPV (i.e., minivan). GM offered an all-new Buick Regal sedan versus Ford's Taurus, which was already about four years old at the time. The Buick nameplate, despite its then reputation for stodginess in the United States, was particularly appealing to the Chinese as historical Chinese figures such as Sun Yatsen, "Last Emperor" Pu Yi and former Premier Zhou Enlai had all owned Buicks.[24] In the end, GM won the competition because it was offering something new and tailored specifically for the Chinese market. GM ultimately implemented 600 changes to the Regal for China, including additional legroom in the backseat and controls for the radio and air conditioner.[25] These changes were overseen by the vice mayor of Shanghai who, according to a former GM insider, "basically engineered the rear seat in 1995–1996."

The memorandum of understanding for the formation of SAIC-GM (SGM) was signed in 1995. The agreement, signed by GM's Rudy Schlais, included the requisite transfer of technology, but GM demonstrated its willingness to go even further than other foreign automakers by setting up a joint venture R&D organization with SAIC called Pan-Asia Technical Automotive Center (PATAC). The establishment of PATAC represented a departure from the standard technology transfer requirement, and the Chinese felt it was the key to the technology they had been lacking. Today, PATAC is run by co-CEOs, one Chinese and one American, both women and both engineers, and it is staffed with approximately 96 percent local hires and a few expatriates. Among PATAC's most prominent projects was design of the new Buick

LaCrosse, which was first released in China and then sold in other markets.

Key to establishment of the GM venture with SAIC was the support and involvement of GM senior management in Detroit. According to Schlais, whenever he encountered an intractable problem, he was able to call GM CEO Jack Smith and request his presence in Beijing. Smith reportedly made the trip to China six times in 1996 to meet Chinese President Jiang Zemin and other state leaders.[26] Smith also demonstrated faith in the venture by approving funding for GM's new factory before the contract had even been approved by the Chinese side.[27] The original SGM factory was built in Shanghai's Pudong district, and since its founding SGM has also opened factories in Shandong and Liaoning provinces. SGM's Buick factory is, according to an executive from a rival automaker with whom I spoke, considered to be "state-of-the-art . . . among the best in the world." SAIC and GM also have an auto financing JV and a JV with OnStar, General Motors' subscription-based wireless communications and security service. GM has also jointly established with Tsinghua University and SAIC, the China Automotive Energy Research Center (CAERC). According to a Shanghai-based GM executive, CAERC is a sort of "think tank for government people to call on for the latest research on various energies such as coal to liquid, biofuels, hydrogen, et cetera." Its goal is to "keep [China's] government from closing the [policy] door to various fuel alternatives before their potential has been fully explored."

The process of negotiating the new JV put GM through difficulties similar to those experienced by AMC and Volkswagen in the 1980s. Prior to the signing of the memorandum of understanding with GM in 1995, SAIC kept both Ford and GM on the hook, constantly competing to out-compromise each other for the reward of the JV contract.[28] The MOU between SAIC and GM was finally signed in 1995, and the final contract was signed in March of 1997, witnessed by U.S. Vice President Al Gore, who happened to be visiting China at the time. Unlike the SVW deal, in which SAIC held only 25 percent, this time the joint venture began as a 50–50 split, with neither SAIC nor GM having absolute control. Each side contributed $350 million in cash, and each assumed responsibility for half of $820 million in bank loans to fund the new joint venture.[29]

Though the JV would not begin full production until April 1999, the first car, a Buick New Century, rolled off the line in December of 1998, and Jack Smith was once again on hand for the celebration. SGM began with a comparatively high parts localization of 47 percent. GM's parts subsidiary, Delphi (which would be spun off in 1999), had already begun local parts production a few years earlier with a wiring harness plant in Anting, home of SVW. By 2000 SGM had already localized 60 percent of parts manufacture.[30] In the ensuing years, the JV introduced different car models including two compact sedans and the now ubiquitous GL8, a China-only minivan which has, surprisingly, become the vehicle of choice for many business executives who use the GL8's comfortable rear seats as a mobile office while their chauffeurs do the driving. In 2010 SGM, for the first time, surpassed SVW as the biggest automaker in China. SGM sold 1.039 million cars to SVW's 1 million.[31]

In 2002, GM joined SAIC in its existing joint venture with the City of Liuzhou in Guangxi province. GM joined with an initial stake of 34 percent while SAIC reduced its stake from 76 percent to 50 percent, and Liuzhou held the remaining 16 percent. The JV was renamed SAIC-GM-Wuling (SGMW). The venture focused initially on building low-end micro-vans and small trucks including the Wuling Sunshine, a popular micro-van that sold in China's hinterlands for about $3,700.[32] GM committed to upgrading the technology of the venture which eventually began to assemble small vehicles for sale both in China and in emerging export markets under the Chevrolet brand.

Toward the end of 2010, SGMW took a step toward the latest trend for joint ventures in China, building "JV brands." The idea behind a JV brand is that the foreign partner contributes to the joint venture older, slightly outdated, yet recognizably foreign, vehicle designs which are then manufactured under a Chinese brand name.[33] In the case of SGMW, the new Chinese brand, *Baojun*, is applied to a design from General Motors' South Korean subsidiary, Daewoo. China auto industry consultant, Michael Dunne, confirms that this trend is being driven indirectly by industry regulators. Foreign automakers that apply for a capacity increase are "indirectly pressured" to include with their applications plans to help their SOE partners develop "indigenous brands."[34] Dunne also wrote in an *Automotive News China* editorial, "Getting involved [with development of indigenous brands] is strictly voluntary, of course. There's no Chinese law requiring formation of an indigenous brand. It's only a recommendation."[35] But, says Dunne, requests from central government officials for production of these brands appear to be connected to requests from foreign automakers for permission to increase production capacity in China. The purpose is to create brands that are JV-owned, but Chinese-branded that will eventually move up-market and compete directly with foreign brands.[36]

Other foreign automakers are, not coincidentally, following a similar strategy in China. Honda and Nissan are both pursuing similar paths, building the Everus and the Venucia, with their respective partners, Guangzhou Auto and Dongfeng. And Volkswagen has been discussing similar possibilities with FAW to create an electric-only JV brand called *Kaili*. This strategy appears to be designed to address the perception gap Chinese consumers have between domestic and foreign brands. The consensus among many of my interviewees is that most Chinese consumers, given the choice, would prefer to purchase a foreign-branded car as they perceive foreign brands to be of higher quality. The JV-brand strategy seems intended to fill this perception gap by offering foreign technology with a Chinese brand. And if Dunne is correct in his assessment, China's central government may be breaking the spirit, if not the letter, of its WTO accession agreement by tying approval of expansion to introduction of these JV brands.

In December of 2009, SAIC and GM announced a surprising change to their joint-venture arrangement. In exchange for $84 million, General Motors agreed to sell 1 percent of SGM to SAIC, leaving GM with 49 percent ownership and SAIC with a majority of 51 percent. At the same time, the two parties announced the formation of a Hong Kong-based investment company intended to be used as a springboard for SGM into India and other emerging markets. Early speculation for this move included the possibility that GM, having gone through bankruptcy earlier in 2009 and emerged $50 billion in debt to the U.S. Treasury, was desperate enough for cash that it was willing to give up control of its most promising subsidiary. However, even if this had been the case, the $84 million GM received would not have come close to paying off GM's $50 *billion* debt to the U.S. Treasury. The deal, by all outward appearances, was not a good one for GM. As 50/50 owners, the two sides were forced to negotiate all important decisions, but with a 51 percent majority, the SAIC side would theoretically be able to take all decisions independently.

A SAIC executive who was close to the negotiations explained to me that the 1 percent ownership shift was part of a much larger plan in which both sides ended up with what they wanted. In short, Shanghai Auto needed two things: to expand abroad and to get bigger, and GM needed access to funding for expansion outside the United States. According to the SAIC executive, SAIC was highly motivated by a need to move up in the *Fortune* Global 500 rankings.[37] Under accounting rules, a company cannot consolidate the top-line revenue of a joint venture unless it owns a majority of the JV's shares. With only 50 percent of SGM, SAIC could only consolidate its share of the joint venture's bottom-line profit. Because the *Fortune* ranking is based on revenue, not profit, SAIC needed a way to consolidate the entire income statement. SAIC got around this requirement in its JV with Volkswagen by establishing a sales organization, SAIC-VW Sales (SVWS), owned 60/40 by SAIC and VW, respectively. The SVW joint venture sells all of the cars it manufactures to SVWS, which then sells them to dealers. Sixty percent of the sales of SVWS are consolidated into SAIC's income statement.

For a few years, SAIC and GM had been in talks about a similar arrangement, but once GM declared bankruptcy and became majority-owned by the U.S. Treasury this was no longer a viable option as this China-specific deal was deemed to be of no benefit to GM's new shareholder, the U.S. Treasury. GM's new shareholder had essentially separated GM into two parts: United States and everything else. While U.S. officials understood that the "everything else" was of value to GM, helping out the "everything else" would not have passed the "*Washington Post* test" of Obama administration auto adviser Steve Rattner. According to Rattner, the question he asked was, "How would the public react to a headline that said [we were] in effect allocating hundreds of millions of dollars to shore up [GM's offshore entities]?"[38] Regardless of who its owner was, as a going concern, GM itself still needed funding for expansion in its most promising global markets, but having recently emerged from bankruptcy, GM lacked access to bank loans. This was where SAIC was able to help. Its solid relationships with banks, both in the Mainland and Hong Kong, would be of benefit to GM.

The other part of the deal, the Hong Kong investment company, provided both companies with an opportunity to expand into another of the world's most important emerging markets, India. GM had already established a presence in India with two vehicle factories and an engine factory. They had also introduced seven models, "none of which," according to the SAIC executive, "had been doing very well." SAIC and GM both felt that some of the micro-vehicles made by the Wuling joint venture (SGMW) would be more suitable for India. GM would contribute its fixed assets in India and the Chevrolet brand; SAIC would contribute cash, and the SGMW joint venture would contribute vehicle designs, including those of the new *Baojun* JV brand.

And the naming of the Hong Kong-based corporate entity through which this would be accomplished also reveals something about the possible future plans of SAIC and GM. The name originally proposed for the entity was "SAIC-GM Asia-Pacific Automotive Investment Co. Ltd.," but in the final agreement, the "Asia-Pacific" portion was dropped. The SAIC executive, who pointed out to me the name change, was noncommittal as to future activities, but did not deny that SAIC and GM had hopes of working together in other markets as well. He also pointed out that the entity's official Chinese and English names are not identical translations of each other. The English name is "SAIC-GM Automotive Investment Co." and the Chinese name is "GM-SAIC Automotive Investment Co." (通用上海汽车投资公司)—almost as if the two partners wanted to remind their respective parent companies of the importance of the other partner.

I asked the SAIC executive why SAIC did not pursue the India venture with their other partner, Volkswagen, which was financially stronger than GM. He responded that "VW's attitude" was an obstacle. "VW has [divided loyalty between] two partners in China, but GM really only has one partner—except for a small JV with FAW, which GM showed enough respect to consult with SAIC on." He further explained that SAIC-GM is *"more of a marriage than a partnership. We are in this for the long-term."* His wording almost exactly matches that of a Shanghai-based GM executive with whom I met on a separate occasion:

They [SAIC] had global aspirations, and we [GM] knew that. They had domestic aspirations, and we knew that. We weren't blinded when we got into it. It's just a matter of how do we make it a win-win. *This is more than a partnership; it's a marriage.* A partnership maybe expires at some point, but a marriage is for life. In a marriage you need to look at things from your partner's perspective. We truly are committed and we think SAIC is as well. What happened over the last six months (July–December 2009) has been a win-win, and it has strengthened our partnership with SAIC.

This may explain why a number of my interviewees in China described SGM as China's "most amicable" or "most harmonious" joint venture. However, as most interviewees were quick to point out, and as the GM executive quoted above intimates, such a close relationship has its costs as well. GM has invested much in China, making China a larger market for GM than the United States, and in the process has, in the views of most interviewees, handed over far more technology to its joint venture partner than any other foreign automaker. With the 2009 1 percent transaction, SAIC now has controlling interest in SGM, and while this may cause no problems for GM as long as the partnership remains amicable, this presents the potential for problems should the partners disagree in the future. However, SAIC has recently shown further commitment to the partnership by purchasing a nearly 1 percent stake in the initial public offering of General Motors in the United States. And GM has also raised its stake in the SGMW joint venture from 34 percent to 44 percent. (SAIC maintains its 50 percent share in that joint venture.)

According to Steven J. Girsky, GM's vice chairman for corporate strategy and business development, it would appear that GM has bet no less than its entire future on China. "China's a big piece of the value of the company...And since we pull cash out of China, it helps fund investments in other parts of the company as well."[39] So while SAIC may be using cash generated from sales of GM cars to fund its R&D pipeline, it now appears that GM is able to accomplish exactly the same purpose with its China operation.

Shanghai Auto is now China's largest automaker. In 2010 the combined entities of SAIC sold a record 3.58 million vehicles.[40] Each of SAIC's joint ventures sold more than one million vehicles in 2010: SGM sold 1.04 million, SVW sold 1.0 million, and SGMW sold 1.23 million.[41] SAIC also sold 160,000 of its own-branded MG and Roewe vehicles, intellectual property of which were acquired from a defunct UK company as well as its merger with Nanjing Auto in 2007, a story that will be covered in Chapter Six. SAIC has already announced its plans to pour $1.5 billion into these domestic brands over the next five years.[42] Much of this development money will come from profits earned by SAIC's joint ventures. And being an SOE, SAIC will continue to enjoy preferential access to bank loans.

Guangzhou-Peugeot

Back in 1988 the fledgling Guangzhou-Peugeot JV was designated as one of China's "small three" automakers intended by the central government to be among the survivors of a massive auto industry consolidation.[43] As the story in Chapter Two described it, that consolidation has yet to take place. And though Guangzhou-Peugeot is no longer in existence (both partners in the JV continue to operate separately in China), the story of this ill-fated JV is instructive from both a political and a managerial perspective.

During the early post-Mao reforms in 1980, Guangdong and Fujian provinces had been designated as areas where the central government wanted to experiment by attracting foreign investment. In a fiscal reform referred to as "eating in separate kitchens" provincial revenue shares would be fixed for five years, and provinces would be required to balance their own budgets without expectations of bailouts from the center. The advantage to the provinces was that they could plan their economies as they saw fit without fiscal targets from the center.[44] In the special case of Guangdong, the province would keep all revenues it collected with the exception of 1 billion yuan it would send to Beijing every year. This special arrangement would have an impact on the Guangzhou-Peugeot joint venture.

In 1981 officials from the city of Guangzhou, Guangdong's provincial capital, approached representatives of the French automaker PSA during an auto exhibition in Guangzhou to discuss the possibility of forming a joint venture.[45] PSA (today known as PSA Peugeot-Citroën) had been founded in 1976 through the merger of two French auto-makers, Peugeot and Citroën. Until this time the Guangzhou city government's auto factory, Guangzhou Automotive Manufacturing or GAM, had only manufactured buses and trucks, and city officials wanted to add passenger cars to the mix. Due to the aforementioned fiscal arrangements, China's central government played very little role in the negotiations, though the head of CNAIC in the early 1980s, Rao Bin, was reportedly supportive of the venture.[46]

Negotiation of this third Chinese-foreign venture took only slightly less time than did that of the JVs in Beijing and Shanghai. By 1985 negotiations were completed for the formation of the Guangzhou Peugeot Automobile Corporation (GPAC). The Chinese side of the JV included GAM (owner of the current truck and bus factory) with 46 percent and the Chinese International Trust and Investment Corp (CITIC) with 20 percent. The French side of the JV included PSA with 22 percent and the French bank, BNP with 8 percent. The World Bank's International Finance Corporation (IFC), an organization that provides advice and funding for private sector investments in developing countries, held the remaining 4 percent (see Figure 4.1).[47]

Unlike the Beijing and Shanghai JVs, the agreement between GAM and PSA included no plans to develop other vehicles as both sides agreed it would be cost prohibitive.[48] The plans were to introduce two French Peugeot models: the 504 light truck and the 505 passenger car which

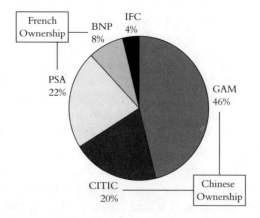

Figure 4.1   Guangzhou-PSA Joint Venture Ownership

came in both wagon and sedan versions. The same concerns Shanghai and Beijing had about foreign exchange and localization were also reflected in the Guangzhou-Peugeot contract, and the expectations were specific and unusually high. The JV would be required to export fully one-third of its production, and within five years of the start of production, the contents of exported vehicles were to reach 90 percent localization, and domestically-sold vehicles were to reach 98 percent localization.[49] Unfortunately, none of these export or localization targets would ever be reached.

Guangzhou-Peugeot produced its first vehicle in 1988, and at first, things seemed to go well. Similarly to the experiences of Volkswagen in Shanghai, PSA had found the factory conditions in Guangzhou to be substandard, but the JV spent two years improving its portion of the GAM factory and training workers. PSA also went to great efforts to teach French to the factory's Chinese workers. And as this was a learning experience for both sides, both demonstrated flexibility in the early years as it became clear that many more Chinese factory workers than had been expected would need to be sent to France for training. Likewise, PSA ended up sending many more French expatriates to Guangzhou than had been planned.[50] Unfortunately, this last move would contribute to some of the JV's early problems.

Eventually the Guangzhou side expressed its concerns about the number of expatriates and their high salaries that were creating some resentment among the Chinese workers. Part of PSA's solution was to suggest that the Chinese factory workers be paid a wage much higher than the national average, but from the perspective of GAM, it would only create additional problems if the JV factory workers were paid a higher wage than GAM's other employees who built the factory's trucks and buses. A survey of employees also revealed many cultural differences between the French managers and the Chinese workers, differences that certainly existed in both the Jeep and VW joint ventures as well, but that, according to the surveys, the French seemed disinclined to resolve. There was resentment that, although the Chinese workers were being taught to speak French, there appeared to be no desire on the part of the French expatriates to learn Chinese. Chinese workers also had difficulties with the strictness of French production methods and felt powerless to explain these difficulties to their French bosses.[51]

In another similarity with the Jeep and VW joint ventures, GPAC also encountered difficulties with localization due to the poor quality of locally made parts. By 1993 the JV had only reached parts localization of 75 percent and 62 percent for the 504 and 505 models, respectively.[52] And the difficulties with localization led to further resentment as money continued to flow back to France for the purchase of parts. Compounding this difficulty was a 110 percent appreciation of the French franc against the *renminbi* from mid-1985 to 1987. Even though the local Guangzhou government, unlike those of Shanghai or Beijing, had plenty of foreign exchange to support the JV, the Chinese side felt that the French were only in China to make a quick profit without a long-term commitment to the venture.[53] Unlike SVW which reinvested any profits earned back into the joint venture, PSA was quick to repatriate any profits back to France. And because the French were disappointed with the quality of assembled vehicles, they were reluctant to export Chinese-made Peugeots for fear of damaging the brand. As a result, this joint venture, which had been expected to export one-third of its cars, never exported any.

The problems that GPAC had with parts localization mirrored those of Beijing-Jeep. In contrast to Shanghai-Volkswagen, which benefited from the efforts of its local government to build a local parts supply network, the Jeep and PSA joint ventures suffered from a *lack* of local government intervention to build a supply network. Eric Thun notes that, while Shanghai's local auto industry was consolidated under a single local government entity, responsibility for Guangzhou's was distributed among six different ministries and bureaus.[54] Though the establishment of the GPAC joint venture early on prompted Guangzhou officials to meet to discuss how their local auto industry might be better coordinated, no agreements were reached because the various ministry heads were more concerned about losing power than streamlining the industry.

Thun's research also revealed that the key to Shanghai's success was the local government's intervention in the market. In Shanghai, prices paid by SVW to the local supply firms "were artificially inflated to give the supply firms a financial cushion" during their early years of development.[55] Supply firms in both Guangzhou and Beijing enjoyed no such cushion. The use by the Jeep and PSA joint ventures of multiple supply firms for each part worked to push down prices resulting in very low margins for the supply companies. Without the benefit of local support in the years of early development, many of Guangzhou's and Beijing's supply firms did not survive, leading ironically to *less* competition. All of this, Thun attributes to an ingrained Shanghai trait of strong local state intervention—traditions which Guangzhou and Beijing lacked. Beijing's city government lacked this tradition because it had always been overshadowed by the central government located in the same city. Guangzhou's city government lacked this tradition because it was located far away from Beijing, right across the border from free-wheeling, *laissez-faire* Hong Kong.

There were also problems with the technology that PSA contributed to the joint venture. Taxi fleets that bought the car complained that the Peugeot 505 suffered from worse fuel efficiency than other available vehicles. Other complaints were that the car's air conditioner, while possibly ideal in France's mild climate, was too weak for the summer heat of Guangdong province. There were also complaints that the Peugeot's electrical system was not designed to operate in an environment as humid as Guangdong's.[56] PSA had apparently made no effort to adapt the technology to the local environment.

Another difficulty faced by GPAC was competition between Guangzhou city and Guangdong province. Harwit points out that, as an "independent planning unit" Guangzhou city reported its economic plan directly to the central government without going through the provincial government.[57] This had the effect of making Guangzhou city and Guangdong province into competitors for resources. Guangdong provincial officials had been opposed to the formation of GPAC from the beginning as the province feared that Guangzhou's auto firm might divert central government funds intended to be shared by the province—a concern that would seem to have been unfounded given Guangdong's special status that allowed it to keep most of its locally collected revenues. Nevertheless, in order to counter the influence of Guangzhou and GPAC, Guangdong province pushed to develop both the Sanxing auto group in the southern Guangdong city of Zhanjiang as well as Panda Motors (another joint venture that would fail even faster than did GPAC).[58] As a result, GPAC did not have the level of support in the central government of SVW or Beijing-Jeep, both represented by their respective provincial level governments to Beijing.

By 1996 GPAC had only produced 100,000 vehicles in nine years of operation, and though the venture had been profitable in some years, altogether it had lost 2.9 billion *renminbi* (US$360 million).[59] As Chrysler had seemed to lose interest in its Beijing-Jeep venture, perhaps PSA, with only a 22 percent ownership share had come to a similar decision about its JV in Guangzhou.

By 1996, the Guangzhou city government, having learned what *not* to do from its GPAC joint venture, decided to change its partner, and moved for an early cancellation of its contract with PSA. The one thing both PSA and Guangzhou could agree on was that the JV was not working out, and PSA sold its interest back to Guangzhou Auto for one French franc. The city then assembled a list of criteria that it wanted its next auto joint venture to deliver and held a competition. Among about half a dozen serious competitors for the new joint venture were BMW, Mercedes-Benz, Fiat, Opel (GM's European unit), Hyundai, and Honda.[60] The selected winner was Honda, and within only five months of completing their agreement in 1998, Guangzhou-Honda's first Accord sedan rolled off the assembly line.

The Guangzhou-Honda joint venture now also makes the Honda Odyssey and the Honda Fit, and (as mentioned above) a JV brand Everus (or *Linian* in Chinese), which is based on the older Honda City platform. Honda also recently entered into another joint venture with both Guangzhou Auto and Dongfeng in which Honda actually owns a controlling 55 percent share.[61] Guangzhou Auto Company (GAC) also subsequently formed a JV with Toyota Motors in 2004.

Together with its Japanese partners, GAC parent Guangzhou Automobile Industry Group (GAIG) is now the sixth largest automaker in China, producing 724,000 vehicles in 2010.[62] GAC was a natural JV partner for the Japanese as there was already a cluster of Japanese auto parts suppliers located in the Pearl River Delta. The location of these suppliers has helped Guangzhou to overcome many of the supplier issues it had with PSA as many of the local Japanese parts makers are wholly Japanese owned, which presumably significantly reduces quality issues. According to an auto industry analyst in Guangzhou, GAC's partnership with the Japanese has brought the company a significant advantage in terms of cost control. And while the Japanese do not excel in brand image (their cars are only "average-looking"), their "relentless cost control" and reputation for quality have finally resulted in a "profitable supply chain for GAC." As an example, the analyst points to the Toyota Camry. "The Camry is now produced in Guangzhou with 80 percent local content, and 100 percent local labor, yet its sales price is 20 to 30 percent *higher* than in the U.S. This gives GAC a *huge* profit margin!"

And thanks to the profitability contributed by its Japanese JVs, GAC has finally been able to introduce its own brand, the Trumpchi. The Trumpchi, first displayed at the December 2010 Guangzhou Auto Show, is based on an old Alfa Romeo design, which, according to a Hong Kong-based auto analyst, "makes sense because GAC has recently signed an agreement to establish a JV with Fiat (owner of the Alfa Romeo brand)." According to the Guangzhou-based auto analyst, the GAC-Fiat JV's factory will be located in Changsha, not coincidentally home to Changfeng, another of China's domestic automakers in which GAC took a 29 percent controlling interest in 2009. This particular merger, details of which will be covered in Chapter Six, is rumored to have been "encouraged" by the central government.

The Guangzhou-Peugeot joint venture, while ultimately a failure, appears to have resulted in learning for both sides. In its JVs with its Japanese partners, GAC has finally established a local supply chain similar to the one that gave Shanghai Auto its early edge. It seems safe to assume that GAC picked its subsequent partners not at random, but because they brought the advantage of local, Guangdong-based suppliers making for a natural fit. Through these JVs, GAC has finally reached a level of profitability in which it can fulfill central government policy by investing in its own brand, and GAC already seems to have turned its joint venture with Fiat into an opportunity for technology transfer. Though China's JV brand trend has yet to demonstrate its ability to wean Chinese consumers away from foreign brands onto Chinese brands, GAC's investments in its Everus brand (with former Honda technology) and its Trumpchi brand (with former Alfa Romeo technology) demonstrate to the central government that Guangzhou Auto is worthy of having been designated in 2009 as one of the "small four."[63]

For their part, the French, having suffered from a lack of flexibility, or apparently even the slightest amount of curiosity, in their initial attempts at a Chinese-French joint venture, have regrouped. In 1992 the Citroën side of PSA formed a JV with Dongfeng Auto, and in 2001,

PSA Peugeot-Citroën reentered China as part of the Dongfeng joint venture. In 2010 PSA-Peugeot Citroën also formed a joint venture with Chang'an Motors of Chongqing, a CSOE that already has JVs with Ford, Mazda, and Suzuki.

Conclusion

These four case studies reveal three important points about the role of foreign automakers in China. The first is obvious, but it is nevertheless important to stress the critical role of the local government in the success or failure of a joint venture. Of the four cases reviewed here, the two most successful joint ventures—indeed, the only two still in existence— are the two Shanghai-based JVs, SVW, and SGM. Not only have Eric Thun's findings, that a locally based supply chain is advantageous to a local automaker, continued to prove true for the two Shanghai-based JVs, but Guangzhou Auto and Beijing Auto appear to have learned the same lessons. Their newer joint ventures, Guangzhou Auto's with Honda and Toyota, and Beijing Auto's with Hyundai, benefit from the kind of highly localized supply chains that Guangzhou-PSA and Beijing-Jeep did not have in the early days.

The second point is that, for all of the central government's insistence that China's automakers develop their own brands, the SOEs have still accomplished very little in this area. Among the more than 3 million vehicles sold by SAIC in 2010, only about 160,000 were of SAIC's own MG and Roewe brands, and SAIC is one of the more successful among the SOEs at building domestic branded sedans.[64] As for Beijing Auto and Guangzhou Auto, these two SOEs have yet to sell a single sedan under their own brands.[65] For China as a whole, the market shares of domestic brands barely budged during 2010. Domestic-branded passenger vehicles increased from 44 percent in 2009 to 45.6 percent in 2010. The subset of domestic-branded passenger cars (sedans) only increased from 30 percent in 2009 to 30.9 percent in 2010.[66]

Since independent automakers such as Chery, Geely, and Great Wall enjoyed sales increases of their domestic brands of anywhere from 36 to 76 percent in 2010, this means that the SOEs most likely experienced a collective *decrease* in domestic brands as a percentage of their total sales during 2010. The important point here is that, while the central government's demands regarding domestic brands have only grown louder, the incentives that drive different behavior between state-owned and private enterprises have yet to change. *It is more profitable in the short-term for SOEs to produce foreign-branded cars than it is for them to pour money into development of their own.*

The recent introduction of JV brands is, however, an interesting development. China's central government appears to be on its way toward killing two, or possibly three, birds with one stone. The pressure being applied when the foreign multinationals apply for capacity expansion—as most of them are doing to take advantage of China's growth potential—is resulting in both a transfer of technology and development of Chinese brands. The multinationals, rather than pour funds into greenfield development of new models appear to be contributing outdated, yet still fairly recent, models, and the resulting cars will all have Chinese names. And in the case of FAW-VW's planned *Kaili* brand, the central government may also be getting a third wish: development of a new energy vehicle.[67]

The final point answers a key question asked toward the end of Chapter Three: Why, if the central government understood by the mid-1990s that the foreign partners were not transferring technology, did joint ventures continue to be formed? The short answer is that the foreign partners still had much to offer. As the data on China's domestic brands indicate, even today, China's market continues to rely heavily on foreign brands. By the mid-1990s, China's auto industry simply was not mature enough to stand on its own, and the fact that the joint ventures had yet to turn Chinese engineers into automobile innovators would not have been a good excuse for kicking the foreigners out. As the joint-venture case studies demonstrate, the early JVs, Beijing-Jeep and SAIC-VW, built their expectations on "wishful thinking," a hope that the proximity of foreign experts would suffice. The Guangzhou-PSA joint venture agreement did not even address technology transfer.

The later joint venture profiled here, SAIC-GM, shows how much the Chinese had learned by the mid-1990s, and it also shows how important the China market had become to foreigners. Not only had the Chinese learned the importance of moving *design* from overseas into China, but foreign automakers also began to realize how important technology transfer was becoming to the Chinese. General Motors not only offered SAIC a car to be modified especially for China, but it offered to build a design center where Chinese and foreign engineers would work side-by-side. And while China may have given up its right to demand technology transfer when it joined the WTO in 2001, this in no way quenched the desire of China's automakers to acquire and modify foreign technology. As investigations into high speed rail, nuclear and wind power industries demonstrate, the price of access to the China market is still technology transfer, but now that competition to enter China has grown so intense, many foreign companies are *voluntarily* handing over their technology for a chance to play.[68] In 2009 Vice Premier Wang Qishan told EU business executives who complained to him about market access, "I know you have complaints...but the charm of the Chinese market is irresistible."[69]

As the story in Chapter Two revealed, the joint ventures have taken on a new role of providing cash flow to assist China's SOEs in conducting their own development, but the central government, though forbidden by its WTO commitment from demanding technology transfer as a condition of approving foreign investment, still expects SOEs to learn from their foreign partners. Table 4.1, which is reproduced (and translated) from a publication of China's Ministry of Science and Technology (MOST), compares four types of auto joint ventures

Table 4.1 Comparison of Extent of Chinese Involvement in Auto Joint Venture Innovation

Model	Role of Chinese Side in Product Development	Typical Enterprises
completely foreign	unable to be involved in R&D work	Beijing-Hyundai
limited modification of foreign technology	limited involvement in R&D work	Shanghai-Volkswagen FAW-Volkswagen
localization and improvement of foreign technology	involvement "depends on attitude of the foreign partner"	Dongfeng-Peugeot Citroën Shanghai-GM
independent R&D	Chinese side has complete control over R&D	Shanghai-GM-Wuling

Source: Ministry of Science and Technology, 2009.

based on the role of the Chinese partner in research and development.[70] The joint ventures are arranged from top to bottom in order of preference, the bottom row being the most preferable.

From the point of view of MOST, the least preferable joint venture is one that imports completely foreign technology that the Chinese side of the joint venture is not allowed to improve upon. This is typified by Beijing-Hyundai which, as confirmed in interviews (see Beijing-Jeep case above) indeed uses completely foreign, unmodified technology. The most preferable joint venture, typified by SGMW, is one in which local Chinese employees are involved in all aspects of R&D. Note that the positioning of the two GM ventures vis-à-vis the two Volkswagen ventures may also give an indication as to why the SAIC executive told me that SAIC preferred the "attitude" of GM to that of Volkswagen (see SAIC-GM case above). GM is, according to MOST, doing a better job than other foreign automakers of teaching its Chinese partners how to design and build cars.

Though none of the cases presented here is specifically about Toyota, this is one foreign brand name that still manages to appear in each of the case studies presented. Despite the fact that Toyota is the world's largest manufacturer of passenger cars, in China it ranks fourth behind VW, GM, and Hyundai, and part of the reason may be Toyota's unwillingness to share technology.[71] As the cases revealed, during early-1980s negotiations with both AMC and Volkswagen, the Chinese also held talks with Toyota, and in both cases, Toyota was not selected, ostensibly due to its apprehension about sharing intellectual property.[72] At the time Toyota was only interested in exporting vehicles from Japan to China, not in building locally. By the late 1990s, however, Toyota had begun to source some parts from southern China in order to remain globally cost competitive. While the location of its suppliers made Toyota a natural fit as a new partner for Guangzhou Auto, there is little evidence that Toyota has lost its reluctance to share technology. Of the three major Japanese automakers currently operating in China (Toyota, Honda, and Nissan), only Honda and Nissan are (so far) working with their partners to introduce Japanese technology under JV brands.

Despite the fact that Toyota was a world pioneer in hybrid technology with the Prius, the company also seems to be having difficulty breaking into China's market for new energy vehicles (NEVs). In June

2010 the NDRC announced a pilot subsidy project for NEVs intended
to spur sales of these vehicles in five (now six) select cities.[73] The idea
was to provide subsidies of up to 50,000 yuan for consumer purchases of
plug-in hybrids (PHEVs) and up to 60,000 yuan for pure electric
vehicles (EVs), as well as smaller subsidies (3,000 yuan) for energy-
efficient gasoline cars with engines smaller than 1.6 liters. The Prius,
which had been manufactured in China by FAW-Toyota since 2005,
unfortunately for Toyota, fits neither category.[74] While the Prius is a
gasoline/electric hybrid, it is not a *plug-in* hybrid, so it does not qualify
for an NEV subsidy.

Toyota also canceled plans to assemble the third generation, plug-in
Prius in China, opting to move production to Thailand instead. The
third generation Prius, as it turned out, would also not be qualified for
even the smaller 3,000 yuan subsidy because its on-board gasoline
engine was increased in size from 1.5 liters to 1.8 liters.[75] Also possibly
reflecting Toyota's ambivalence about sharing technology, Prius production in China only consisted of assembly of components shipped
from Japan.[76] Toyota never attempted to localize parts production for
the Prius, much less R&D.

In summary, local governments have an important role in ensuring
the success of their joint ventures, and JVs continue to be absolutely
critical to the development of China's automobile industry—for now.
Not only is the output of domestic-branded vehicles woefully insuffi-
cient to meet demand, but the innovative skills of China's backbone
SOEs are far from adequate to drive the design of uniquely Chinese
brands. Furthermore, selling foreign-branded cars is still a much more
profitable activity than is pouring resources into development of
Chinese brands. And even though Chinese demands for technology
transfer are no longer explicit, the rush by foreign automakers to gain
a foothold in China have led to an environment in which a voluntary
offering of technology and learning opportunities has become *de rigueur*
in most of China's competitive industries.

Notes

1. Jim Mann, *Beijing Jeep: The Short, Unhappy Romance of American Business in China* (New York: Simon & Schuster, 1989).

2. Ibid., 48.
3. Ibid., 68.
4. Kelly Sims Gallagher, *China Shifts Gears: Automakers, Oil, Pollution, and Development* (Cambridge, MA: MIT Press, 2006), 47.
5. Mann, *Beijing Jeep*; Eric Harwit, *China's Automobile Industry: Policies, Problems, and Prospects (Studies on Contemporary China)* (Armonk, NY: M.E. Sharpe, 1995).
6. Harwit, *China's Automobile Industry*, 87.
7. Ibid., 75–76.
8. Gallagher, *China Shifts Gears*, 57.
9. Ibid., 54–55.
10. Photos comparing BAIC's Qishi with the Jeep Cherokee may be viewed at www.designateddrivers.co.
11. Zhongguo qiche jishu yanjiu zhongxin, 中国汽车工业年鉴 [China automotive industry yearbook] (Beijing: Zhongguo qiche gongye xiehui, multiple years), 2009, 501. Hereafter, *CAIY*.
12. "First BAIC Sedan, BC301Z, Rolls Off Production Line in Zhuzhou, Hunan," *ChinaAutoWeb*, December 28, 2010, http://chinaautoweb.com/2010/12/first-baic-sedan-bc301z-rolls-off-production-line-in-zhuzhou-hunan/.
13. Hyundai ranks third behind Volkswagen and General Motors brands, and ahead of Toyota in China. JD Power statistics, December 2010. *Automotive News China* website, www.autonewschina.com.
14. *CAIY*, 2009, 497.
15. At the end of 2010, BAIC was a distant fifth place behind SAIC, Dongfeng, FAW and Chang'an. (See market share graph in Figure 6.1.)
16. For a more in-depth look at the early experiences of Volkswagen in China, I would recommend Martin Posth's highly readable chronicle, *1,000 Days in Shanghai: The Story of Volkswagen: The First Chinese-German Car Factory* (Singapore: John Wiley & Sons, 2008).
17. Harwit, *China's Automobile Industry*, 95.
18. Posth, *1,000 Days in Shanghai*, 8–9.
19. Posth, *1,000 Days in Shanghai*.
20. Ibid., 91. Note that, at the time these discussions were taking place between Volkswagen and FAW (October of 1987), Chrysler had already bought AMC and was thus responsible for the Beijing-Jeep JV. From Zhu's point of view, a Chrysler JV with FAW would not have been anticompetitive as the new JV would produce sedans, not SUVs. A Volkswagen JV with FAW, again, from Zhu's point of view, *would* have been anticompetitive as both major sedan JVs in China (at the time) would have been partners with the same foreign company, Volkswagen.
21. Ibid., 93. The (black) Audi 100 would go on to become the car of choice for Chinese officials.

22. Eric Thun, *Changing Lanes in China: Foreign Direct Investment, Local Government, and Auto Sector Development* (New York: Cambridge University Press, 2006), 24–34.
23. See Michael Dunne's recent book for a well-researched and highly engaging in-depth account of the GM experience in China. Michael J. Dunne, *American Wheels, Chinese Roads: The Story of General Motors in China* (Singapore: John Wiley & Sons [Asia], 2011).
24. William Holstein, *Why GM Matters: Inside the Race to Transform an American Icon* (New York: Walker, 2009), 173.
25. Ibid.
26. Holstein, *Why GM Matters*, 174.
27. By December of 1996 GM had already spent $100 million on the plant even though the contract would not be signed for another three months.
28. Michael J. Dunne, *American Wheels, Chinese Roads*, 46.
29. Gallagher, *China Shifts Gears*, 65.
30. Gallagher, *China Shifts Gears*, 69.
31. "GM's China Sales Run Down," *China Car Times*, January 5, 2011, www.chinacartimes.com/2011/01/05/gms-china-sales-run-down/.
32. Steve Schifferes, "Cracking China's Car Market," *BBC*, May 17, 2007, http://news.bbc.co.uk/2/hi/business/6658583.stm.
33. Norihiko Shirouzu, "In China, Making Cars on a Budget," *wsj.com*, December 20, 2010, http://online.wsj.com/article/SB10001424052748704610904576031293046766076.html.
34. Personal email communication, March 22, 2011.
35. Michael Dunne, "Launch a New Brand in China—Whether You Like It or Not," *Automotive News China*, April 12, 2011, www.autonewschina.com/en/article.asp?id=6807.
36. Ibid.
37. This was no off-the-cuff remark. The SAIC executive emphasized to me his company's *Fortune* ranking as a primary motivation on two separate occasions. Also, recall from Chapter Three that the 2004 Auto Industry Development Policy included the aim to establish Chinese automakers large enough to be listed in the *Fortune* ranking.
38. Steven Rattner, *Overhaul: An Insider's Account of the Obama Administration's Emergency Rescue of the Auto Industry* (Boston: Houghton Mifflin Harcourt, 2010), 203.
39. David Barboza and Nick Bunkley, "GM, Eclipsed at Home, Soars to Top in China," *The New York Times*, July 21, 2010, www.nytimes.com/2010/07/22/business/global/22auto.html.
40. China Association of Automobile Manufacturers.

41. Jianshe Kong, "SAIC Sold Record 3.58 Million Vehicles in 2010," *ChinaAutoWeb*, January 6, 2011, http://chinaautoweb.com/2011/01/saic-sold-record-3-58-million-vehicles-in-2010/.
42. "SAIC Invests $1.5 Billion to Boost Own-Brand Car Capacity," *Reuters*, December 27, 2010, www.reuters.com/article/2010/12/27/retire-us-saic-idUKTRE6BQ0IS20101227.
43. See Chapter Three. The "big three" were FAW, SAW, and SAIC, and the "small three" were Beijing-Jeep, Guangzhou-Peugeot, and Tianjin Auto.
44. Susan L. Shirk, *The Political Logic of Economic Reform in China* (Berkeley: University of California Press, 1993), 166–167.
45. Harwit, *China's Automobile Industry*, 117.
46. Ibid.
47. Juan Fernandez and Liu Shengjun, *China CEO: A Case Guide for Business Leaders in China* (Singapore: John Wiley & Sons, 2007), 78.
48. Harwit, *China's Automobile Industry*, 118.
49. Ibid., 119.
50. Ibid.
51. Fernandez and Liu Shengjun, *China CEO*, 84–85.
52. Harwit, *China's Automobile Industry*, 121.
53. Fernandez and Liu Shengjun, *China CEO*, 80.
54. Thun, *Changing Lanes in China*, 143.
55. Ibid.
56. Fernandez and Liu Shengjun, *China CEO*, 83.
57. Harwit, *China's Automobile Industry*, 127.
58. Ibid., 127–128.
59. Fernandez and Liu Shengjun, *China CEO*, 76.
60. Ibid., 91.
61. *CAIY*, 2008, 38. This is, so far, the only Chinese-foreign auto joint venture in which the foreign partner owns more than 50 percent. The reason for this exception is that the 2004 auto policy allowed for foreign partners in auto JVs to hold more than 50 percent if the JV makes autos primarily for export. Honda also has a 50–50 JV with Dongfeng Auto in Wuhan that produces the Honda CR-V.
62. China Association of Automobile Manufacturers.
63. See discussion of the "big four, small four" toward the end of Chapter Three.
64. Kong, "SAIC Sold Record 3.58 Million Vehicles in 2010."
65. Though, as mentioned above, BAIC continues to sell SUVs descended from its old Soviet designs, and both BAIC and GAC have introduced Chinese-branded sedans which the companies had planned to offer to the market in 2011 or 2012.
66. And interim 2011 figures indicate that domestic-branded passenger cars may have actually lost market share in 2011. Guowuyuan fazhan yanjiu zhongxin,

中国汽车产业发展报告 [China automotive industry development report] (Beijing: Shehui kexue wenxian chubanshe, multiple years), 2010, 29. Xinhua News Agency, January 14, 2011.

67. Jianshe Kong, "FAW-VW to Launch 'Kaili' Brand EV," *ChinaAutoWeb*, May 9, 2011, http://chinaautoweb.com/2011/05/faw-vw-to-launch-kaili-brand-ev/.

68. Norihiko Shirouzu, "Train Makers Rail against China's High-Speed Designs," *wsj.com*, November 17, 2010, http://online.wsj.com/article/SB10001424052748704814204575507353221141616.html; John Gapper, "China Takes a Short-Cut to Power," *Financial Times, FT.com*, December 8, 2010, www.ft.com/cms/s/0/d3da8b78-0309-11e0-bb1e-00144feabdc0.html; Dexter Roberts and Stanley Reed, "China Wants Nuclear Reactors—Fast," *BusinessWeek: Online Magazine*, December 2, 2010, www.businessweek.com/magazine/content/10_50/b4207015606809.htm; Keith Bradsher, "To Conquer Wind Power, China Writes the Rules," *New York Times*, December 14, 2010, www.nytimes.com/2010/12/15/business/global/15china wind.html.

69. Richard McGregor, *The Party: The Secret World of China's Communist Rulers* (New York: Harper, 2010), xvi.

70. Tang Jie, Yang Yanping, and Zhou Wenjie, 中国汽车产业自主创新战略 = *China Auto Industry Indigenous Innovation Strategy* (Beijing: Kexue Chu-banshe, 2009), 85. Note: the original table contained four columns, one of which contained redundant information when translated into English.

71. 2010 ranking, JD Power, China.

72. At least this is what those involved in the negotiations have said. There also exists the possibility that Toyota was brought into the negotiations by the Chinese as a foil to "encourage" AMC and Volkswagen to be more generous in their negotiations.

73. See discussion of this pilot project in Chapter Three.

74. In the years 2007–2009, only 3,465 Priuses were sold in China. *CAIY*, 2007, 485; 2008, 512; 2009, 493.

75. "Prius Does Not Qualify for China's Green Car Subsidies," *ChinaAutoWeb*, June 24, 2010, http://chinaautoweb.com/2010/06/prius-does-not-qualify-for-chinas-green-car-subsidies/. "New Toyota Prius Won't Be Made in China Due to Government Policies," *China Car Times*, November 1, 2010, www.chinacartimes.com/2010/11/01/new-toyota-prius-wont-be-made-in-china-due-to-government-policies/.

76. Yoshio Takahashi and Kazuhiro Shimamura, "Toyota to Make Prius in Thailand," *wsj.com*, October 21, 2010, http://online.wsj.com/article/SB10001424052702304023804575566062996581490.html.

Chapter Five

The Independents

The hope of China's auto industry still lies with the private sector. This is a competitive process: First, SOEs compete with foreign capital, and the SOEs lose. Then, foreign capital competes with private [Chinese] enterprises, and the private enterprises win.

—Geely Chairman Li Shufu
March 2009 (Ding Yang, "李书福： 我不奢望太多
[Li Shufu: My expectations are not excessive],"
Economic Observer, March 8, 2009)

R ecall from the opening case in Chapter One that Chery, an independent, local state-owned automaker, had to get its start under the radar. Once Chery had its factory up and running, the central government stepped in to suggest to Chery a path to legality. Though Chery relied heavily on copying foreign models, it eventually proved worthy of the central government's support by developing its own brands and becoming China's largest exporter of automobiles.[1]

The five automakers whose stories I tell in this chapter highlight similar themes. Geely, BYD, and Great Wall are all nominally private firms that sell cars under their own brands. Case studies on these companies will demonstrate the critical role of entrepreneurs partnering with local government to get their companies off the ground. They also raise some questions about innovative ability and, in one case, possible illicit privatization of state-owned assets. These are followed by a case study on Brilliance China, an automaker that is no longer independent, though at one time it was—or, at least some people think it may have been. This story will demonstrate how one entrepreneur got his relationships with both central and local government wrong and paid a heavy price. And finally, Sichuan Tengzhong is a company no one had ever heard of and may very likely never hear of again. This brief case will demonstrate the importance of policy adherence to an independent automaker's existence.

I should also note that the word *private* does not necessarily have the same connotation in China as it does in the West. In the West, a "private" company is one whose shares are not publicly traded. In China, a "private" company is one that is not state-controlled; however, just because a Chinese company is nominally private, this does not mean that it is beyond the influence of the state. And while private companies in the West are also subject to state regulation, in China, the nature of state influence over private companies often goes beyond simple regulation. As the research of both Kellee Tsai and Bruce Dickson has demonstrated, involving entrepreneurs in Party and government institutions is a method of co-optation whereby the Party helps to ensure support for the political status quo.[2] Dickson's survey indicates that the Party targets only the largest and most successful entrepreneurs for membership, thereby ensuring that the members of society most able to assemble enough resources to challenge the Party's leadership are kept firmly within its grasp.[3]

In the auto industry in particular this is evidenced by the fact that the leaders of China's four largest private automakers have each been appointed to political positions. Geely Chairman Li Shufu is a delegate to the Chinese People's Political Consultative Conference (CPPCC) and a deputy to the Taizhou People's Congress in Zhejiang Province. BYD Chairman Wang Chuanfu is a member of the Standing Committee of the Shenzhen Municipal People's Congress. Great Wall CEO, Wang Fengying is a member of the National People's Congress. And Lifan Chairman Yin Mingshan was previously a member of the CPPCC and a standing committee member of the Chongqing Political Consultative Conference. Among these four chief executives, Li Shufu and Wang Fengying are also both full-fledged members of the Communist Party.

The key points to look for in these stories are the struggles of entrepreneurs to establish their enterprises and gain access to funding, a shift in the central government's attitude toward independents from one of antagonism to one of tolerance, the contribution of independents to achievement of key central government objectives, and the efforts of the independents to become more innovative companies. The very fact that the independents exist is evidence that the central government is not getting its wish for consolidation of the industry, but this may not be such a bad thing: the central government, and indeed, China's entire auto industry, is gaining something else in return.

Geely

Geely is perhaps best known outside China for having recently bought Volvo from Ford, but inside China it is best known for being China's first and largest privately-owned automaker. In business and political circles, Geely is also known for its charismatic and indefatigable chairman, Li Shufu.

Li was born in Zhejiang Province where his company, Geely Automobile Holdings, is headquartered. Li got his start in the business world by buying a camera to take posed photographs of tourists, and, according to an auto consultant who is well-acquainted with him, to this day, Li continues to call on his photography skills, taking an active role in staging photographs for PR purposes. In the early 1980s, Li combined money earned from his photography business with money borrowed from relatives to start a company that made components for refrigerators. By the late 1980s he had progressed to manufacturing complete refrigerators, which were sold nationwide. Unfortunately, due to a tightening in industrial regulations, he had difficulty obtaining permits to continue with his business and was forced to close his factory.

Only a few years later, Li turned to motorcycles. The area around Li's hometown, Taizhou, Zhejiang Province was well-known for expertise in plastic molding, and Li took advantage of this local expertise to begin manufacturing small "step-through" scooters in 1994, soon becoming one of the largest motorcycle manufacturers in China. But all the while his ambitions were to do more. Li wanted to build cars, and he took every opportunity he could to learn about auto manufacture and talk to anyone who would listen.

Li's timing was unfortunate as China's 1994 auto industry policy clearly stated that no new passenger car manufacturers would be approved during the near term, and despite his numerous appeals to the Ministry of Machine Building, he continued to come away empty handed. As Chapter Three showed, the central government was reluctant not only to approve new auto manufacturing ventures, but also to allow private firms into the industry. According to several auto executives and consultants who were active in China's auto industry at the time, the belief in Beijing was that only state-owned firms had the access to capital necessary to afford the plant and equipment needed to manufacture automobiles.

Even though Li Shufu had been successful with his motorcycle venture, he had difficulty finding sympathy in Beijing for his plans to build cars; however, being a typical Chinese entrepreneur, Li chose to stop confronting his obstacle head-on and to find a way around it. In 1997 Li became aware of a prison-owned auto factory in Deyang, Sichuan that was on the verge of bankruptcy.[4] Though this factory did not produce passenger cars (it produced small vans and micro-buses) this factory possessed something Li needed: permission to manufacture vehicles. By buying the company, Li would take possession of the factory's official vehicle production certificate. The fact that the certificate only allowed production of vans and buses (not cars), and it only allowed production in Sichuan were only minor quibbles that Li would worry about later.

Li's greatest desire was to produce a luxury car based on a Mercedes-Benz, so he bought two Mercedes sedans and had them disassembled and studied by engineers only to learn that the cost to produce such a complex and sophisticated vehicle—even by copying those already in existence—was beyond the capability of his small company. The difficulty, however, was moot as he was unable to get permission from the Ministry of Machine Building to build a luxury car. Undaunted, Li then turned his focus toward smaller economy cars. Setting aside his wish to copy a Mercedes, Li chose models from Xiali, an automaker in Tianjin that manufactured small Daihatsu cars under license from Toyota. For reasons that are not entirely clear (though most interviewees insisted the Zhejiang provincial government was instrumental in helping Li in this regard), Li was able to get permission, not only to build the smaller cars, but also to open a factory in his home province of Zhejiang. The first Geely-produced car, the *Haiqing*, rolled off the assembly line of Geely's Linhai, Zhejiang factory in August 1998.

In a pattern that will reveal itself among China's independent automakers, Geely found itself the subject of a lawsuit in 2003. For its *Meiri* (or "Merrie") sedan, Geely chose a logo that looked very similar to Toyota's familiar logo.[5] In a move that was watched as a litmus test for whether Beijing was serious about protecting the intellectual property of foreign businesses, Toyota filed suit in a Chinese court seeking restitution of nearly 14 million yuan.[6] In the end the court ruled against Toyota and ordered it to pay Geely's court costs. The court said that it "did not recognize Toyota's logo as a well-known brand in China requiring protection," leaving other foreign businesses to wonder how safe their designs and logos would be in China.[7] Despite its close call with the Toyota logo early in its life, Geely exhibited no qualms borrowing liberally from the designs of others.[8]

Over the following years, Geely quickly moved up the ranks of China's largest automakers because it chose to compete on the bottom end of the scale, where the foreign joint ventures had little to offer, and in Tier 3 and 4 cities, where the foreign producers had yet to tread. By producing small, fuel-efficient cars, Geely, along with several other builders of domestic-branded cars, was able to capture the attention of the largest segment of consumers in China just as they were becoming able to afford cars of their own.

In another pattern that will reveal itself among other independent producers, Li Shufu was only able to fund his company's initial growth by relying on loans from relatives. As the company grew, Geely was later able to survive on cash generated by its earlier non-automotive-related businesses, and in 2004 Geely launched an initial public offering (IPO) on the Hong Kong Stock Exchange.[9] In September of 2009 Geely also benefited from a $334 million investment by Goldman Sachs.[10]

However, loans from China's state-owned banks, with one important exception, have been largely off limits to privately held Geely. From the banker's point of view, a state-owned business is a safer bet than a private company, as the SOE's ultimate owner, the state, will guarantee the loan. The banker has no such guarantee for loans made to a private firm. But the lack of access to loans may also have a positive effect on the longer-term prospects of the private company. Whereas state-owned firms could lose money in perpetuity (as some do) and continue to be supported by soft loans from state-owned banks, private firms, having no such recourse, have no choice but to become profitable and to remain that way. In Geely's case, cash generated by a successful business manufacturing motorcycles allowed Geely to move upstream to automobiles.

To be fair, however, new automakers, whether state-owned or private, are able to rely on another source of help, and that is the local government. Local governments, incentivized as they are to achieve both local economic growth and social stability, tend to find automobile factories an irresistible source of both. Accordingly, local governments in China—not unlike local governments in the United States and other developed countries—are usually eager to provide all manner of inducements to new or existing firms who will build in their localities. However, local governments in the developed world tend to be unable to simply transfer state-owned assets to private businesses.

The local government in Taizhou, Zhejiang was an important partner during Geely's startup phase. They sent officials to Beijing to lobby on Geely's behalf and organized visits and tours by officials from auto industry research institutes and government think-tanks.[11] The local government also sold land use rights to Geely at a below-market price such that soon after purchase, the value of the land immediately increased Geely's balance sheet by over one billion yuan (about $128 million at late-1990s rates).[12] Geely was also able to sell some of its land use rights to real estate developers. In addition, Taizhou provided tax breaks to Geely worth more than 80 million yuan ($10.2 million) per year.[13]

We saw in the previous chapter that Shanghai's government protected auto parts firms in their startup phases by allowing them to charge above-market prices, thereby allowing these fledgling companies to build both equity and experience faster than would have been possible without such protection. The same principle was at work in Taizhou's treatment of Geely. The local state essentially transferred public wealth to Geely during its critical startup phase, thereby allowing the company to grow faster than would have been possible. In both Shanghai and Zhejiang, the local government ultimately benefited from higher employment and taxes. Without exception, every person interviewed for this project confirmed the universal assumption in China that local governments provide substantial help to local businesses, whether state-owned or private, including, but not limited to: tax breaks, inexpensive or rent-free land, inexpensive or free utilities, paving of roads to factories, and even, to the degree they exercise influence over local state-owned banks, low-interest loans.

The involvement of the *central* government in supporting any given auto company is, however, less certain. In short, it depends on the company and the degree to which it is able to capture the central government's attention. In the spring of 2009 Premier Wen Jiabao paid a visit to a Geely plant, met with Li Shufu, and was quoted in the press as saying, "I am asking Geely to submit a special report to the State Council again after six months. [At that time] I will . . . give instructions to continue to support Geely's industrial development."[14] The fact that a Prime Minister is involving the State Council in the strategic planning of a nominally private enterprise is not insignificant. The auto industry is a pillar industry, so the central government has an interest in the activities of all major automakers, regardless of ownership.

This degree of state involvement in a private company's planning process serves to illustrate just how blurry the line is between "public" and "private" in China. It also indicates that Geely is viewed as large and important enough to merit the central government's attention. But whether this is viewed as good or bad by the company itself, one senior Chinese auto executive explained to me how important central government support can be:

All auto companies have the support of their local governments, but the central government offers a kind of support that no local government can give. The central government is the only government that controls national media—local government only control local media—and favorable news stories about a car company can have a big influence on [consumer perceptions].

That same executive went further to explain that, while local government support is absolutely essential to the startup and ongoing well-being of an auto company, central government support is needed if a company is to survive in the long term. Without this support, a company will have little or no access to bank loans, nor can it list on mainland stock markets. And one of the best ways that an automaker can gain the support of the central government is to be seen carrying out its wishes in a significant way.

Though it appears that Geely has the support of the Premier, Li Shufu has all along been quite vocal about the lack of a level playing field with SOEs, particularly in terms of access to bank loans from centrally-controlled banks. In a 2006 interview with China's *21st Century Business Herald*, Li complained, "Geely has never received help from the national level in terms of capital support. We have had to rely on our own strength as we develop step-by-step . . . If the government wants to support independent development (自主创新), it should focus [funding] on private enterprises."[15] And more recently, Li told the *Economic Observer* in 2009, "Fairness is all we ask . . . As a private company, simply getting into the industry is worth thanking God over."[16] And despite the fact that Geely received a bank loan to aid in its recent acquisition of Volvo, Li Shufu has nevertheless continued to complain publicly about the lack of access to funds, complaining to the state-owned China News Service in September 2010 that domestic banks are still unwilling to lend money to Geely.[17]

So while Geely appears to have difficulty getting funding from the state, the fact that Geely has received any state funding at all (for its purchase of Volvo, as I explain in the following passage) indicates that getting such funding is not an impossibility. When I asked a Geely executive why he thought the company was able to obtain bank financing for the Volvo purchase when it had not on many other occasions, his (somewhat predictable) answer was, "this was purely a commercial transaction. The bank judged that it was a good business opportunity, so they invested." However, other industry experts believe that the reason was much deeper. Because China's central government has, since 1999, had a "going out" policy in which Chinese enterprises are encouraged to invest abroad, and, more specifically, because the auto policy has repeatedly called for Chinese automakers to acquire foreign technology, the central government was highly supportive of Geely's Volvo transaction.[18]

But Volvo was not Geely's first overseas transaction. In 2006 Geely took a 23 percent position in UK-based Manganese Bronze Holdings, becoming the company's largest single shareholder. Together the two companies formed a China-based joint venture to build the iconic London Black Taxi, which is now exported from China in the form of SKDs for assembly in the UK.

In 2009 Geely spent $55.8 million to purchase struggling Australian automatic transmission maker DSI International. This was a major purchase for Geely, the significance of which may not have been appreciated outside of China. Automatic transmissions are among the most complex parts of an automobile and have always been a technological deficiency for the Chinese auto industry. According to Geely's press release at the time of the acquisition, 99 percent of automatic transmissions used in Chinese-made cars in 2008 were bought from foreign companies—these foreign firms, according to Geely, held a "technological monopoly [that] led to high prices . . . which blocked the development of Chinese [automatic transmission] technology."[19] By adopting nationalist rhetoric to describe this transaction, Geely's PR department was merely repeating the same rhetoric it had been hearing from the central government. Geely and DSI now have three factories operating in China building the very technology for which Chinese automakers had previously depended on foreign suppliers. Through DSI Geely is also developing more complex eight-speed, double-clutch, and continuously variable transmissions.

If the Manganese Bronze and DSI transactions had not been enough to capture the support of the central government, the Volvo purchase most certainly was. Volvo, a luxury brand based in Sweden, has a reputation as a leader in vehicle safety. In 1999 Ford Motor Company bought Volvo to add to its "Premier Automotive Group" that included its earlier purchases of British brands Jaguar and Aston Martin. (In 2000 Ford also added Land Rover to this group.) As the American auto industry fell on hard times during the 2000s, Ford, having lost $24 billion from 2005 until late 2008, disbanded the Premier Automotive Group and gradually sold off the brands: Aston Martin in 2007, Jaguar and Land Rover in 2008. Toward the end of 2008, Ford also announced its intention to sell Volvo, hoping to recoup something close to the $6.45 billion it had paid in 1999.

Though it went unreported at the time, Li Shufu traveled to Detroit in early 2007 to discuss a possible purchase of Volvo with Ford's CFO who did not take Li's offer seriously. Then, in December of 2008, British automobile news website Autocar.co.uk first reported that people from Geely had visited Volvo in Sweden in early 2008, months before Ford announced its plans to sell.[20] Throughout the spring and summer of 2009, news of Geely's interest in Volvo, confirmed by "unnamed sources," persisted, as did the denials of both Ford and Geely. Finally, in the fall of 2009, Geely confirmed its intention to bid for Volvo, and Ford announced that Geely had been selected as the "preferred bidder" for Volvo.

By the end of 2009, a deal had yet to be reached between Ford and Geely as a preponderance of auto industry experts expressed their doubts as to Geely's ability to either marshal the funds or ultimately run Volvo. One Chinese auto executive with whom I spoke told of a meeting that took place in southern China earlier in 2009 in which Li Shufu personally went, hat in hand to ask a gathered group of auto executives and entrepreneurs for cash to help finance his purchase of Volvo. Yet another Chinese auto executive expressed his doubts to me before the Volvo transaction had yet to be completed. As he explained it, an auto company not only needs to fund research and development for new models, but it also requires about $1 billion of R&D a year for each existing product line, just to keep the models fresh and to introduce incremental changes from year to year. (The figure seemed high to me, so I asked again, and he repeated the number, "$1 billion.") He further explained that Geely did not have enough cash to complete the purchase and would have to rely on loans, which would most likely come from state-owned banks.

If Geely is going to rely on the government for at least half of a comparatively small purchase of Volvo, how can Geely possibly fund Volvo's ongoing R&D pipeline? Add to this the likelihood that Ford has underinvested in Volvo over the past few years. I'm not sure Li Shufu fully understands what he is getting into.

But while industry insiders were, at best, skeptical, if nothing else, Geely had, in the process of bidding for Volvo, become very well-known. Li Shufu had managed to keep the name of his company in the Western press for over a year, which, even if Geely had never managed to buy Volvo, was a kind of publicity that Geely's PR budget could never have bought. Many of my interviewees remarked about Li Shufu's savviness in public relations (though some held the opinion that this was the *only* skill Li brought to the company).

Ultimately, Geely was successful in its bid for Volvo, paying $1.5 billion in August of 2010 for an asset Ford had bought for $6.45 billion 11 years earlier. Zhejiang Geely Holding Group ("Geely Group"), a shell company controlled by Li Shufu, gave Ford a $200 million note and paid the remaining $1.3 billion in cash. Of the $1.3 billion in cash paid to Ford, $100 million came from a loan and $1.2 billion came from a special purpose entity named Shanghai Geely Zhaoyuan International Investment Corporation, a company registered in the Jiading District of Shanghai and whose registered owners are Geely Group (51%), Daqing City (37%), and Shanghai Jiading District (12%).[21]

The "Geely Group" involved in this transaction is not to be confused with Geely Auto Holdings, the Hong Kong-listed company that controls all of Geely's auto factories. Geely Group is a shell company owned 90 percent by Li Shufu that, as of this writing, controls 50.97 percent of Geely Auto Holdings (thus giving Li Shufu majority control over Geely). The significance of this distinction is important as it means that Li Shufu controls both Geely Auto Holdings and Volvo, but Geely Auto Holdings was not a party to the Volvo purchase.[22] (This also means that the holders of Geely's HK-listed shares have no participation whatsoever in the future success or failure of Volvo—except to the extent that Volvo technology may leak over to Geely, which Li Shufu says won't happen: "Volvo is Volvo and Geely is Geely."[23]) Daqing is a city located in northeast China's Heilongjiang Province, known

primarily for its oil fields. Shanghai's Jiading District is located outside the Shanghai metropolitan area and home to Anting City, location
of the SAIC-Volkswagen factory, numerous parts factories, and
Shanghai's Formula-1 raceway.

What did these two local governments get aside from the satisfaction
of owning part of a company that had been losing money for years? The
same thing Shanghai got for protecting its local supply chain in the early
days, and the same thing Taizhou City got for selling Geely land below
market value: jobs and taxes. As Geely revealed not long after the
purchase had been settled, the company planned to open three Volvo
factories in China. Not surprisingly, Daqing and Jiading will both be
getting factories; the third will be in Chengdu.[24] Chengdu and Jiading
are not surprising choices as both cities already have auto factories and
experienced labor forces. Daqing, on the other hand, has no experience
with auto manufacture. In absence of its 37 percent contribution to the
special purpose entity, Daqing, it is fair to assume, would not have been
considered as a factory location.

This case demonstrates the importance of a charismatic entrepreneur
to a privately held enterprise. It would be difficult to argue that Geely
would even exist in the absence of Li Shufu's energy and audacity. At
the same time, this case illustrates the critical role of local government at
every important step along the way. Taizhou City helped to swell the
nascent Geely balance sheet with equity in the early days, and years later,
Daqing and Jiading stepped in to support Geely's (actually, Li Shufu's)
purchase of Volvo. And while there can be no doubt that Li Shufu
appreciated the $100 million bank loan for the Volvo purchase, he
continues to ask the central government for more support for the Geely
side of his organization, not just in terms of access to funds, but also
through a level playing field in its ability to compete with SOEs. As it
appears now, however, the central government is more willing to
approve a loan for the purchase of a struggling foreign brand (Volvo) than
they are to support the growth of a profitable Chinese brand (Geely).

In late 2010, a mild furor was raised when the assistant director
of the State Council's Development Research Center, Liu Jieshi
suggested that it was time for China to consider dropping the 50 percent
ownership limit for foreign companies doing business in China's
auto assembly industry. (The 50 percent limit only applies to vehicle

assembly; parts manufacturing ventures may be wholly foreign-owned.) Liu's comments were made during the China-Europe Auto Manufacturing Forum, reports from which indicated that, while all of the foreigners in attendance nodded their heads in agreement, the Chinese were vehemently opposed.[25] The Chinese arguments echoed those made prior to China's joining the WTO: the Chinese auto industry is not yet mature enough to compete head-on with the foreign automakers. If restrictions were to be lifted, they argued, foreigners would completely occupy China's market to the exclusion of the Chinese manufacturers. There was, however, at least one Chinese auto company leader who voiced his strong *support* for Liu's suggestion: Li Shufu.

> Only complete lifting of the restrictions [on foreign investment] will help the development of the Chinese auto industry. The current policy of the 50 percent limit on foreign investment is disadvantageous; it does not protect the Chinese auto industry at all. On the contrary, it restricts foreign car companies from entering China.[26]

Reflecting his continued refrain, Li continues to be so confident in his company's ability to compete with foreign producers that he welcomes increased competition. What Li most likely expects is that increased foreign competition within China would more quickly drive out the weaker competitors. That, of course, is anathema to the central government. Since an overwhelming majority of China's automakers are state-owned, it logically follows that an overwhelming majority of the weaker players are state-owned. The central government may have recently learned to appreciate the contributions of the private players, but that still has not changed the "pillar" status of the auto industry.

Recall that the 2004 auto policy contained the new rule that, henceforth, no auto company would be allowed to sell its certification to a non-automobile-related company (see Chapter Three). This rule was put in place, some of my interviewees believe, specifically to prevent private companies like Geely from getting into the auto business. However, as this case has demonstrated, by 2009, the central government seems to have taken a more positive attitude toward Geely. The same may be said of BYD.

BYD

Like Geely, BYD did not begin life as an automaker. BYD was formed in 1995 by Wang Chuanfu, its current chairman, as a manufacturer of batteries, a natural outgrowth of Mr. Wang's educational background. BYD did not enter the auto industry until, also like Geely, it rescued a struggling automaker from bankruptcy. Many observers may be surprised to learn that BYD only began to make cars in 2003. Outside of China, BYD did not start to draw much attention until a unit of Warren Buffett's Berkshire Hathaway announced plans to take an ownership share in this "electric car company" in the fall of 2008.

Wang Chuanfu was born into a poor family in 1966 and was raised by an older brother, as his parents both died before he finished high school. He later went on to earn both bachelor's and master's degrees in metallurgy and physical chemistry, and worked as a government researcher at the Beijing Nonferrous Research Institute from 1990 to 1995. During this time he was assigned to be General Manager of the Institute's *Bi Ge* Battery Company in Shenzhen where he grew increasingly impatient with the lack of money to adequately fund research. "It was difficult to do anything [inside the SOE]," he said.[27]

This led him to "jump into the sea" in 1995 and start his own company, BYD, to manufacture rechargeable batteries to compete with the likes of Sony and Sanyo. Wang felt that there was great opportunity in mobile phones, and that China's new business elite would eventually find mobile phones to be an indispensable tool for business. Wang, together with his cousin, Lu Xiangyang who had worked for Bank of China, pulled together a small amount of startup capital, hired about 20 young engineers and rented space in Shenzhen to begin making batteries. The name BYD is an acronym of the company's Chinese name, 比亚迪 *(bi ya di)*, which actually has no meaning. Wang has joked in the past that BYD stands for "Brings You Dollars," and only recently adopted "Build Your Dreams" as the company's motto.[28]

Wang's key competitive advantage over his Japanese rivals in battery manufacture was cost. Instead of employing robots and expensive clean rooms as the Japanese did, Wang hired thousands of laborers and developed a manufacturing process that avoided the expense of clean rooms and large amounts of purified water. Wang claims that his simplified process results in batteries equal in quality to those of the Japanese.[29] Because of the large number of employees, BYD's productivity is lower than that of its Japanese competitors, but the unit cost of a Japanese battery is still five or six times higher than that of BYD.[30] Wang's approach proved successful as by 2000 BYD had become the world's largest manufacturer of mobile phone batteries.[31] In 2002, the company launched an IPO on the Hong Kong Stock Exchange, using the proceeds for R&D, repayment of loans and for future acquisitions. Meanwhile, BYD expanded further into handset components such as LCD screens, cases and keyboards, and eventually into designing and assembling mobile phones for Motorola, Nokia, and Samsung, among others.

BYD's plunge into automobiles did not come until 2003, and according to Wang, it was only after a process of elimination that autos seemed to be a good fit for BYD. The company had done very well manufacturing batteries and was sitting on about 1.2 billion yuan (approx. $160 million) in cash. Wang considered various investment possibilities including making home appliances or mobile phones under its own brand or investing in real estate. Cars seemed to fit the bill because there were, according to Wang, relatively fewer players in the industry, barriers to entry were relatively high and the degree of competition, as he saw it, was not too intense.[32]

It was around this time that a friend of Wang's just happened to mention to him that a state-owned automaker in Xi'an was looking for a buyer. Qinchuan Auto was one of four auto companies that had years earlier been spun off from a state-owned weapons company (兵器总公司), each of which had been given permission to manufacture the "Alto," a small car based on blueprints licensed from Japan's Suzuki.[33] Despite its contract to supply the local taxi business in Xi'an, Qinchuan had difficulty achieving scale and began seeking a buyer. Its first suitor, in 2002, was none other than Geely, but Geely, which would not be launching its own IPO for another two years, could not raise enough cash for the transaction. Next, Brilliance China, a New York Stock Exchange listed automaker in Shenyang threw its hat into the ring, but soon withdrew as the company became distracted by a falling out between its chairman and the government of Liaoning Province.[34] (See the Brilliance case study later in this chapter.) BYD was next in line.

Wang negotiated an initial purchase of a 77 percent stake that required government approval as BYD was listed on the Hong Kong Stock Exchange and thus considered to be a "foreign" entity.[35] The purchase cost BYD more than the value of Qinchuan's 77 percent stake as investors in Hong Kong sent BYD's shares tumbling 20 percent on the day the intention to purchase was announced. Analysts were skeptical that a company with no auto experience could successfully manage an auto company.[36] BYD's purchase of Qinchuan, which it soon renamed BYD Auto, immediately made BYD China's second-largest private automaker behind Geely. BYD, which was initially the majority partner in Qinchuan with local state-owned entities maintaining a minority stake, eventually increased its ownership to 99 percent.[37] Because BYD followed established procedures for "foreign" investment, and because the target of its investment, Qinchuan, was on the verge of bankruptcy, approval from Beijing does not appear to have been a difficult hurdle. However, as Chapter Three revealed, the Auto Policy to be released in the following year, 2004, closed this loophole that had allowed a private company take over a state-owned automaker.

Part of the attraction in buying an automaker was, for Wang Chuanfu, the prospect of merging the battery technology BYD had already mastered with transportation. In his view, not only was electric vehicle technology achievable in China, but it was necessary. Though China still had comparatively few cars on the road, Wang saw a future of crowded, polluted streets, and envisioned the electric vehicle (EV) as a potential solution. Furthermore, Wang saw the EV as an opportunity to leapfrog foreign multinational corporations in terms of technology. Wang was aware that GM had tried electric vehicles in the 1990s with its EV1 project, which it later abandoned.[38] He understood that China was behind the foreigners in terms of traditional internal combustion engine (ICE) technology, and saw EVs—*his* EV—as a way to close the gap and take the lead.

And it was Wang's pursuit of EV technology that ultimately drew the attention of Warren Buffett's Berkshire Hathaway whose Mid-American Energy unit announced its intention to purchase nearly 10 percent of BYD in the fall of 2008. As BYD's stock soared over the next year due to Buffett's investment, Wang Chuanfu grabbed headlines with an audacious goal: by 2015, BYD would become the largest

companies had signed "a strategic cooperation framework agreement to support BYD's pillar industries and development of new energy technology."[45]

BYD's success to date, according to a 2010 exposé by *Caixin* magazine is due primarily to two factors: relentless cost control and copying.[46] So far, the extent of BYD's development cost for automobiles has been that of disassembly and reverse-engineering of competitors' cars, a charge to which BYD officials readily admit. And though most auto companies go to great lengths not to build cars that look like those of their competitors, a former GM official in China told me that, "it is an open secret that all car companies buy and disassemble each others' cars." But, according to *Caixin*, reverse-engineering has, until recently, been the extent of BYD's R&D for automotive design.

Another way that BYD has thus far managed to keep costs under control is to gradually bring parts production in-house. According to a BYD manager with whom I spoke, as of the end of 2009, a staggering 80 percent of BYD auto parts were made in-house. "Except for glass, tires, and some electronics like CD players, we make everything." The *Caixin* article reveals that BYD both "delights and frightens" its suppliers: "BYD typically makes one or two serious, large orders of models, materials, or components but never orders again. That's because it just starts making whatever it bought."[47] However, the *Caixin* article also quotes BYD managers as saying that the company now "borrows" from others a lot less than before, and China-based auto blogs now offer confirming opinions that BYD's newer models are coming from unique designs. Perhaps BYD's move toward its own designs comes none too soon as the F3, BYD's flagship sedan, sold fewer models in 2010 than in 2009.[48]

As we have seen thus far, BYD has benefited from support, not only from the local governments in Shenzhen and Guangdong province, but also from the central government, in the form of a very large line of credit. In 2010, however, BYD found itself caught in the middle of a political battle between central and local governments, and suffered for its lack of political foresight. This episode began in July of 2009 when BYD signed an agreement with the Xi'an High Tech Zone to build a factory that would expand production by 200,000 vehicles per year.[49] That same month, two different village governments in Huxian County (in the Xi'an area) appropriated 725 acres of land for BYD's project, and, as required by law, compensated the people who were being moved off the land. Huxian County later asked the Xi'an city government to approve an expansion of the BYD project land to about 807 acres (90 percent of which was arable land). Xi'an city then passed this request up to the Shaanxi Provincial government, which approved the request in November of 2009. By the following month, BYD had begun construction on seven factory buildings including a dormitory, a mixing plant, and surrounding roads on about 121 acres of land, 92 percent of which was arable.

All of this came to light in July 2010, when the Ministry of Land and Natural Resources ordered a halt in construction and launched an investigation into illegal development of arable land. The fact that this land was arable was not just a minor detail. Misuse of arable land had become a serious issue in China, drawing much discussion at the previous National People's Congress in March of 2010. China's law states that any potential nonfarm use of arable land, anywhere in China, must be submitted to China's State Council (the Cabinet) for approval. By agreeing to BYD's use of arable land for factory construction, the Shaanxi Provincial government granted the company permission it lacked the authority to give.

BYD, for its part, thought it had covered all its bases. It went to the local government and filed its request, and within a few months, it received the approval it wanted. And though this kind of behavior by BYD and local governments was not out of the ordinary, the Ministry of Land and Natural Resources did not see it that way. It fined BYD nearly $500,000 and confiscated all of its illegally constructed buildings. And since an entire hierarchy of local officials from village to county to city to province had granted approvals, Beijing handed out punishments to them as well, meting out fines, warnings, and demerits to 14 officials at various levels. The fact that both BYD and local officials were punished was a clear signal from Beijing that this law in particular was not to be broken. Despite the fact that BYD was favored enough to receive a massive credit line from a state-owned bank, it lacked sufficient clout with the central government to have this violation overlooked.

This came during an especially humbling year for BYD. At the beginning of 2010, BYD had set for itself an ambitious goal of selling

800,000 vehicles. This would have represented a 79 percent increase over its 2009 sales of 448,000. By mid-year, BYD had to admit that sales were not materializing as hoped, so it scaled back sales projections to 600,000, only to find this number out of reach as well. Sales for 2010 reached only 519,800, or a growth rate of 16 percent. While this still would have qualified as outstanding growth in any of the world's developed auto markets, it was only half that of China's auto market as a whole which grew by 32 percent in 2010.[50] Though Warren Buffett's investment in BYD is still profitable on paper, as of this writing, his profit is now only about half as large as it was at its peak.[51]

During my interviews in China in the early part of 2009, BYD was still flying high on its reputation as a technology leader, but most of my interviewees, presciently, it now seems, expressed skepticism about BYD's technological claims. I asked a design engineer and former senior Chinese auto executive which Chinese company showed the greatest promise in EV technology, and he replied, "none of them." "Not even BYD?" I asked. "Not even BYD." Being led by an optimistic entrepreneur, cultivating close relations with local government and being seen to carry out central government policy, while all positive attributes of a private auto company, can only take an automaker so far. Eventually, the company must be seen to deliver on its reputation for high technology, and, eventually, the company must evolve away from merely copying the designs of others.

Still, despite the fact that BYD's public relations seem to have run too far ahead of its capabilities, the company continues its push to develop, not only new energy vehicles, but also the infrastructure to support them. In May of 2010, BYD and Daimler of Germany formed a 50:50 JV "research and technology center" to design an electric vehicle for the China market. The JV has announced that it intends to introduce a car in China in 2013. BYD is also actively supporting China's "going out" policy, having recently established a relationship with the City of Los Angeles whose Housing Authority has taken delivery of a fleet of ten F3DMs for testing.[52] Though the scale is small, BYD has in effect become the first Chinese company whose cars are driven daily in America, but the E6 electric vehicle BYD had been planning to introduce in California in 2010 has been indefinitely postponed.

The slowness to bring new energy vehicles to the consumer market seems to be due to both cost considerations and scale. According to Wang Chuanfu,

> The current price of an E6 is 300,000 yuan . . . If we can reach production capacity of 200,000 vehicles, the price of an E6 will be cut in half. And for the F3DM model, there are currently more than 200 orders a month in Shenzhen. But we can provide no more than 100, mainly because battery production capacity can't keep up.[53]

But Wang also blames a lack of consistency in China's policies supporting new energy vehicles for his company's continued reliance on traditional ICE technology. This is apparently a case in which he would rather see a uniform, nationwide policy than the current mishmash of local experimentation:

> A bottleneck for industrializing new-energy vehicles still lies in the policy environment. Policies surrounding new-energy vehicles need to have a system, for example, for a purchase tax, vehicle and vessel tax and consumption tax. Setting these tax rates at zero would be a big help. But right now, policies are not coordinated. In places such as Beijing and Shanghai where there are restrictions on new license plates, couldn't new-energy vehicles be exempted? And then there are road tolls and other things.[54]

Still, Wang must certainly be pleased with the level of support BYD has received from his local government in Shenzhen. One BYD manager with whom I spoke described BYD's relationship with the local government as "*feichang, feichang, feichang hao*" or extraordinarily—three times—good. "Without such support, BYD would not even exist." He says BYD's early success was also considered to be an "achievement (业绩) of local government officials" who subsequently earned promotions based on their association with BYD. A lot of local Shenzhen officials "grew up" with BYD and have benefited from the company's success, and Shenzhen has returned the favor by providing BYD with "all the land it needs—either free or very cheap." BYD is also, according to the BYD manager, well-liked by the central government. Several senior leaders, including Hu Jintao, Wen Jiabao, and Jiang Zemin, have visited to show their support. BYD has attracted their support, he says, because it pursues government-mandated policies such as new energy vehicles and energy-saving/carbon-reducing technologies. "BYD is successful because of government support, and the government supports it because it is successful. It is hard to say which came first."

Whereas BYD has been able to count on its local government for help when needed, this next company started life as *part of* its local government, which still maintains a minority interest.

Great Wall

Great Wall Motor Company is unique among China's private auto-makers in that it began life as a collective enterprise (also known as a township and village enterprise or TVE), and only later did it sell a stake to private investors.[55] It is located somewhat off the beaten path in Baoding City, Hebei province, where it is the largest employer in the city. The company is best known in China as one of the largest makers of pickups and SUVs, only in recent years adding sedans to its product mix. The company was listed on the Hong Kong Stock Exchange in 2003, and today, the company is controlled by its Chairman, Wei Jianjun, who holds 38.1 percent of the company's equity. The Nandayuan Township still holds 24.1 percent, and public shareholders hold a total of 37.7 percent.[56]

In a radical contrast with Geely and BYD, Great Wall is a remarkably quiet company in that it does not often make news. In the words of one auto consultant with whom I spoke, "Great Wall is quiet and reserved . . . doesn't draw attention to itself . . . focuses on making cars, not news." The company does not have a widely recognized entrepreneur-spokesman like Geely's Li Shufu or BYD's Wang Chuanfu. Instead, it is typically represented, not by its controlling owner, but by its female General Manager, Wang Fengying, who became the company's CEO in 2002 at the relatively young age of 31. Great Wall was founded as a collective enterprise in 1976 by the Nandayuan Township of Baoding City, and, similarly to Geely and

BYD, did not start out as an automaker. Its initial business was in repairing agricultural vehicles and equipment, adding vehicle modification to its services during the 1980s. By 1990 the company neared bankruptcy and had dwindled to only 60 employees.

During the 1980s many Chinese SOEs had adopted an "enterprise contracting system" (承包经营责任制) whereby state owners would contract with managers to run an enterprise and hand all profits, up to a certain percentage, over to the owners. The remaining profit would be retained by management.[57] The local state leaders of Great Wall actively sought an individual manager who would implement a similar contract with Great Wall to rescue the firm and return it to profitability. The manager who stepped up to accept the contract was Wei Jianjun, a local Baoding native who was only 26 years old at the time.

Wei Jianjun was not unfamiliar with industry. His father, Wei Deyi, had founded the Baoding-based Taihang Group, a manufacturer of industrial equipment, and his uncle was a senior manager at Great Wall. Wei had worked in several factories in both Beijing and Baoding, and most recently had been general manager at a local water pump factory.[58] In 1990 Wei Jianjun signed a five-year contract with Great Wall in which he would hand over a percentage of profits to the collective owners and retain the rest for himself.[59] Great Wall returned to health under Wei's leadership, but the national catalogue established under the 1994 Auto Industry Policy (see Chapter Three) effectively ended Great Wall's business in vehicle modification as none of the company's vehicles qualified to be listed in the catalogue. Wei made the decision to enter the auto assembly business, but the company lacked sufficient capital to begin producing sedans. However, he noted that none of the major Chinese automakers was building pickup trucks, and identified this as the niche in which Great Wall could make its entry.

The company's first pickup, the "Deer," rolled off the assembly line in 1996, and in the following year, Great Wall began exporting pickups to the Middle East. By 1998 Great Wall had become the leading producer of pickup trucks in China. Assessing the trend toward larger SUVs (sport-utility vehicles) that had taken the United States by storm during the latter half of the 1990s, Great Wall noticed that there were few SUV makers in China and released its first SUV, the "Safe," in 2002. Within a few years, Great Wall had also become the largest SUV maker in China and one of China's largest exporters of vehicles. On the back of this success, in December of 2003 Great Wall Motors became the first among China's "private" automakers to complete an H share listing in Hong Kong, raising HK$1.7 billion in an offering that was 682 times oversubscribed.[60]

In the following years, the company released its very popular "Hover" SUV (which has since been renamed "Haval"), and in 2008 released its first two sedan models after having applied to the NDRC for permission to expand its product mix.[61] Though Great Wall's exports suffered during the global financial crisis, they rebounded to more than 55,000 units in 2010, keeping Great Wall among the list of China's largest vehicle exporters with sales to more than 100 countries and regions worldwide. More importantly, by year-end 2010, Great Wall had 12 factories located overseas assembling kits shipped from its factories in China. As of this writing, Great Wall also has the distinction of being China's only automaker successfully to have sold vehicles in developed auto markets. Australia and Italy are among Great Wall's export markets for SUVs.[62]

I asked a senior manager at Great Wall how his company had been able to penetrate a few of the developed overseas markets where other Chinese automakers had continued to fail. He said Great Wall had set foreign standards for safety and emissions as its goal years before, and to demonstrate its commitment to these goals, invested in a world class testing facility. Whereas many other Chinese auto companies had to send their vehicles to a government organization for crash testing, Great Wall had built its own 250-meter crash-test track that, at the time I visited, was the longest in China.[63] Great Wall had the advantage of knowing its cars would pass before they were tested by the government, and eventually, the government began to accept Great Wall's test results. The company also rents its facility to automakers that do not have their own test facilities.

The senior manager whom I interviewed said that, as a private company, Great Wall also had the advantages of flexibility and cost control. "For example," he said, "a typical SOE might have 50 people in its purchasing department, whereas a private company can do the job with five. SOE workers see all money as the government's so they are not so concerned about waste, but, of course, the SOE has the advantage of government funding." The manager also noted that Great Wall's employees are taught from day one the importance of managing costs and looking for ways to improve in everything they do: "Our Chairman's favorite slogan is to 'improve a little every day' (每天进步一点一点)." Indeed, I later found this slogan on little brass plaques above the urinals in the men's room at Great Wall headquarters.

In interviews with auto industry analysts, consultants and journalists, I always asked for their opinions as to which automakers are among the best in China, deliberately leaving unclear what I meant by "best." Most would name three or four companies. Their answers, of course, often conflicted as each person weighed certain factors as more important than others, but I was surprised to find Great Wall mentioned more consistently than any other. And the typical reason given was that Great Wall is "well-managed." Some also praised Great Wall as a company that is "quiet" and "not led by a flamboyant leader" who constantly seeks the spotlight. "They just focus on making vehicles." One interviewee, who is an auto consultant with years of experience in senior management of auto companies in both the United States and China, also praised Great Wall's production skills: "They are surprisingly good at making engines and body panels. Unlike others they manufacture their own die sets for stamping sheet metal. This speeds up their cycle time because stamping is in the critical path."

I asked the Great Wall manager whether the company's relationships with local or central government had any influence on the company's operations, and he described the relationships as "two-way." The local government is a partial owner in Great Wall, holding 24 percent of the company's equity, but, the manager was quick to point out, the local government has no managerial control. "Local government likes the fact that Great Wall employs thousands of workers, so it gives the company breaks on its electricity, water, and land." At the same time, "the local government also sees Great Wall as a welfare factory (福利工厂), so it expects the factory to maintain employment levels in exchange for subsidies and policy support." As for the central government, the manager said there are "constantly people from Beijing coming around to ask questions and conduct surveys. They ask, 'if we pass a certain kind of policy, how would this affect you?'" He said Great Wall does not often have a reason to contact the central government as the local government is more important in helping with day-to-day issues. "Auto experts from MIIT (Ministry of Industry and Information Technology) will visit and conduct an assessment when we want to add a new product line or build a new factory, and we also frequently have visitors from the Ministry of Commerce and NDRC as well—especially during the financial crisis. They all wanted to know how we were affected."

All has not been smooth sailing for Great Wall, however. Like Geely, Great Wall has also found itself the target of lawsuits by foreign automakers. In 2003 Nissan reportedly considered a suit because the front end of one of Great Wall's SUV models bore a resemblance to one of Nissan's. The president of the Dongfeng-Nissan JV in China said that, though he was sure Nissan had a valid case, "the Toyota ruling [against Toyota in its suit versus Geely] may discourage us."[64] And apparently it did, because Nissan ultimately decided not to pursue charges. More recently though, the Italian automaker Fiat sued Great Wall because Great Wall's Peri sedan appeared to be a copy of Fiat's Panda model. After first suing Great Wall in Chinese courts and losing, Fiat brought the suit in Italian court and won a ruling forbidding Great Wall from selling the Peri in the EU. The following year, Great Wall countersued Fiat alleging corporate espionage. Citing photographic evidence Fiat had presented in Chinese court to protect its intellectual property, Great Wall said that Fiat had taken unauthorized photos, thereby infringing Great Wall's commercial secrets. Great Wall sought an apology and unspecified compensation.

As mentioned above, Great Wall is now controlled by its Chairman, Wei Jianjun, who holds 38.1 percent of the company. The township government that formerly owned Great Wall now only controls 24.1 percent of the company. How or why control of Great Wall was allowed to be switched from the township to Wei is not entirely clear. In 1998 the company reorganized from a collective enterprise to a joint-stock company. According to an article in China's *21st Century Business Herald*, a publication known for investigative reporting on China's business sector, Wei took his first ownership share at the time of the company's 1998 reorganization.[65] In that year Wei received a bonus from the company of 2.14 million yuan (about US$260,000), which he then used to buy a 25 percent stake in Great Wall.

Then, in 1999 and 2001, Wei Jianjun and his father, Wei Deyi (who is still chairman of Baoding Taihang Group), in two separate transactions, invested a total of 16 million yuan (about US$1.9 million) to buy another 30 percent stake in the company. This gave the Wei family majority control of Great Wall with a 55 percent stake. (At the time, Wei Jianjun held 46 percent and his father held 9 percent of the 55.) The Nandayuan township government held 44 percent, and the remaining 1 percent was held by company employees. The Great Wall manager with whom I spoke offered no explanation as to how control came to shift from the township to Wei Jianjun, nor have I been able to find documentation, either official or in Chinese or English media, as to what precipitated these transactions. According to the *21st Century Business Herald*, the director of the Enterprise Department of Nandayuan Township, says that Great Wall is not state owned, but individually owned, and that the township's share of the company now consists only of the land use rights it has transferred to the company. The article also quotes Wei Deyi as saying that his portion of the company was paid for with cash, but that he did not know whether his son's portion was paid for with cash or loans.[66]

Regardless of how Wei Jianjun came to be the controlling owner of Great Wall Motor Company, the parties involved all recognize that Wei is indeed the company's controlling owner. In China, corporate control is not a trivial matter. According to Wei, "we do not have control issues like other companies. I bear unlimited responsibility for Great Wall."[67] He said these words in 2003 around the time that Great Wall prepared to launch its IPO in Hong Kong, presumably to assure investors. But why volunteer such a statement at that time? Perhaps it was because another of China's nominally "private" automakers, Brilliance China, had in the previous year experienced a drastic shakeup due to a lack of clarity around who controlled the company.

Brilliance China

Brilliance China Automotive Holdings, Ltd. (华晨中国汽车控股有限公司) is a state-owned automotive conglomerate based in Shenyang, Liaoning province. Its major auto assembly subsidiaries include a joint venture with Germany's BMW and Jinbei Auto, one of China's largest manufacturers of micro-vans. So why am I including a case about an SOE with a foreign partner in a chapter about independent automakers? Because it used to be private—more or less. Like most of the other independent automakers, Brilliance involves the ambitions of an entrepreneur, but in this case, the entrepreneur eventually found himself at odds with the local government and paid a steep price.

Brilliance has its foundations in the late 1980s when the former Shenyang Automotive Industry Corporation reorganized itself, combining more than 90 enterprises into a single, joint-stock, group company named Jinbei Automobile Company. According to both *People's Daily* and the *China Automobile Industry Yearbook* of 1988, the reorganized company had "state-owned, collective and individual shareholders," and was the first truly large-scale industrial enterprise in China to undergo enterprise reform.[68] Individuals were encouraged to invest in the newly corporatized automaker through either common stock or preferred stock that carried a 14 percent dividend rate. The group company was primarily in the business of building micro-vans, also known as *mianbao che* or "bread vans," (because they are shaped like a loaf of bread with wheels), along with their engines and many of their parts. The company also built Toyota HiAce minivans under license. The combined enterprises were technically insolvent prior to the reorganization which was seen as a way to raise capital that the local government in Shenyang did not have. In the following years, Jinbei enjoyed somewhat improved performance, and even formed a joint venture with General Motors to make S10 pickups and SUVs from kits.

In 1990 a 32-year-old businessman from Anhui province named Yang Rong registered a company named *Huachen* (or 华晨, known as "Brilliance" in English) in Bermuda.[69] Exactly how Yang made his initial connection with Jinbei is not clear, but in July of 1991, his Hong Kong-based Brilliance Financial Group formed a joint venture with Jinbei to produce "Sea Lion" micro-vans.[70] In 1992 Yang launched a strategy that would lead to Brilliance's ownership of Jinbei Automobile and an initial public offering (IPO) on the New York Stock Exchange. According to investigative reporting by the *South China Morning Post*:

He convinced [Jinbei's] managers that he would be able to obtain a listing for them, on condition that they sold him a substantial portion of the shares. They sold him 46 million shares or 40 percent of the total . . .

Where did Mr. Yang get the money to buy the Jin Bei shares? According to yesterday's *Beijing Youth Daily*, he borrowed US$12 million from Hainan Hua Yin International Trust and Investment Corp, a non-bank financial institution set up by the Hua Yuan Group, the Beijing branch of the Bank of China and the China Institute of Finance, his former employer. Once he had listed the company in New York, he paid back the money to Hua Yin, leaving him with a handsome profit.

His next step, in May 1992, was to set up the China Financial Education Development Foundation, as a vehicle to take a controlling share in the listed company, with a registered capital of 2.1 million yuan, of which Brilliance held 2 million. The other three shareholders were Hua Yin Trust and Investment, China Finance College and the education division of the People's Bank of China.[71]

Brilliance China Automobile (ticker symbol CBA) was listed in New York in October of 1992, becoming the first-ever PRC-based company to list outside of Greater China. Following the listing, Zhao Xiyou, Chairman of Jinbei (which was now a Brilliance subsidiary) went to Beijing to report on the IPO to President Jiang Zemin who likened the Brilliance IPO to a "pipeline connecting China with the financial world."[72] While the public were able trade 28.75 percent of the listed company's shares, apparently the celebration over China's first foreign IPO overshadowed the fact that an educational foundation no one had heard of and a division of China's central bank were also part owners of this New York-listed company.

Brilliance used proceeds from the IPO to fund expansion during the 1990s. The Jinbei unit formed a joint venture with First Auto Works to produce Jiefang branded trucks, and the Brilliance unit began designing its own-branded sedan. The company later raised even more funds by launching IPOs in both Hong Kong and Shanghai in 1999.

But not all was rosy. *People's Daily* reported in 1999 that tax authorities shut down a Jinbei factory and seized 300 vehicles as compensation for unpaid taxes of 18.8 million yuan.[73] And in the same year, though this would not come to light until 2002, China's Finance Ministry internally decreed that Brilliance rectify its ownership status by transferring the 55 percent share held by the Chinese Financial Education Development Foundation to Zhongjin Fengde, a state-owned asset management company.[74] There is no indication that Yang Rong took any steps to comply with the Finance Ministry's wishes.

Meanwhile, Yang went about his business and launched discussions with numerous foreign automakers, looking for ways to increase output. Among the companies with which Brilliance opened talks were the London cab company, Manganese Bronze (with which Geely ultimately formed a JV), MG-Rover of the UK (which was ultimately sold to Shanghai Auto) and Germany's BMW. Brilliance's growth prospects added to both Yang Rong's wealth and his reputation as a business leader. In 2001 he was number three on *Forbes'* list of the wealthiest individuals in China with estimated net worth of $840 million, and in 2002 he was listed among China's top-ten most notable entrepreneurs.[75]

In the spring of 2002, while Brilliance was still in discussions with Manganese Bronze, MG-Rover, and BMW, rumors of irregularities within Brilliance began to surface. The Finance Ministry's 1999 decree to clarify ownership soon came to light and added further to the rumor mill while Yang Rong maintained silence. By the end of June, Yang Rong had resigned as chairman of Brilliance, and trading in the company's shares was halted on both the New York and Hong Kong exchanges. According to analysts quoted by the *New York Times*, Yang had been making use of the Chinese Financial Educational Development Foundation as a vehicle for his personal control of Brilliance, and he had "frequently presented himself as the main owner of the company."[76] Even the new Chairman who took over following Yang's resignation, Wu Xiaoan, claimed in the wake of Yang's departure that Brilliance was not a state-owned company.[77]

The following week news surfaced that Yang had dumped shares representing 2.2 percent of Brilliance's share capital and fled the country.[78] Within a few more weeks, Yang was indeed discovered to have left China (allegedly using falsified travel documents), and landed in Los Angeles, where his wife and son already lived. From Los Angeles, Yang finally began to speak out. Yang told a Chinese weekly newspaper, *Yazhou Zhoukan*, that provincial officials had been trying for years to take control of a larger share of "his company" by claiming assets in Brilliance Holdings in addition to the province's rightful state-owned portion in the Jinbei subsidiary. Yang claimed that he had controlled the group from the beginning because he had set it up, funded it, and managed it for a decade. He had been tipped off in early June 2002 that he would be arrested and charged with financial crimes, so he fled to the United States, fearing for his safety.[79] In fairly short order, Liaoning province seized full control of Brilliance by buying the Educational Development Foundation's portion of Brilliance shares for the bargain-basement price of HK$144 million (US$18 million)—a 93 percent discount to the market price in Hong Kong.[80]

Following Yang's accusations, then governor of Liaoning province, Bo Xilai struck back, publicly denouncing Yang Rong as a "fraud" and "not a private entrepreneur at all, but an agent entrusted by the government to run state-owned assets . . . "[81] In response, Yang's attorney in the United States claimed that the province had seized control of Yang's business in retaliation for Yang's discussions with BMW that involved setting up a joint venture factory in Ningbo, Zhejiang province.[82] Several of my interviewees also indicated that Bo and Yang had a falling out because Bo insisted that all of Brilliance's factories remain in Liaoning province. According to an investigative report by the government of the UK into the disposition of a British company (which will feature in the SAIC-Nanjing merger case in Chapter Six), the BMW subsidiary with which Brilliance had been in negotiation in 2001 and 2002 was MG-Rover. One of the MG-Rover principals, Nick Stephenson, had the following to say about the reason MG-Rover's negotiations with Brilliance did not result in a joint venture:

> Whether [Yang Rong] ever did anything illegal or not truthfully by Western standards we will never know, in my view. But sure as hell what he did wrong was he got on the wrong side of an incredibly influential political individual, who was called [Bo Xilai]. [Bo Xilai] amongst other things was head of

the Liaoning province and that is of relevance to Brilliance because their factories were in the Liaoning province.

We think the reason he got on the wrong side of [Bo Xilai] was the project he was doing with us was not in Liaoning province, it was in Ningbo, which was [in] a different province.[83]

Both sides ended up suing the other, Yang in U.S. court and Liaoning province in Beijing, but neither suit resulted in any actions. Perhaps this was because the rat's nest of nearly 300 companies and subsidiaries that comprised both Brilliance and Mr. Yang's business empire proved too difficult for any courts to sort out.

Was Yang, as Bo Xilai claimed, a "fraud" who deceived everyone into believing that state-owned assets belonged to him, or was he a legitimate entrepreneur whose property rights were violated by an envious local governor? Yang's claim was that he had established the Educational Development Foundation and funded it himself in order to give the *appearance* that Brilliance was state-owned. Without this veneer of state ownership, he claimed, he would not have been able to gain approval from Beijing to take the company public in New York. His mistake, then, seems to have been in doing nothing in the early years following the IPO to clarify his ownership, and then in ignoring the Finance Ministry's decree in 1999. He then tempted fate again in 2002 by suggesting that Brilliance's BMW factory be located in Ningbo over the objections of Liaoning provincial officials.

While courts in neither China nor the United States have sorted out the competing claims, Yang's role in establishing Brilliance and pushing it into the top-ten among China's automakers is unassailable. Even a July 2001 *People's Daily* editorial listed Brilliance among China's "privately owned" automakers (独资民营).[84] At a minimum, Yang appears to have taken personal risk to borrow money, make a profit from those funds, use that profit to take a stake in Brilliance and then repay the loans. Whether this should have resulted in a controlling stake, we may never know.

The fact now is that Liaoning Province is the controlling share-holder of the Hong Kong-listed Brilliance. (The company was delisted from the New York Stock Exchange in 2007 due to lack of trading volume.) And though the company went on to establish a successful joint venture with BMW following the ownership turmoil, the company continues to make most of its money from minivans and from lackluster sales of its own-brand Zhonghua sedans that were first introduced when Yang Rong was still in charge. Since 2002, Brilliance has endured difficult times, going through four different CEOs and losing three other key senior managers. It also rebuffed potential mergers with Guangzhou Auto in September 2010 and FAW in March 2011.[85] Though some knowledgeable industry observers report that Brilliance is making efforts to improve, this locally state-owned enterprise continues to struggle to gain footing and may be a good candidate for eventual consolidation.

As for Yang Rong, he has become a permanent resident of the United States and has not lost his enthusiasm for the auto business. In 2009 he founded Hybrid Kinetic Motors, a Hong Kong-listed company with plans to build "new energy vehicles" at one or more factories in the United States. And, despite the fact that there was at one time a warrant for his arrest in China, Yang's company has been discussing possibilities of forming joint ventures with auto companies in China.

Sichuan Tengzhong

If Brilliance is not an *independent* automaker, Sichuan Tengzhong looks even more out of place in this chapter: it's not even an *automaker*. But it wasn't for lack of trying. The same crisis that pushed Ford to unload Volvo also pushed General Motors to unload a number of brands, one of which was Hummer, the maker of the civilian version of the iconic "Humvee" military vehicle. (The military version of the Humvee is produced by a different company, AM General.) The only serious contender to purchase Hummer from GM was Sichuan Tengzhong, a privately owned maker of heavy industrial equipment that few people had ever heard of. Not even fellow automakers in China had heard of Tengzhong at the time it announced its intention to buy Hummer.[86]

As news of Tengzhong's interest emerged in June of 2009, most auto industry observers were scratching their heads, wondering why a heavy equipment manufacturer with no experience in the auto industry would be interested in buying Hummer. In the absence of corroboration from GM, no one would have been likely to take the news seriously, but James Taylor, CEO of GM's Hummer brand, expressed optimism that Tengzhong would be able to rescue his company along with its main assembly plant located in Shreveport, Louisiana.[87] While the media beat a path to Tengzhong's factory gate about an hour south of Chengdu in Sichuan province, few reporters came away with any answers. One prominent auto analyst with whom I met a few weeks after the announcement told me that the owner of Tengzhong, Yang Yi, was one of the wealthiest people in Sichuan. Having made his fortune in coal mining, Yang was well acquainted with many of China's coal miners, and their companies were also frequent buyers of Tengzhong's heavy equipment. Because many of the coal mine bosses also drove imported Hummers as their personal vehicles, Yang jumped at the opportunity to bring Hummer to China and get a license to produce them locally.

Unfortunately for Hummer, Tengzhong encountered resistance from Beijing right away. Not only was the hulking, inefficient SUV not in line with the central government's policy trend toward cleaner, more efficient vehicles, but this possible entry of yet another private auto-maker also ran counter to the policy supporting consolidation in the industry. While Tengzhong received approval from Sichuan provincial authorities, final approval lay with China's Ministry of Commerce which is responsible for approval of foreign investment, as well as the NDRC which, as China's economic planner, holds a veto over major investment decisions within any pillar industry. The fact that Tengzhong was a private firm had no bearing on whether it could undertake this transaction. In fall 2009, the NDRC bowed out of the decision saying that, because Tengzhong had dropped plans to localize production, approval did not fall within the NDRC's purview.

As time ran out for Hummer in early 2010, China's Vice Minister of Commerce, Wang Chao made the baffling announcement that the Ministry had yet even to receive an application for the transaction—a clear indication that approval was not forthcoming.[88] Tengzhong attempted a last minute end-around by announcing it would establish an offshore entity to acquire Hummer, a move that would free Tengzhong from the need for Beijing's approval.[89] This idea must have been a non-starter for GM as it announced less than 24 hours later that it would be winding down Hummer and would no longer seek a buyer.

Just as quickly as it had emerged from obscurity to capture the spotlight with its audacious bid for Hummer, Tengzhong returned to the obscurity from whence it had come. While General Motors was not specific as to why it rejected Tengzhong's suggestion of an offshore entity, it is difficult to imagine GM would wish to jeopardize its positive relationship with China's authorities (see SAIC-GM case in Chapter Four) by helping Tengzhong to avoid official approval.

Conclusion

This survey of several of China's most prominent independent automakers helps to explain the outcomes of the story in Chapter Two, and it also reveals several important factors that affect business–government relations and the position of private enterprise in China. (Note: Though the Chery case study was presented at the beginning of Chapter One, as it may be categorized among China's independent automakers, I will summarize that case along with those presented in this chapter.) I will proceed here according to the central government's key objectives presented in Chapter Two.

Consolidation

One of the central government's key policy actions to bring about consolidation in China's auto industry was first to prevent the establishment of new auto assembly firms, but the very fact that some of these independent automakers even exist is an indication that the central government's actions have not been entirely successful. In most of these cases we can see how a local government and a local automaker (or aspiring automaker) worked together to find ways around the central government's prohibitions.

The founder of Chery Automobile was also a local government official in the City of Wuhu, Anhui, who was in a position to build a factory, recruit engineers, install an assembly line, and begin assembling cars before the central government even knew what was happening. But rather than shut down Chery, which was operating in clear violation of the rules, a central government official offered a solution by which Chery could continue in operation under the wing of Shanghai Auto.

This was all for show, of course, because Shanghai Auto did not have to put up any money for its stake in Chery. In effect, the central government, not wanting to close a factory that was employing people in one of China's poorer provinces, created political cover that allowed a local government to continue violating policy.

Geely and BYD both entered the industry under circumstances somewhat different from Chery's—by buying production certificates from bankrupt automakers—but again, with help of local governments, they managed to enter an industry in which the central government had already made it clear that they were not welcomed. And after it became clear that BYD had found a loophole that allowed a nonautomaker to enter the auto industry, the central government erected a policy barrier preventing any other company from exploiting the same loophole.

Each of these cases illustrates how the central government has made a decision to subordinate its goal of building a globally-competitive auto industry to its goal of maintaining social stability. However, one could also argue that, even though the central government did not get its wish to keep upstarts out of the auto industry, the presence of these upstarts has still helped the central government to achieve some of its other objectives.

Technology Acquisition

Since the independent automakers, by definition, lacked foreign partners, they also lacked a lot of the same opportunities for technology transfer. They either had to buy foreign technology or copy it, and most (possibly all) of them started out by copying. But as their capabilities have improved, some of the independents have begun to introduce more unique designs that are less blatantly "borrowed" from other car companies. And the larger, more successful among the independents have also grown to a point that they are beginning to buy, not just technology, but entire companies. Geely's purchases of Australian transmission manufacturer DSI and Swedish automaker Volvo are examples of this new acquisitiveness.

Chinese Brand Development

Another positive side effect of not having access to a foreign partner that the independents brought to the industry was self-development of their own brands. And while early attempts at brand development at times relied on creating logos with amazing similarity to those of famous foreign brands, over time, China's larger independents have begun to develop their own brand identities in China. Only toward the end of the 2000s did the central government begin to realize that the independents, though unwanted, were contributing to the accomplishment of one of the central government's important objectives. Though the central government has taken no steps to place the private sector on an equal footing with the SOEs, it has provided token support in the form of access to bank loans for some of the larger private firms, including both BYD and Geely.

New Energy Vehicle Development

There is no question that the leading Chinese automaker in terms of NEV development has, until now, been BYD. And though it has experienced difficulties in getting its plug-in hybrids and pure electric vehicles to market (there is isn't much consumer demand for them), it is still far ahead of any other Chinese automaker in this regard. The central government has also belatedly recognized this and has rewarded BYD with support for its contribution toward this important central government objective. Among the other large automakers that are close to having a NEV ready for the market is Chery.

There is a Chinese idiom, 塞翁失马 *(sai weng shi ma)*, that describes a story in which a fictitious man named Sai Weng loses his horse, but each point of bad news in the story is followed by a positive outcome. In the end, the fact that Sai Weng lost his horse ended up being a good thing. Perhaps this idiom also describes the presence of independent automakers in China's auto industry. The central government did not want any new automakers to be established, but they were established anyway. Fortunately for the central government, this was not the end of the story. These independent automakers, while initially unwanted, provided several things the central government wanted. First of all, they employed a lot of people, and this fact alone has mostly likely kept the central government from shutting them down. Second, these independent firms have accomplished far more than the SOEs in terms of developing Chinese brands and NEVs—a fact that the central government has only recently begun to appreciate. But that is not the end of the story either. Unfortunately for the private automakers, they still must struggle to compete against SOEs that enjoy a far greater level of support from the central government—a central government that still, at best, only tolerates the presence of private automakers.

Other Key Points

These case studies also highlight several additional noteworthy points on the development of China's auto industry. First, as did Chapter Four, these case studies demonstrate the critical nature of the local government relationship to a firm's existence and the critical nature of the central government relationship to a firm's success. Second, they demonstrate that, though the central government has belatedly accepted the presence of private firms in the auto industry, not just any independent automaker will be allowed into the industry. Ownership lines must be clear, a company's activities must adhere to policy, and to truly draw the support of the central government, firms need to demonstrate a certain level of creativity and survivability. Finally, we see that, though the central government has rewarded independent automakers for their innovation, even the most innovative of China's independent automakers have relied heavily on copying, cost control, and public relations to give the appearance of innovation.

Like the previous chapter on joint ventures, this chapter illustrates well the importance of local government in the startup and functioning of a local automaker; however, whereas Chapter Four highlighted the importance of local government competence or industrial planning ability, this chapter shines more light on the business–government relationship itself. Recall that Chery continues to enjoy the patronage of its local Party Secretary who was also the founder and former chairman of the company. As de novo private enterprises, both Geely and BYD have benefited from cheap or free land as well as local government support in gaining their respective licenses to produce cars. And while Great Wall's local government continues to hold, if not a controlling interest, certainly a sizeable portion of the company's equity, it is also in a position to reward Great Wall (and thus, itself) with breaks on various expenses. Furthermore, as the senior Great Wall manager with whom

I spoke emphasized, such help is not a one-way street. Local governments appreciate these private auto firms because of what these firms
provide in return: employment and taxes. Accordingly, these firms are
expected to maintain their employment levels through both good times
and bad.

Such ties, however, are not unique to the auto industry. David
Wank's landmark study, *Commodifying Communism*, documented the
importance of local government ties among businesses in Xiamen.[90] He
found that property rights, while important, pale in comparison to a
business owner's relationship with local government. Though China's
property rights have been strengthened since the time of Wank's
research (e.g., by enshrining individual property rights in article 13 of the
PRC constitution), all indications are that ownership still matters less
than one's relationship with local government.

This mirrors the observations of dozens of auto industry insiders
with whom I spoke. In China the local government relationship is a
real-life equivalent of "passing GO" in the Monopoly board game.
Without it, an auto company (or indeed *any* company), no matter how
well-led or organized, no matter what kind of technology it possesses,
has practically no chance of success. As the corollary to this maxim,
several of my interviewees brought up the negative example of Yang
Rong and Brilliance. Though some were sympathetic with Yang's
plight, and questioned whether the charges against Yang were legitimate, my interviewees unanimously drew the lesson that part of Yang's
mistake was in trying to thwart the wishes of the local government by
attempting to locate factories outside of Liaoning province. Had he not
fled China, Yang most certainly would not have "passed GO." He
would have gone directly to jail.

And while this chapter further confirms the absolute importance of
the local government, it also illustrates that automakers cannot neglect
their relationships with the central government either. BYD's difficulties
expanding in Xi'an are a case in point. Though BYD already had a good
relationship with the local government (built on BYD's having rescued
its near-bankrupt auto factory), and BYD took steps to ensure that its
proposed expansion would be approved locally, BYD failed to ensure
that the central government would also approve. The facts that BYD
had been visited by several senior central government leaders and had

even been granted a very generous $2.2 billion credit line by the state-owned Bank of China, were not enough to ensure BYD could get away with breaking the central government's land use policy.[91]

The second key point highlighted by this chapter is that, while the central government accepts the contributions of the private firms, not just any private firm will be allowed to enter the industry. There are several unwritten rules that these case studies highlight. First of all, regardless of who owns a firm, ownership needs to be clear. Perhaps Yang Rong could be excused for making the decision in 1992 to apply the veneer of state ownership so that Brilliance could launch its IPO, but his later failure to remedy the situation—particularly after being ordered by the Finance Ministry to do so—placed him in an untenable position. Secondly, regardless of who owns a firm, that firm's intentions must adhere to policy. Tengzhong's problem with getting approval for the Hummer purchase had nothing to do with its status as a private firm. Though Tengzhong may have credibly argued that by purchasing Hummer it was following the central government's "going out" policy, it was guilty of running far afield of the policy urging the auto industry to move toward cleaner, more efficient vehicle technology. And third, regardless of who owns a firm, it seems that a key to attracting central government support lies in demonstrating a certain creativity and sur-vivability. In any business, success tends to breed success, and though Chery, Geely, and BYD had to find back doors into the industry, the fact that they not only survived, but thrived could not have failed to have had an impact on central government support for their businesses. Though Chery, Geely, and BYD have made their share of mistakes, few other automakers even come close to achieving their policy successes in terms of domestic brands, exports, new energy vehicles, energy-efficient vehicles, and foreign investment.

In all fairness to Yang Rong, we should recognize that his assumption in 1992 that a private firm would not have been allowed by Beijing to list in New York was probably sound. But by 1997 the landscape had already begun to change. The shift of the Premiership from Li Peng, an economic hardliner, to Zhu Rongji, an economic pragmatist, very likely created a more sympathetic attitude toward independent automakers in Beijing. Li Shufu's efforts to obtain a pro-duction license in 1997, and Wang Chuanfu's in 2003, came in different times and under different circumstances from those of Yang Rong. Furthermore it also seems plausible that location had an impact on these three entrepreneurs' startup activities. Whereas Yang Rong operated from a more conservative province, Liaoning—located in China's so-called "rust belt"—Li Shufu and Wang Chuanfu both had the luxury of operating from China's richest province (Zhejiang) and richest city (Shenzhen), respectively. One could argue the same for Chery. While its location in relatively poor Anhui may have been expected to work against Chery, the fact that Anhui was also the site of China's earliest experiments with privatization in the late 1970s, very likely worked in the company's favor.

The final key point that this chapter highlights supports the findings in Chapter Four that Chinese automakers have, thus far, demonstrated little innovative capability. Since the apparent uncertainty of winning an intellectual property lawsuit has probably dissuaded some foreigners from bothering to file lawsuits, it seems that all of the independent automakers have in some way borrowed liberally from the creations of others. And BYD, presumably the most innovative among the independent automakers, has yet to introduce a new energy vehicle that fully delivers on its claims. On the other hand, BYD has introduced some incremental innovations in terms of its business model. The company's longer-term view toward building an integrated "zero-emissions eco-system," though admittedly unable to deliver the short-term profits most equity investors seek, may be setting the company up for a more successful future. Only time will tell whether Wang Chuanfu's audacious goals, and Warren Buffett's investment, will pay off.

Recall that the Tenth Five-Year Plan in 2001 included a policy provision urging China's automakers to pursue development of hybrid and electric vehicles (see Chapter Three). Though BYD was not the only company to attempt to follow this central government policy—all of the major players now have EV projects—BYD was the only one that appeared to own the technology necessary to make it happen. Wang Chuanfu commented on the EV projects of the other automakers:

> Most of these projects are speculative. Some have taken state money to fund research projects, and build an [electric] car to gain publicity so that they can get more state money to fund

more research. Our motivation is completely different. Of course, they have to claim that what they are building is good, otherwise, how else could they get more money for research?[92]

I will address in the final chapter whether Wang's claims about the technological capabilities of the other automakers was accurate, but the important issue here is that BYD set out from the beginning to establish itself, not as an automaker, but as an *electric* automaker. The reality, of course, is different, but in China, appearances are important, and for most of its life as an automaker, BYD has deployed considerable PR resources to maintain this high-tech image.

Central government policy appears to have driven much activity among independent automakers. Policy called for Chinese brands, and independent automakers were the first to make it happen. Policy called for new energy vehicles, and independent automakers, BYD chief among them, were the first to make it happen. Only very recently, after the independents began to reap token support from the central government, have we begun to see action by the SOEs along these policy lines. Would Chery, Geely, BYD, and Great Wall have developed their own brands in the absence of central government policy urging them to do so? Of course they would have: without foreign partners, if they wanted to sell cars, they could only do so under their own brands. Would they have developed new energy vehicles? Perhaps. Though Chery, Geely, and Great Wall have their own NEV projects underway now, it seems that only BYD's Wang Chuanfu truly had intentions of developing NEVs in absence of a major government push.

From the point of view of the central government, the independents are on the leading edge of innovation in China's auto industry, and by rewarding them for their policy adherence, the central government sends a signal to the SOEs that this is the kind of behavior the central government wants to see. China's auto industry remains a pillar industry, which means the state will continue to insist on a preponderance of influence, but perhaps the presence of a few successful independents in this industry allows the central government to have its cake and eat it too.

As earlier chapters have stressed, another important policy focus for the central government is in pushing consolidation so that China's fragmented auto industry will develop the scale and industrial might eventually to take on the foreign multinationals in their own markets. The next chapter looks at how the industry has consolidated thus far.

Notes

1. Because Chery is also an independent automaker, it will be summarized at the end of this chapter along with the five case studies to be presented here.
2. Bruce J. Dickson, *Wealth into Power: The Communist Party's Embrace of China's Private Sector* (Cambridge: Cambridge University Press, 2008); Kellee S. Tsai, *Capitalism without Democracy: The Private Sector in Contemporary China* (Ithaca, NY: Cornell University Press, 2007).
3. Dickson, *Wealth into Power*, 99.
4. Tang Hongqiong, "浙江吉利汽车有限公司李书福简介 [Zhejiang Geely Auto and Li Shufu, Introduction]," *Business World—Financial Watch* (商界财视网), December 5, 2008, www.caistv.com/html/2008–12–05/113110 .shtml; Tian Weihua and Li Min, "生死李书福 [Li Shufu, life and death]," *Sina Finance* (from 中国企业家), March 3, 2005, http://finance.sina.com .cn/leadership/crz/20050303/13501400563.shtml.
5. Photos comparing Toyota's logo with Geely's Merrie logo may be viewed at www.designateddrivers.co.
6. Mark O'Neill, "Toyota Loses Logo Suit in China," *South China Morning Post*, November 25, 2003.
7. "Car Sector Attempt to Stop Plagiarism in China Fails," *Expansion*, November 25, 2003.
8. Photos comparing the Mercedes-Benz C-Class with Geely's Merrie may be viewed at www.designateddrivers.co.
9. Geely's HK listing came via a "back-door" purchase of an already-listed Hong Kong property company into which Geely eventually injected many of its mainland assets. Jane Cai and Candy Wong, "Geely's Aspirations Stuck in Low Gear," *South China Morning Post* (Hong Kong, March 11, 2009).
10. "Geely Shares Jump on Goldman Sachs Fundraising," *MarketWatch*, September 22, 2009, http://www.marketwatch.com/story/geely-shares-jump-on-goldman-sachs-fundraising-2009–09–22.
11. Tak-Wing Ngo, "Rent-Seeking and Economic Governance in the Structural Nexus of Corruption in China," *Crime, Law and Social Change* 49, no. 1 (February 2008): 37–38.
12. Ibid.
13. Ibid.
14. Here I have translated "give instructions" from the Chinese "批示"(*pishi*), the same term used to describe handwritten instructions from China's senior

leaders in the margins of policy documents sent back down to the various ministries. See explanation of the term *pishi* in Chapter Three. "温家宝考察吉利: 国家要支持 企业要努力 [Wen Jiabao inspects Geely: The state will give support . . .]," *Wangyi Caijing (from Dongfang Ribao),* June 15, 2009, http://money.163.com/09/0615/05/5BQTUVOM00252KFB.html.

15. "吉利汽车李书福: 自主创新60%资金应投向民间 [Geely's Li Shufu: 60% of funds for independent development should go to private enterprise]," *Sina Auto (from 21世纪经济报道),* March 22, 2006, http://auto.sina.com.cn/news/2006–03–22/0942174875.shtml.

16. Liu Zhaoqiong, "Private Business Sidelined by China's Stimulus," *Economic Observer,* March 16, 2009, www.eeo.com.cn/ens/Industry/2009/03/16/132582.shtml.

17. "李书福: 国内银行不愿借钱给吉利 [Li Shufu: Domestic banks unwilling to lend money to Geely]," *China News Service,* September 13, 2010, www.chinanews.com.cn/auto/2010/09–13/2529099.shtml.

18. A summary of China's "going out" (走出去) policy (in Chinese) may be found on the central government website, www.gov.cn/node_11140/2006–03/15/content_227686.htm.

19. "Geely to Set Up DSI Transmission Factory in Jining," *China Car Times,* June 12, 2010, www.chinacartimes.com/2010/06/12/geely-to-set-up-dsi-transmission-factory-in-jining/.

20. "Geely Interested in Volvo," *Autocar.co.uk,* December 15, 2008, www.autocar.co.uk/News/NewsArticle/Volvo-XC60/236484/.

21. Wang Jing, "吉利成功迎娶北欧新娘李书福的三道必答题 [Geely successfully escorts its Scandinavian bride, three questions Li Shufu must answer]," *Sina Auto (from 中国经济报),* August 7, 2010, auto.sina.com.cn/news/2010–08–07/1006635977.shtml.

22. This is confirmed in a document posted by the Board of Directors of Geely Auto Holdings on the Hong Kong Stock Exchange website: www.hkexnews.hk/listedco/listconews/sehk/20100803/LTN20100803009.pdf.

23. Keith Bradsher, "Volvo in a Deal to Be Sold to Company in China," *New York Times,* March 28, 2010, www.nytimes.com/2010/03/29/business/global/29auto.html.

24. "Volvo's New Factory to Settle in Chengdu, Shanghai, Daqing," *People's Daily Online,* November 11, 2010, http://english.peopledaily.com.cn/90001/90778/90860/7196280.html.

25. Zhao Yi, "外资欲越持股50%红线, 中方担忧车企空心化 [Foreigners want to surpass 50 percent ownership, Chinese worry about hollowing out of their auto industry," *Yicai.com (First Finance),* November 1, 2010, http://auto.ifeng.com/news/domesticindustry/20101101/454675.shtml.

26. Ibid.

27. "The Stars of Asia—Entrepreneurs: Wang Chuanfu," *Bloomberg Business Week,* June 9, 2003, www.businessweek.com/magazine/content/03_23/b3836610.htm.

28. Marc Gunther, "Warren Buffett Takes Charge," *Fortune*, April 13, 2009, http://money.cnn.com/2009/04/13/technology/gunther_electric.fortune/index.htm.

29. Li Xiang, "王传福：成本创新之王 [Wang Chuanfu: The king of cost innovation]," 金融界 [Finance World (from Economic Observer)], December 27, 2008, http://finance.jrj.com.cn/people/2008/12/2702123179514.shtml.

30. Hua Wang and Chris Kimble, "Betting on Chinese Electric Cars?—Analyzing BYD's Capacity for Innovation," *International Journal of Automotive Technology and Management* 10, no. 1 (2010): 79.

31. "Wang Chuanfu: Building Electric Dreams in China," CNN.com, April 20, 2009, www.cnn.com/2009/WORLD/asiapcf/04/20/byd.wangchuanfu/index.html#cnnSTCText.

32. Zheng Xianghu, 比亚迪之父王传福 [*Wang Chuanfu, Father of BYD*] (Beijing: Zhongyang bianyi chubanshe, 2009), 68–69.

33. The four spinoffs were Qinchuan in Xi'an, Chang'an in Chongqing, Jiangnan in Hunan Province and Jiangbei in Jilin Province.

34. Zheng Xianghu, 比亚迪之父王传福 [Wang Chuanfu, father of BYD], 69–70.

35. According to the *China Automotive Industry Yearbook*, the Ministry of Commerce is responsible for approvals of foreign investment. Zhongguo qiche jishu yanjiu zhongxin, 中国汽车工业年鉴 [China automotive industry yearbook] (Beijing: Zhongguo qiche gongye xiehui, multiple years), 2007, 15. Hereafter, *CAIY*.

36. Winston Yau, "BYD Draws Flak over Purchase of Carmaker," *South China Morning Post* (Hong Kong, January 24, 2003).

37. Zheng Xianghu, 比亚迪之父王传福 [Wang Chuanfu, father of BYD], 64–65.

38. Li Jiayi, 王传福与比亚迪 [Wang Chuanfu and BYD] (Hangzhou: Zhejiang Renmin Chubanshe, 2008), 71.

39. Li Fangfang, "BYD Guns for Top Slot before 2015," *China Daily*, September 17, 2009, www.chinadaily.com.cn/bizchina/2009–09/17/content_8701553.htm.

40. Norihiko Shirouzu, "Safer Battery Technology Gives China an Edge in Developing Affordable Electric Cars," *WSJ, China Real Time Report*, March 23, 2009, http://blogs.wsj.com/chinarealtime/2009/03/23/safer-battery-technology-gives-china-an-edge-in-developing-affordable-electric-cars/.

41. Photos comparing BYD's F3 with the Toyota Corolla may be viewed at www.designateddrivers.co.

42. "比亚迪奇瑞获银行贷款与政府采购支持 [BYD and Chery gain support from bank loans and government purchases]," *Nanfang Daily*, December 15, 2008, http://finance.nfdaily.cn/content/2008–12/15/content_4769078.htm.

43. "New Energy Vehicle Sales in China Disappoint Automakers," *Global Times*, December 6, 2010, http://autos.globaltimes.cn/china/2010–12/599331 .html.
44. Brad Berman, "China's BYD Aims for Total Zero Emissions Solution," *Plugincars.com,* October 18, 2010, www.plugincars.com/china-byd-aims-global-zero-emissions-solution-94288.html.
45. "比亚迪与中国银行签150亿元战略合作协议 [BYD and Bank of China sign 15 billion yuan strategic cooperation agreement]," *China News Service*, December 4, 2009, www.chinanews.com/auto/auto-zxzz/news/2009/12–04/1999651.shtml; "BYD Gets $2.2 bln in Credit from Bank of China," *Reuters*, December 3, 2009, www.reuters.com/article/idUSPEK209770 20091203.
46. Liang Dongmei et al., "How Manufacturing's Mockingbird Sings," *Caixin Online*, February 10, 2010, http://english.caing.com/2010–02–10/100117245.html.
47. Liang Dongmei et al., "How Manufacturing's Mockingbird Sings."
48. JD Power China, *Automotive News China*, www.autonewschina.com.
49. Parts of this story were previously published (with linked references) on the ChinaBizGov blog. G. E. Anderson, "In China, Not All Politics Is Local," *ChinaBizGov*, October 19, 2010, http://chinabizgov.blogspot.com/2010/10/in-china-all-politics-is-not-local.html.
50. Tian Ying, "China 2010 Auto Sales Reach 18 Million, Extend Lead," *Bloomberg BusinessWeek*, January 10, 2011, http://www.businessweek.com/news/2011–01–10/china-2010-auto-sales-reach-18-million-extend-lead.html.
51. A GaveKalDragonomics special report speculates that Buffett's interest in BYD may more related to BYD's energy storage solutions than its cars. "BYD: China's electric car pioneer," GaveKalDragonomics, September 2009.
52. Brad Berman, "L.A. Housing Inspector Logs First 300 Miles in China's BYD Plug-in Hybrid," *Plugincars.com*, January 24, 2011, www.plugincars.com/la-housing-inspector-logs-first-300-miles-byd-plug-hybrid-106717.html.
53. Lu Yanzheng and Liang Dongmei, "BYD Dream Story, in Wang Chuanfu's Words," *Caixin Online*, February 15, 2011, http://english.caing.com/2011–02–15/100225767.html.
54. Ibid.
55. Township and village enterprises are collectively-owned and typically non-agricultural businesses that grew in rural areas beginning in the late 1970s. See: Barry Naughton, *The Chinese Economy: Transitions and Growth* (Cambridge, MA: MIT Press, 2007), Chapter 12.
56. Great Wall Motor Company annual report, 2009.
57. On the enterprise contracting system, see: Jinglian Wu, *Understanding and Interpreting Chinese Economic Reform* (Mason, OH: Thomson/South-Western, 2005), 146–148.

58. Dong Changhong, "民企第一桶金:长城汽车突破产权困局 [Private enterprise's first pot of gold: Great Wall Motors breaks through property rights deadlock]," *21st Century Business Herald*, December 8, 2003, http://finance.eastday.com/epublish/gb/paper282/1/class028200001/hwz1355668.htm.

59. Neither a senior Great Wall manager with whom I spoke, nor any public documentation I have found, reveals the profit percentage that Wei was required to turn over.

60. Great Wall Motors 2003 Annual Report. Note that, when BYD launched its IPO in 2002, it was not yet an auto company.

61. Subsequent to this time, the authority to approve new vehicle models was handed over from the NDRC to MIIT, which was formed in 2008.

62. Figures in this paragraph from Great Wall Motors 2003 Annual Report.

63. Government testing is carried out by the China Automobile Technology and Research Center (CATARC) located in Tianjin. A photo of Great Wall's crash test track may be viewed at www.designateddrivers.co.

64. James Kynge, "Nissan Alleges Chinese IP Theft," *Financial Times*, November 28, 2003.

65. Dong Changhong, "民企第一桶金:长城汽车突破产权困局 [Private enterprise's first pot of gold: Great Wall Motors breaks through property rights deadlock]," *21st Century Business Herald*, December 8, 2003, http://finance.eastday.com/epublish/gb/paper282/1/class028200001/hwz1355668.htm.

66. Ibid.

67. Xu Feng, "长城汽车上市倒计时 [Great Wall Motors listing countdown]," *21st Century Business Herald*, November 27, 2003, www.21cbh.com/HTML/2003–11–27/12813.html.

68. Yang Jicai, "经济体制改革触角伸向所有制领域, 沈阳成立金杯汽车股份公司 [The tentacles of economic system reform stretch into the ownership arena, Shenyang establishes Jinbei Automobile Company]," *People's Daily*, May 19, 1988; Zhongguo qiche jishu yanjiu zhongxin, *CAIY*, 1988, 30.

69. Yang Rong (仰融) is also known as Yung Yeung or Benjamin Yeung.

70. *CAIY*, 1994, 39.

71. Mark O'Neill and Winston Yau, "Brilliance Shrouded," *South China Morning Post*, June 25, 2002.

72. *CAIY*, 1993, 31.

73. Li Jianxing, "欠税一千八百八十万元, 金杯公司被查封货车三百台 [Jinbei owes 18.8 million yuan in taxes, 300 trucks seized]," *People's Daily*, January 5, 1999.

74. "Brilliance China Auto execs under asset-stripping probe," *The Business Times of Singapore*, June 1, 2002.

75. Forbes 2001 China Rich List: www.forbes.com/global/2001/1112/032_8.html. "中国企业十大新闻揭晓 [Top Ten Chinese Enterprises announced],"

People's Daily, January 28, 2002. Incidentally, listed at number two on the Forbes list that year was Yang Bin (no relation), a business magnate who had made a fortune in tulips, operated a miniature "Dutch town" in China, had been designated as "governor" of a special economic zone in North Korea that never got off the ground, and was subsequently arrested and convicted of tax evasion. He is still in prison.

76. Keith Bradsher, "2 Exchanges Suspend Trading in Shares of Chinese Auto-maker," *The New York Times*, June 22, 2002.
77. Winston Yau, "New Brilliance chief denies state ownership," *South China Morning Post*, June 29, 2002.
78. Anthony Tran, "Brilliance Ex-Chairman Disposes of 79M Shares," *The Standard*, July 3, 2002.
79. Winston Yau, "Ex-Brilliance Chief Hiding in US Alleges Persecution," *South China Morning Post*, September 30, 2002.
80. Winston Yau, "Provincial Government Grabs Brilliance for $144m," *South China Morning Post*, December 20, 2002.
81. "Bo Xilai Refutes Yang Rong's Private Entrepreneur Identity," *China.org.cn*, September 30, 2003, www.china.org.cn/english/MATERIAL/76473.htm.
82. Mark O'Neill, "Law Being 'Manipulated,' Says Yang," *South China Morning Post*, October 1, 2003.
83. Gervase MacGregor and Guy Newey, "Report on the Affairs of Phoenix Venture Holdings, Limited, MG Rover Group Limited and 33 Other Companies" (Department for Business Innovation and Skills, appointed by the Secretary of State for Trade and Industry, United Kingdom, 2009), 462–463.
84. Jiang Shijie, "轿车需要市场竞争 [The Auto Industry Needs Market Competition]," *People's Daily*, July 15, 2001.
85. Yang Jian, "Should Brilliance China Find Itself a Buyer?," *Automotive News China*, September 3, 2010, www.autonewschina.com/en/article.asp?id=5724; "FAW-Brilliance Auto Merger Off – Liaoning Governor," *Reuters*, March 5, 2011, www.reuters.com/article/2011/03/05/faw-china-idUSTOE72401320110305.
86. Norihiko Shirouzu, "Hummer Bid Puts Spotlight on Obscure China Firm," *wsj.com*, June 4, 2009, http://online.wsj.com/article/SB124407220644583089.html.
87. The initial press release announcing the intended transaction may be found online at PR Newswire: http://news.prnewswire.com/DisplayReleaseContent.aspx?ACCT=104&STORY=/www/story/06–02–2009/0005037241&EDATE=.
88. Liang Dongmei, "How Tengzhong Won by Losing the Hummer Deal," *Caixin Online*, March 4, 2010, http://english.caing.com/2010–03–04/100122668.html.

89. Yan Fang and Jacqueline Wong, "Tengzhong May Buy Hummer via Off-shore Vehicle," *Reuters*, February 23, 2010, www.reuters.com/article/2010/02/23/us-hummer-tengzhong-idUSTRE61M1OY20100223.
90. David L. Wank, *Commodifying Communism: Business, Trust, and Politics in a Chinese City*, Structural analysis in the social sciences (Cambridge, UK: Cambridge University Press, 1999).
91. Note that, in 2011, BYD was subsequently able to cut a deal with the central government whereby it was able to resume construction, but the company still had to pay the fine.
92. Li Jiayi, 王传福与比亚迪 [Wang Chuanfu and BYD], 73.

Chapter Six

The Mergers

Since the country has resumed auto production . . . the number of factories has increased . . . This will once again bring about waste, low quality and high costs. Historical experience tells us this road is a dead end.

—Wu Facheng, director, Policy Research Office
China National Automotive Industrial Corporation
October 1984 (汽车强国之梦 [Dream of an automobile superpower], 2009)

This chapter focuses on a single central government objective: industrial consolidation. The accepted wisdom for almost any national industry is that an excessive number of domestic competitors dilutes that industry's ability to compete on a global scale. Early in China's auto industry renaissance, the economic planners in Beijing were already keenly aware of the need to reduce the number of industry players so that the remaining enterprises could better compete with the multinational firms of the developed world. But Deng Xiaoping's reforms apparently created a fertile environment for auto assemblers whose numbers more than doubled from 55 in 1978 to 114 by 1985.[1] As Chapter Three demonstrated, the call for consolidation has been one of the most consistent elements of China's auto policy since the mid-1980s. From the "big three, small three" of 1988 to the "big four, small four" of 2009, the pressure from Beijing for consolidation has not abated.

However, despite the pressure for consolidation and restrictions on market entry, the number of assemblers in the industry has remained remarkably stable since the mid-1980s. Though the number of auto assemblers peaked at 124 in 1992, it had only fallen to 117 by 2008.[2] Though a handful of mergers has taken place over the past decade, for each company that has disappeared into a larger entity through merger, at least one newer, smaller player has sprung up to take its place in the industry.[3] And the mergers that *have* taken place could probably be more accurately termed "combinations" as they did not result in the plant closures or layoffs typical of most mergers. When two firms in the same industry merge, the purpose is typically to take advantage of economies of scale. Because the combined companies no longer need, for example, two accounting departments, two purchasing departments, or two headquarters buildings, mergers often result in job elimination and sales of redundant assets. None of this has happened in any of China's auto company mergers that have taken place to date.

The fact that very few of the expected mergers have taken place, and that new players have entered the industry against Beijing's wishes gives at least the *appearance* that the central government is powerless to get its way when it comes to restructuring the auto industry. And the fact that all but a handful of the major industry players are state-owned makes this phenomenon all the more interesting: would an authoritarian government not have complete power to merge state-owned enterprises with each other?

But does the central government truly have no influence over industry structure? When I put this question to interviewees in China, the consensus answer was that, while the central government does indeed have the power to make consolidation happen, in general, the central government prefers that consolidation be market-driven.

However, a few went further to explain that, as long as China's auto market continues to grow quickly, many of China's smaller automakers will have no reason to consider merging with another. As long as they produce a minimally positive cash flow, they can remain independent, and their respective local governments will have no incentive to seek rescue through mergers.

But what would happen if growth were to slow? Several of my interviewees commented that the brief slowdown China's auto industry experienced in 2008 could have led to layoffs, closures and mergers—the very consolidation the central government had been hoping for—but just as many automakers reached a point where critical decisions needed to be made, the central government rode to the rescue with its stimulus package. So while the central government may prefer that the market drive most merger decisions, there are boundaries within which the market is allowed to operate. Markets are great—as long as they do not lead to instability.

The cases in this chapter support the claims of my interviewees that the central government does indeed have influence, but that it has chosen thus far to use that influence only sparingly. Though the central government has had a hand in "encouraging" some of the few mergers that have taken place in recent years, it has largely chosen to limit its role to one of selective intervention in order to correct mistakes or enforce policy provisions.

Even though the central government has insisted—for nearly three decades—that consolidation was necessary, only four major mergers (and a few minor ones) have taken place among passenger car assemblers. Chief among the strategic reasons motivating the acquir*ees* in these mergers was the need to survive. Chief among the strategic reasons motivating the acquir*ers* was increasing competition among China's largest automakers. As Figure 6.1 shows, China's automakers were grouped relatively tightly around the middle of the past decade, but as the auto market grew, we can see a smaller group of four or five automakers that begin to break away from the rest of the pack. Some of this growth was indeed driven by the combination of two or more automakers.

This chapter reviews three major auto industry mergers that have occurred over the past decade. The first, between First Auto Works (FAW) and Tianjin Xiali Auto took place in 2002 when FAW sought to

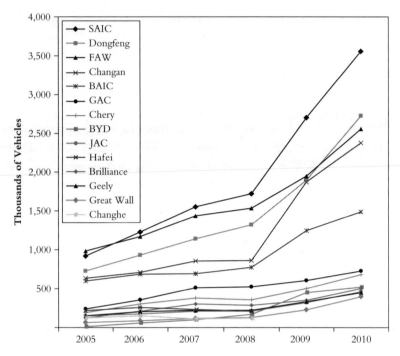

Figure 6.1   Annual Vehicle Sales by Manufacturer 2002 to 2010: The "Big Four" Break Away from the Pack
Sources: *China Auto*, Tianjin, 2006–2009; *China Automotive Blue Book*, 2010; CAAM.

keep pace with the other major automakers and Xiali sought a rescue from near-bankrupt conditions. The second, between Shanghai Automotive Industry Corporation (SAIC) and Nanjing Auto (NAC) took place in 2007 following a series of strategic mistakes and the intervention of the central government to repair the resulting situation. The third, between Guangzhou Automobile Group Company (GAC) and Changfeng happened in 2009 as GAC tried to gain the favor of the central government while Changfeng sought a partner with a complementary product mix. I will also briefly review two additional mergers: Chang'an's purchase of Hafei and Changhe, and GAC's purchase of GoNow Auto.

FAW–Tianjin Xiali Merger

The 2002 purchase of Tianjin Xiali by First Auto Works (FAW) was the first significant auto merger in China. At the time the merger was

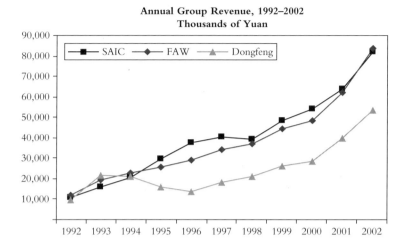

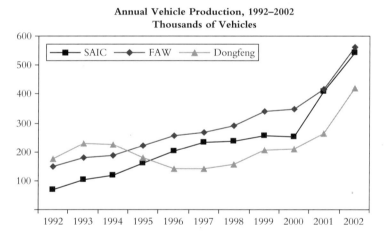

Figure 6.2 Top Three Automakers' Revenue and Production, 1992 to 2002
Source: CAIY, 1993–2003.

finalized in June of 2002, FAW, a central state-owned enterprise
(CSOE), was China's largest producer of vehicles, and Tianjin Xiali, a
local state-owned enterprise (LSOE), was also listed among China's top
ten. However, FAW had lost its spot as the largest generator of revenue
to Shanghai Auto (SAIC) back in 1995 (see Figure 6.2). With its purchase of Xiali, FAW returned to the top of the list in terms of both

revenue and vehicles produced, if only briefly. While there is evidence that the central government influenced at least two of the mergers that have taken place in China's auto industry over the past decade, the central government has generally allowed the market to influence merger decisions. In this case the evidence demonstrates that the FAW–Xiali merger was driven by considerations of competition and survival. Whether the central government attempted to force this merger or not—and I have found no evidence that it did—its influence was not needed.

FAW, as its name implies, is considered to be the PRC's first automobile *company* (even though the auto factory at Nanjing was founded a few years earlier). FAW began producing trucks from Soviet plans in 1953 and the home-grown *Hongqi* limousine in 1958. Until forming its joint venture with Volkswagen in 1991, FAW's primary line of business was production of *Jiefang* brand commercial trucks. In the early 1990s, the FAW-VW joint venture began producing the Audi 100, a semiluxury sedan favored by government officials, and later added the Volkswagen Jetta sedan to its mix.

Recall from Chapter Three that FAW had been listed among the "big three" automakers, along with SAIC and Dongfeng, in the 1988 policy formulation. By the early 1990s, due to its later start with its sedan-producing joint venture, FAW, though still among the "big three," found itself being challenged for the first time for the top spot among Chinese automakers by both SAIC and Dongfeng. In the late 1990s, FAW went through four difficult years of reforms, begun during the Premiership of Zhu Rongji, in which the company cut staff by an astounding 80 percent, while increasing profits sixfold from 1998 to 2001.[4] Despite the wrenching reforms, FAW continued to find its leadership challenged, particularly by SAIC, which in 2000 had begun production in its JV with General Motors, and which in 2001 bought a 76 percent stake in Liuzhou Wuling, adding over 50,000 commercial vehicles and nearly 40,000 sedans to its total production in that year.[5] Figure 6.2 illustrates tight competition among China's "big three" in terms of both revenue and vehicles produced.

Tianjin Xiali Automotive was owned by the local government of Tianjin, a provincial-level municipality that reports directly to the central government. It was among the earliest of China's automakers to establish relations with a foreign multinational automaker. The main subsidiary of Tianjin Automotive, Tianjin Xiali, had since the mid-1980s been producing small Daihatsu Charade cars under license from Toyota. Tianjin Auto was also listed among China's "small three" in the 1988 policy formulation. The "Xiali," as the small car was called in China, became nearly ubiquitous on the roads of China as it was the first small car to be produced there. At its peak in the 1990s, the little red Xiali held over 80 percent of the taxi market in Beijing.[6]

Production of Tianjin Auto peaked at 158,000 vehicles in 1997, but began to fall as newer auto models began to usurp the increasingly stale Xiali model's once dominant position. The company reacted with significant staff cuts of approximately 16 percent *each* in 1999 and 2000, but the expense cuts failed to keep pace with the company's decline in revenue.[7] Meanwhile, Xiali took advantage of its relationship with Toyota to pursue talks about forming a joint venture, and in 1999, the two companies announced plans to produce jointly a small car based on Toyota's Echo platform beginning in 2002. Prior to this time, Toyota's only production in China took place in two commercial vehicle JVs: one with Sichuan Wagon Company and one with Brilliance (Jinbei). The Tianjin JV would be Toyota's first venture to produce sedans in China.

Before the Xiali-Toyota venture could even begin production, China's impending accession to the World Trade Organization (WTO) prompted preemptive price cuts among Chinese automakers. In January 2002, Tianjin Xiali cut the prices of its sedans by as much as 30,000 yuan (US$3,627), representing 25 to 80 percent of the price of its cars.[8] It would cut prices twice more in the following year.

It was in this climate that Xiali began to look for a rescuer. Following 2001 sales that were 63 percent below those of its peak in 1997, Xiali began actively to reach out to the larger auto companies in China to discuss "possible capital tie-ups or asset restructurings."[9] This revelation from Tianjin Auto, that it had initiated talks with FAW and other potential suitors, seems to defy the logic that local governments are resistant to mergers for fear of losing local employment and tax revenue. We must then assume that the local government of Tianjin was either unwilling or unable to come to the rescue of Tianjin Auto and, therefore, gave it permission—or possibly even ordered it—to pursue other options.

As the other two "big three" automakers were themselves also the subjects of merger rumors around the same time, it is not difficult to imagine that FAW, in an effort to keep pace, would have been open to talks with a willing seller. SAIC was rumored to have been in discussions with Nanjing Auto, and SAIC's joint venture with GM and its majority stake in Liuzhou Wuling were both paying off with increased revenue and production. Also, Dongfeng Motors was rumored to have been discussing a possible merger with Beijing Auto, the China partner of Daimler-Chrysler. And Beijing Auto itself was also known to have been discussing establishment of a JV with Hyundai of South Korea.[10]

Despite the fact that FAW's majority shareholder is the central government, I have uncovered no evidence that the central government, aside from its customary policy focus on consolidation, pressured either FAW or Tianjin Xiali into a merger. While my inability to find evidence cannot conclusively rule out central government interference, the available evidence provides reason to believe that such pressure would not have been necessary. This merger was a true win–win, and it appears to have been driven by both competitive and survivalistic pressures. FAW benefited in several ways. First, FAW was able to add small cars to its portfolio. As a result of China's WTO entry, demand for small, affordable cars, which had grown steadily throughout the 1990s was beginning to explode. With its trucks, *Hongqi* limousines and only the beginnings of a self-developed midsized sedan (under the brand name Besturn), FAW had been ill-prepared to capitalize on what would become China's fastest-growing auto segment. Xiali gave FAW the small car it lacked.

Second, the purchase of Xiali instantly gave FAW a joint venture with one of the world's most highly respected automakers, Toyota. And within less than three months after purchasing Xiali, FAW launched talks with Toyota that resulted in a folding in of Toyota's existing venture with Sichuan Wagon as well as extension of the Xiali JV into a JV with FAW that would include more Toyota models (including Corolla and eventually, Prius). Said Zhu Yanfeng, General Manager of FAW, "Co-operation will enable us to gain Toyota's advanced technology, models and management know-how to provide better products to Chinese consumers."[11]

And a third benefit of the merger to FAW was that it would allow FAW to keep up with the other members of the "big three." As Figure 6.2 above showed, with this transaction, FAW did indeed regain its top position in 2002 in terms of both revenue and vehicles produced.[12] Recall my conversation in which a SAIC senior manager expressed to me the prime importance of growing bigger as a company goal. (See SAIC-GM case in Chapter Four.) As the central government has continued to include FAW among the favored larger automakers, from the 1988 "big three, small three" to the 2009 "big four, small four," this listing in itself has served as a kind of pressure on FAW and the others to keep growing. An engineer who formerly managed a design team at FAW confirmed to me that FAW was at least partially driven by pressure to keep up. "Even the company's name [First Auto Works] places pressure on corporate leaders . . . When they bought Xiali, this immediately made FAW bigger and more competitive."

While there may be future emphasis on improving efficiency, for now, efficiency is trumped by size in official policy. Size is easily measured and is a very visible and tangible way for the central government to measure the success of its auto companies in pursuit of the goal of global competitiveness. Several interviewees confirmed that CEOs of large SOEs know their job performance will be measured primarily by how big their empires become under their watch, and only secondarily by how profitable they are.

The benefits of the merger to Xiali were also quite clear. This is a company whose primary product, the old Daihatsu Charade-based sedan, had not been updated in years, and as other newer, fresher sedan models became available in China, its sales fell off rapidly. Not even a determined effort to cut expenses—Tianjin Auto had cut over 18,000 jobs in the three years *prior* to the merger—was enough to keep the debt-ridden, loss-making company off the slippery slope toward insolvency.[13] While its impending joint venture with Toyota offered some hope, apparently it was not enough to keep Xiali management from actively seeking a rescue.[14]

At the time of this merger, the combined partners made promises of continued significant staff cuts at Tianjin Xiali in order to improve efficiency. The company said that it would decrease its workforce by 75 percent within two years of the merger.[15] Given Xiali's 2001 year-end employment of about 39,000, this would have represented a cut of about 29,000 employees. The cuts did not happen. Though Tianjin Auto's workforce declined by a total of about 9,600 in 2002 and 2003, employment began to increase again in 2004.[16] Most of the company's cuts had already happened in the years prior to the merger. The merger benefited Xiali by making it a part of a stronger group company, but it did not result in significant expense cuts to achieve economies of scale.

The FAW-Xiali merger was a merger that offered clear benefits to both parties. It demonstrates that the leadership of one of China's largest SOE automakers thought strategically enough to see the value Xiali would bring, both in terms of product mix and overall size. It also demonstrates that a local government was motivated to seek a merger when poor managerial decisions had brought its local auto company to the brink of insolvency. While we cannot see the hand of the central government in this particular case, the following case reveals a SAIC-Nanjing merger that grew from a more complex situation requiring overt coordination from Beijing.

SAIC-Nanjing Merger

Shanghai Auto (SAIC) has already figured prominently in this book—as a partner in one of China's earliest auto joint ventures (SAIC-VW), as a partner in one of China's most "harmonious" auto joint ventures (SAIC-GM), and as an early caretaker of Chery Auto. So it seems somehow appropriate that SAIC was also a party to China's largest auto merger to date. The company that SAIC acquired to create China's largest auto group in December 2007 was Nanjing Automobile Corporation (NAC), a smaller LSOE located in neighboring Jiangsu province. In this particular case, the merger comes at the end. The interesting part of the story is of how these two partners got together; it revolves around a formerly British-owned automaker with a long and storied history, MG Rover Group. First, a brief history of the three players.

SAIC is not only China's largest automaker, but it is also considered to be among the strongest of China's state-owned automakers. Its roots go all the way back to the Shanghai Car Plant that began producing

Phoenix brand sedans in 1958.[17] SAIC's major joint ventures are with Volkswagen and General Motors (see SVW and SGM cases in Chapter Four) and in 2010, its combined subsidiaries sold nearly 3.6 million vehicles, more than any other automaker in China.[18] SAIC was also among the earliest of China's SOEs to begin venturing outside China. In 2002 it tested the waters by purchasing a 10 percent stake in GM Daewoo of South Korea, and in 2004, it took a controlling stake in Ssangyong Motors, also of Korea. SAIC's investment in Ssangyong seemed to go well for the first several years, but a combination of management-labor difficulties and the global financial crisis sent Ssangyong into bankruptcy resulting in SAIC relinquishing managerial control of Ssangyong in 2009.

Nanjing Automobile Corporation (NAC) has its roots in a factory founded in 1947 to make commercial trucks. Until the mid-1990s, NAC had been consistently listed among China's top-10 automakers, but its decision to partner with Italy's Fiat is widely seen to have been a mistake. Prior to the SAIC merger, the NAC-Fiat JV had not been able to produce more than 40,000 sedans in a year, and, according to a veteran China auto journalist, "their sedans had been a miserable failure."[19] However, NAC's truck building joint venture, set up in 1995 with another Italian company, Iveco, has been largely successful. The inability of NAC to gain momentum in the rapidly growing sedan segment led the government of Jiangsu province to change corporate management. But rather than bringing in an auto industry veteran, the province appointed Deputy Party Secretary of Jiangsu Province, Wang Haoliang, as the company's chairman. Wang's mission was to turn the company around and gain a foothold in China's increasingly competitive sedan market.[20] Within two months of his appointment, Wang's NAC would make a bold move that would shock the industry.

The MG and Rover brands that made up MG Rover Group were, along with Mini Cooper, Austin Healy, Jaguar, and Land Rover, formerly part of the state-owned British Leyland, which was privatized under British Prime Minister Margaret Thatcher in the 1980s. In 1989 Detroit-based Ford bought Jaguar, and in 1994 BMW of Germany bought the remaining brands. In 2000 BMW sold off all of the former British brands, except for Mini, which it still owns. BMW sold Land Rover to Ford (which in 2008 sold both Jaguar *and* Land Rover to Tata of India).

The remaining brands MG, Rover, and Austin Healy, collectively, MG Rover Group (MGRG), were sold by BMW to Phoenix Corporation, a consortium of four British auto executives who had hoped to revive the brands and keep them in the United Kingdom. An investigation by the United Kingdom's Department of Trade and Industry (DTI) subsequently concluded the four partners in Phoenix Corporation paid themselves "tens of millions of pounds" while failing to generate a profit.[21] The poor performance of MGRG led Phoenix to begin seeking a buyer for the automaker in fairly short order. As early as 2002, MGRG made it to the threshold with Brilliance China, only to have its hopes dashed as Brilliance Chairman, Yang Rong, had a falling out with the government of Liaoning province and fled China for the United States to avoid possible criminal charges (see Brilliance case study in Chapter Five). The British DTI reports that, over a five-year span, Phoenix Corporation held discussions to sell all or parts of MGRG to companies in Malaysia, Iran, Poland, India, and China. And in addition to Brilliance, Phoenix held discussions with a virtual who's who of Chinese automakers: Geely, Chery, FAW, Chang'an, Lifan, Beijing Auto, Guangzhou Auto, NAC, and most promisingly, SAIC.[22]

By 2004, SAIC had risen to the top of the list of potential buyers for MGRG. To assist in the negotiations with the Chinese, Phoenix Corporation engaged the services of a Dr. Qu Li, a native-born Chinese woman with an engineering PhD who was then living in the United Kingdom.[23] In the fall of 2004, SAIC agreed, in what was to have been a good faith measure, to pay £67 million (about $120 million) for the designs of two auto models, the Rover 25 and Rover 75, along with the intellectual property rights to an engine. This £67 million payment was to have been part of a total purchase price of approximately £192 million (about $345 million), and in late 2004, it seemed that SAIC and Phoenix were well on their way toward a deal.[24]

During the winter and spring of 2005, the two sides continued to negotiate, both bringing in auditing firms, investment banks and attorneys to agree on a valuation and come to terms on a final price. But the negotiations began to lengthen as uncertainty about the company's recent historical cash flow, not to mention future projections, began to raise doubts. At one point, SAIC even brought NAC back into the deal as a potential junior partner to the acquisition.[25] As the negotiations dragged on, it became obvious that MGRG's financial condition was far worse than either side had anticipated, to the extent that MGRG was in danger of running out of cash before the discussions could be concluded. One of Phoenix's directors, Nick Stephenson, attempted at one point to threaten SAIC with declaring bankruptcy, a strategy that the British DTI's investigation concluded seemed to kill any possibility of a deal.

In a last minute effort to avoid bankruptcy, Phoenix, unable to obtain bank credit, appealed to the DTI for a bridge loan to sustain the company until a sale to SAIC could be finalized. After conducting its own analysis, DTI agreed to provide the bridge loan, but only under the condition that a deal could first be concluded with SAIC. Unknown to Phoenix at this time, SAIC had apparently already decided not to go through with the purchase, but SAIC nevertheless claimed that it could not agree to finalize the purchase until the British government came through with the bridge loan. It was under this apparent standoff that MG Rover Group was declared insolvent, entering administration in April of 2005. Within a few days, the company laid off its 6,500 workers and the court administrator moved to liquidate the company's remaining assets including its brands and its 100-year-old Longbridge factory at Birmingham, England. While the DTI investigation demonstrated no conclusive proof of this, it cannot have escaped the attention of SAIC that MGRG's individual pieces would have been worth more than the whole. In the event of a bankruptcy, SAIC would have its pick of the remaining assets without having to assume £410 million (US$780 million) in unfunded pension obligations.[26]

In the early summer of 2005, MGRG's administrator, PricewaterhouseCoopers (PwC), conducted an auction of the company's remaining assets. As expected, SAIC was among the three bidders, and only a few days before the expected announcement of the auction winner, *People's Daily* ran a story explaining that SAIC was about to buy MGRG's Longbridge plant and hire back approximately one-half of the company's laid-off workers.[27] But on July 22, PwC announced that the highest bid had been submitted, not by SAIC, but—surprise!—by its earlier proposed junior partner, Nanjing Auto. SAIC was stunned by the outcome. In a statement, SAIC said, "we express our regret at the decision . . . we will use legal measures to strenuously protect our legal right to the intellectual property rights to the 25 and 75 series, including the complete series of engines."[28]

When the dust settled, it still was not clear exactly who had bought which pieces of MGRG, though the consensus seemed to have been, according to a retired senior Chinese auto executive, that "NAC had bought the hardware [the plant] and SAIC had bought the software [the designs]." Perhaps SAIC had been less concerned about a clear identification of exactly which assets it was buying for £67 million in the fall of 2004 because SAIC had planned eventually to buy the rest of MGRG. Regardless, SAIC and NAC would spend the next two years bickering over their respective pieces of MGRG.

How could this have happened? And, more importantly, how could Beijing have *allowed* this to happen? It seems that NAC had benefited from a recent relaxation in the approval process for external investment. The central government had recently decided to allow outbound investments of less than $1 billion to be approved by regional governments, in this case, leaving the governments of Shanghai and Jiangsu province to bid against each other.[29] The central government's liberal behavior was rewarded with an embarrassing and untenable situation: neither SAIC nor NAC had full control of the assets of MGRG.

SAIC's initial inclination was to attempt legal maneuvers to gain control of the bits of MGRG it did not already own, but this attempt was eventually abandoned. SAIC initially claimed that it had managed to buy 98 percent of the Rover and MG models and that NAC had only bought two percent, but this claim was refuted by the administrator, PwC who averred that SAIC had got its percentages backward; it was NAC that owned the 98 percent.[30] Within a few months of NAC's win, both SAIC and NAC set about to make what they could of what they had bought.

NAC's initial plan had been to reopen the Longbridge factory in Birmingham, England, and rehire about half of the company's 6,500 laid-off workers, but this plan was quickly abandoned as NAC had difficulty raising the necessary funds. Over the remainder of 2005, it seemed that NAC had fully intended to follow through on its commitment to restart the factory, but as the return to production continued to be delayed, discussion in the United Kingdom turned to whether all NAC intended to do was dismantle the factory's equipment and ship it to China. These fears were realized in September of 2005 when the British press reported a "lift and shift" operation in which NAC did in fact plan to ship equipment to Nanjing while NAC continued to insist to an increasingly cynical British public that it intended to reopen Longbridge and produce up to 100,000 MGs a year.

By mid-2006, however, despite discussions with several potential partners, NAC continued to struggle to find funding and further scaled back its plans, announcing that the Longbridge factory would only be used to assemble cars from kits produced in China, and that only 250 workers would be needed. For this project NAC received help with funding from several Jiangsu provincial asset management companies. *People's Daily* also began to question how NAC would make anything of its purchase of "only the hardware."[31] NAC also pursued the possibility of opening an MG factory in the U.S. state of Oklahoma in hopes that it could take advantage of MG's positive brand image in America, but after months of talks, the proposal went nowhere.

Meanwhile, SAIC also moved forward with its plans to begin producing Rover models, first choosing the Rover 75 platform to develop a midsized sedan. Development took place between SAIC's PATAC joint venture R&D arm with General Motors and about 100 former MG Rover engineers SAIC hired in the United Kingdom.

By the end of 2006, SAIC was ready to introduce its first "own brand" Rover 750 sedan when it encountered yet another obstacle. As it turned out BMW still owned the Rover brand name, but rather than selling it to SAIC, it allowed Ford the right of first refusal since Ford already owned the Land Rover brand. Once Ford took possession of the Rover name, this left SAIC with a no-name car. As it prepared to launch its new sedan, SAIC decided to give it the "English" name of Roewe (pronounced "roh-way"). While the Roewe name may have left a few China-based expatriates scratching their heads, the Chinese name, 荣威 (pronounced *rong wei*), seemed to carry more prestige among Chinese consumers (even if the Chinese pronunciation sounded like "wrong way" in English). SAIC's Roewe 750 rolled off the assembly line in February 2007. Not to be outdone, one month later NAC introduced its first "own-brand" sedan, the MG7, also based on the Rover 75 platform.[32]

It was apparently at this time that the central government decided this untenable situation had gone on long enough. Despite the fact that central policy had called for consolidation, here were two Chinese companies, one of which (NAC) had persisted near bankruptcy for years, and both of which owned pieces of the same car company. These two companies should be cooperating, not competing. According to a number of my interviewees in China, it was the central government that finally took action to solve the dilemma by forcing SAIC and NAC to merge. One former SAIC executive said that, despite the fact that SAIC very much wanted to own the remainder of MG Rover Group, SAIC "did not want to merge with Nanjing [Auto]," which SAIC considered to be "a piece of dog shit." A retired senior executive from Nanjing Auto verified that pressure did indeed come from the central government, specifically from Premier Wen Jiabao. But Wen was, according to this executive, influenced by two local officials who were on the verge of being elevated to the Politburo, Xi Jinping and Li Yuanchao. For a brief time in 2007 (the year the merger occurred), following the Chen Liangyu scandal in Shanghai, Xi Jinping served as Shanghai's provincial party secretary.[33] At the same time, Li Yuanchao was serving as Jiangsu's provincial party secretary. According to the former Nanjing Auto executive with whom I spoke, Xi and Li took the idea of a merger to Wen Jiabao who approved.

News first surfaced in June of 2007 that SAIC and NAC were in merger talks, and by September, the merger appeared all but inevitable. In December the merger was finalized with SAIC paying 10.6 billion yuan in cash and stock. In order to make the transaction more palatable to the Jiangsu provincial government, SAIC further agreed, over the following three years, to invest in the Nanjing factory and increase production capacity by three times. SAIC also committed not to reduce the Nanjing factory's profits or tax payments to the local government during that time.[34] These concessions were necessary in order to allay the fears of Jiangsu officials that their agreement to a merger would lead to a decrease in local GDP, one of the most significant factors used in measuring the performance of local officials. By locking in these terms for three years, Shanghai and Jiangsu officials effectively pushed these concerns into the future when they would only affect the job prospects of their successors.

Since the merger, the combined SAIC-NAC company has continued to sell both the Roewe 750 and the MG7, and the company has also introduced new models under both brands. Roewe have introduced the 550, a very sharp PATAC-designed coupe, and the 350, a hatchback with an entertainment and navigation system powered by Google's open-source Android operating system. In addition to the MG7, the NAC side of SAIC now offers the MG3, a small hatchback, the MGTF, a midengine roadster descended from the old MGB that is assembled at the Longbridge factory in Birmingham, and more recently, the MG6 which is built on the same platform as SAIC's Roewe 550.

There is no word yet on whether SAIC has kept its promise to leave profits and taxes in Nanjing, but the parent company recently announced the allocation of $1.5 billion in R&D funds to support the growth of SAIC's "indigenous" brands.[35] Even though the Rover and MG brands were not truly developed by SAIC and NAC—the initial models were only "improved" foreign designs—among the large SOE automakers that have foreign JV partners, the combined company has become one of the more successful at introduction of indigenous brands.

Guangzhou-Changfeng Merger

Guangzhou Auto Company (GAC) first appeared in Chapter Four as a party to one of China's earliest Chinese-foreign auto joint ventures, the now defunct Guangzhou-Peugeot. Since that time it has enjoyed success as one of the primary China partners of the Japanese manufacturers Toyota and Honda. GAC's newest joint venture, with a reinvigorated Fiat of Italy (new owner of Chrysler), is currently building a new factory, but according to most accounts, if not for GAC's 2009 purchase of a controlling stake in Changfeng of Hunan province, the Fiat deal would never have happened.

Changfeng Automobile, located in Changsha, Hunan, was founded in 1950 to build vehicles for the People's Liberation Army (PLA). It was then known as Factory Number 7309. In 1982 the company began to make four-wheel drive vehicles, but operated largely unnoticed until the mid-1980s when Mitsubishi of Japan paid three billion yen ($25.4 million) for an equity stake of approximately 16 percent in Changfeng.[36] This was only the second foreign automaker (after Suzuki) to take a direct equity stake in a Chinese company.[37] The agreement required

Mitsubishi to provide manufacturing technology, equipment, and technical support to Changfeng which would assemble the Mitsubishi Pajero (known in the United States as the Montero) under license. In 1996 Changfeng was reorganized as a shareholding corporation, but it remained under PLA control until September of 2001 when ownership was transferred to Hunan province. In 2004 Changfeng was listed on the Shanghai stock exchange, but Hunan province SASAC (State-owned Asset Supervision and Administration Commission) remained the company's largest shareholder and Mitsubishi remained its second largest.

Throughout the early- to mid-2000s, Changfeng enjoyed steadily increasing production, introducing several SUV models under its own brand while continuing to assemble Mitsubishi SUVs. Its Cheetah *Feiteng* (猎豹飞腾) model even won *MotorTrend China's* SUV of the Year award for 2004. Changfeng was also among the earliest of Chinese automakers to show their vehicles at the Detroit Motor Show, following Chery and Geely to exhibit four SUV models along with a concept car in January 2007.

Along with the rest of China's auto industry, Changfeng's sales were significantly affected by the global downturn during 2008. The company sold only 27,000 of its own brand vehicles in 2008 (40,000, including Mitsubishi models), up only four percent from the previous year, and its profit decreased by 23 percent.[38] Even though the company had returned to the Detroit Motor Show that year and boldly announced it would enter the U.S. market in 2009, Changfeng's leaders increasingly believed that the company's product lineup of only SUVs would not provide the growth the company needed to remain competitive in years to come.[39]

In March 2008, the company released a small sedan, the Qiling, but it was not well received by the market. Not only did Changfeng introduce its sedan during a difficult economic time, but there was already established competition in the small car segment from the likes of BYD, Lifan, Geely, and Chery. Changfeng's relationship with Mitsubishi was also becoming strained as Mitsubishi became distracted by a competing partnership with SouEast Motors of Fujian. Changfeng had wanted to expand into sedan production with Mitsubishi, but was disappointed when Mitsubishi chose to produce its sedans at SouEast instead.[40]

Unable to raise the capital it needed to expand on its own, Changfeng began talking to other automakers about the possibility of a joint venture or equity partnership. Further pressure was added as, according to a former senior auto executive who now runs an auto industry think tank, Changfeng wanted to develop a new midsized sedan, but the company was unable to get permission from the central government to introduce the new product unless it agreed to be acquired by a larger company. Under the threat of bankruptcy *and* pressure from the central government, the company reportedly held discussions with nine other automakers, both Chinese and foreign. By April 2009, the list had been narrowed to only two: Guangzhou Auto (GAC) and Beijing Auto (BAIC).[41]

In the meantime, China released its 2009 Auto Industry Adjustment and Stimulus Plan (see Chapter Three), which had, for the first time since the late 1980s specified the companies that the central government wished to see become the ultimate winners as the industry consolidated into fewer and larger players. This formulation was known as the "big four, small four." The remaining two suitors for Changfeng, GAC and BAIC, were both listed among the "small four," meaning that the central government encouraged these two companies to expand through *regional* mergers. Both companies had begun to express interest in Changfeng as early as 2007, a year in which both GAC's and BAIC's Chairmen paid visits to the company in Changsha.[42]

BAIC, not previously known as one of China's more acquisitive or innovative automakers (see Beijing-Jeep case in Chapter Four), apparently began to hold talks with any auto or auto-related company it could in 2008 and 2009. At various times, BAIC was mentioned as a potential partner of Opel, Saab, and Volvo, and domestically, it had been linked with Dongfeng, Lifan, SouEast, and Changfeng. Though BAIC had enjoyed solid growth by assembling Hyundai and Mercedes sedans, during the time it was talking with Changfeng, BAIC had yet to introduce a sedan under its own brand (though it is preparing to do so in 2012). Changfeng just happened to be developing a new midsize sedan under its own brand at the time, making it a viable target for a BAIC wishing to add a Chinese-branded sedan to its own product mix.

Unfortunately for BAIC, there were several objections to its proposed purchase of Changfeng, and they came from both the central government and Changfeng itself. First, the central government, having designated both GAC and BAIC as companies it wanted to see conduct *regional* mergers, favored GAC over BAIC because Changfeng is located in southern China, much closer to Guangzhou than to Beijing.[43] Second, Changfeng leaned toward GAC for several reasons of its own. According to a Changfeng spokesman, after conducting its own analysis, Changfeng felt that BAIC's financial resources were limited, their product lineup was not complementary with Changfeng's, and BAIC's previous cooperation with Mitsubishi through SouEast Motor had not been sufficiently "harmonious."[44] As Changfeng's product lineup consisted almost entirely of SUVs, it favored GAC, which produced mostly sedans, over BAIC, which was already making SUVs. Changfeng also assessed that "GAC was more market-driven than BAIC."[45]

Another provision in the 2009 Auto Industry Stimulus and Adjustment Plan was also key in producing this merger between GAC and Changfeng. In addition to the "big four, small four" formulation, this plan also stated that if any auto enterprise wanted to establish a new venture, it would first be required to buy an existing domestic enterprise.[46] According to both a senior think tank executive and a Chinese auto analyst with whom I spoke (on separate occasions), GAC's most pressing strategic move had been to complete its JV agreement with Fiat, but GAC had been pressured by the central government to conduct a domestic merger first.

On May 21, 2009, GAC and Changfeng conducted the signing ceremony for the formation of GAC-Changfeng. GAC would take a controlling 29 percent share in the company for 1.2 billion yuan, the second largest shareholder would be Hunan provincial SASAC with a 22 percent share, and Mitsubishi would remain as the third largest shareholder with a 15 percent share. The remaining 34 percent would float on the Shanghai Stock Exchange.[47]

In November 2009, GAC finally got the prize it had most coveted, a joint venture with Italy's Fiat. The GAC-Fiat factory is currently under construction in Changsha, and the company has announced plans to build midsized sedans, MPVs and SUVs for the China market. Changfeng, meanwhile, received the permission it had been seeking from MIIT to introduce its midsized sedan (which, auto aficionados agree, is the spitting image of a Volvo S40—a development that has likely disappointed Geely's Li Shufu).[48] The new Changfeng *Zhuoyue*, rolled off the line in 2010.

This merger illustrates some of the various pressures to which commercial ventures are subject in China, particularly those that are part of China's "pillar" industries. While GAC, like probably any other SOE, would have been motivated to conduct a merger for the sake of growing its revenue, it is clear that the real prize for GAC was its pending joint venture with Fiat. With comparatively little investment, an SOE can establish a JV with a foreign partner that, because of its eagerness to tap the Chinese market, is willing to bring its own designs. In this case we can see the central government applying pressure to bring about consolidation. GAC and Changfeng both needed central government permission—GAC to form its JV with Fiat, and Changfeng to introduce its midsized sedan—and the central government was able to "encourage" the two to get together as the price for granting the permissions they sought.

But this merger was not completely designed from the top down. Changfeng, after talking with a number of potential acquirers found GAC to be the most suited to Changfeng's strategic direction. At the same time, GAC had also been considering a merger with SouEast motors, but found SouEast's various joint ventures with other companies to present a structure that was "too complicated."[49] If GAC had to conduct a regional merger (a decision that was made for it by the central government), then Changfeng made more sense to the management of GAC.

This merger also highlights a somewhat different focus of decision making from that of the larger "big four" SOEs. Recall from the SAIC-GM case (Chapter Four) that SAIC was highly motivated to move up on the *Fortune* Global 500 listing—to the extent that it purchased a one percent share from GM that would allow it to consolidate SAIC-GM's revenue for that express purpose. This seems to have been of less concern to GAC, currently the sixth largest Chinese automaker by volume. GAC initially took only a 29 percent stake in Changfeng. While I have found no documentation as to the reason GAC was satisfied with an initial stake of only 29 percent, it seems likely that GAC was less motivated by being listed among the *Fortune* Global 500 than by getting this small merger done so it could move on to completing its JV with Fiat.

Subsequent Mergers

Since the time of the mergers detailed above, there have been a few other notable mergers. Toward the end of 2009, Chang'an Auto of Chongqing announced it would buy the automobile division of AVIC, a central state-owned aviation company. Chang'an is also a subsidiary of a central state-owned enterprise, China South Industries Group, which is in the primary business of weapons manufacture. AVIC sold five of its auto subsidiaries, including automakers Hafei Auto of Heilongjiang and Changhe Auto of Jiangxi, to Chang'an in exchange for a 23 percent stake in Chang'an. With both Chang'an and AVIC being owned either directly or indirectly by central SASAC, this merger seems to conform to SASAC's directive that its companies focus on their core businesses and shed noncore businesses, and it was undoubtedly much easier to make this particular merger happen as there was no local government involvement. While AVIC no longer has managerial responsibility for its former auto businesses, it still gets to participate in their future success by virtue of its investment in Chang'an. And Chang'an, with this purchase, remains solidly among China's "big four" automakers. Figure 6.1 (near the beginning of this chapter) shows a very clear jump in production for Chang'an in 2009 as it consolidated Hafei's and Changhe's production, putting it within striking distance of both Dongfeng and FAW. With this merger, Chang'an demonstrated that it belongs among China's "big four."

Another recent merger is interesting because it involved the purchase of a private company by an SOE. Guangzhou Auto (of GAC-Changfeng fame) bought 51 percent of privately held, Zhejiang-based GoNow Auto at the end of 2010. GoNow was founded only in 2003, and by 2009 was producing about 40,000 own-branded SUVs a year, mostly for export. The attraction of GoNow to GAC was GoNow's three auto factories in eastern China with a capacity of 300,000 vehicles a year. As GoNow had depended primarily on exports, the global downturn in 2008 and 2009 significantly dented GoNow's sales and the company reportedly began to seek a strategic investor or buyer to keep the company afloat. Post-merger, GAC retained GoNow's management team, including its Chairman, Liao Xuezhong, who is now the CEO of GAC-GoNow. This was the first takeover of a private auto company in China by a state-owned auto company.

How Fragmented Is China's Auto Industry?

Recall the analysis presented in Chapter Two comparing the cumulative market shares of the top five automakers in both the United States and China. For convenience, it is reproduced in Table 6.1.

An issue that is of particular concern to China, and that is not captured in this analysis of the top five, is the fact that China still has a large number of auto assemblers with very small annual production. So while Table 6.1 indicates that China has already achieved a "developed country" level of consolidation among its top five, the overall statistics indicate that there is still a problem at the bottom of the list. And as Figure 6.1 (at the beginning of this chapter) demonstrated, while China has four, possibly five, manufacturers that are beginning to achieve significant scale, there is still, even among the top 12, a cluster of also-rans at the bottom that lack the momentum of the those at the top. And unfortunately for China, that group of also-rans includes, with a couple of exceptions, independent automakers that are known exclusively for producing Chinese-branded vehicles: Chery, BYD, JAC (Jianghuai Auto), Geely, and Great Wall.

Assume that China still has about 117 auto assemblers that collectively produced China's 18 million vehicles in 2010. If we remove the top-five listed above along with their combined 2010 production of 12.7 million vehicles (70.4 percent of 18 million) from the list, we are left with about 112 companies that produced the remaining 5.3 million vehicles in 2010—an average of about 48,000 vehicles per company. The automobile industry has a "minimum efficiency scale" (MES) of 250,000 vehicles per year.[50] (In other words, an auto factory would need

Table 6.1 Cumulative Market Shares in U.S. and China Markets, 2010 Auto Sales

	United States	China
Top company	19.1%	19.7%
Top 2 companies	35.6%	34.8%
Top 3 companies	50.9%	49.0%
Top 4 companies	61.5%	62.1%
Top 5 companies	70.8%	70.4%

Sources: United States: Ward's Auto; China: CAAM.

to produce a minimum of 250,000 vehicles to break even.) This means that the vast majority of those remaining 112 cannot possibly be profitable, though many are likely producing a positive cash flow. I asked a veteran China auto industry executive how many cars a Chinese automaker needed to assemble to break even on a cash flow basis. He replied with all seriousness, "one." But he hastened to add, "realistically, though, a company would probably need to make at least ten to twenty thousand cars a year on an ongoing basis to make it worth the local government's time." Still, the fact that an automaker producing only a few thousand cars could conceivably manage to produce a positive cash flow would make local governments less likely to withdraw their support.

Further assume that, among China's 117 or so automakers, the top 10 are competitive enough to form the basis of a vibrant auto industry. And assuming another 30 to 40 are builders of specialty vehicles such as ambulances, buses, fire trucks, and garbage trucks that can charge a premium for their vehicles, then, conservatively, that still leaves about 70 to 80 small firms that, in a truly market-driven economy, would not exist. In any given year, many of these companies probably break even on a cash flow basis, which means that their local governments are absorbing the costs of their capital. The reason the local governments continue to support these small companies is that they employ anywhere from a few dozen to perhaps a few hundred people, and local governments are disinclined to add to their unemployment problems. For the same reasons, the central government is probably also disinclined to intervene.

So if we accept that some of these small players are part of a welfare system that keeps people gainfully employed—not necessarily a bad thing if China's local governments can afford it—then China's leaders should at least be satisfied that, at the top of its auto industry, China appears to have the makings of an increasingly strong and competitive industry. But that is not exactly the case either, and the next set of figures reveals why. Table 6.2 shows the top five companies in both the United States and China along with their respective market shares.

What is most notable about Table 6.2 is that each of the companies on the U.S. side also corresponds with a brand (or group of brands), but each of the companies on the Chinese side is a large state-owned

Table 6.2 Top Market Shares by Group Company in U.S. and China Markets, 2010 Auto Sales

Rank	United States		China	
	Company	Mkt. Share	Company	Mkt. Share
1	GM	19.1%	SAIC	19.7%
2	Ford	16.5%	Dongfeng	15.1%
3	Toyota	15.3%	FAW	14.2%
4	Honda	10.6%	Chang'an	13.2%
5	Chrysler	9.3%	BAIC	8.2%

Sources: United States: Ward's Auto; China: CAAM.

enterprise that primarily assembles cars for foreign companies. SAIC makes most of its money selling VW and GM cars. Dongfeng sells Nissan and Citroën. FAW sells Toyota and VW. Chang'an sells Ford, Mazda, and Suzuki. BAIC sells Hyundai and Mercedes. While each of these companies also sells some cars under its own brand, the numbers are comparatively small. Overall, only 30.9 percent of sedans sold in China in 2010 were of local brands—up only slightly from 30 percent in 2009.[51]

Herein lies the essential problem that China's leaders have with the structure of the industry. The problem is not that production of cars is too fragmented. The problem is that production of Chinese-*branded* cars is too fragmented. While this chapter is concerned primarily with the central government objective of consolidation, this analysis demonstrates how interrelated the central government's various objectives are. Yes, the central government wants China's largest automakers to become larger, an objective it is apparently very close to achieving, but to the degree these SOEs still make most of their money by selling foreign-branded cars, the central government is still very far from achieving its overall goal of a competitive auto industry.

Conclusion

When I questioned my interviewees in China about why significant consolidation had yet to happen, they tended to offer two reasons:

market influence and social stability. The most commonly offered reason was that the central government wanted to allow the market to influence merger decisions and it was therefore disinclined to simply push automakers together for the sake of reducing the number of companies. These case studies have revealed that market influence is indeed at work in the few mergers that have happened, but also that the central government has the ability to intervene when it believes it necessary to do so. The central government has demonstrated that it is willing to engage in a sort of *selective* intervention, in cases such as SAIC-NAC, in which a mistake needs to be corrected, or in cases such as GAC-Changfeng, in which specific policy measures (GAC's *regional* status) need to be enforced.

At the same time, there were valid market-driven reasons supporting each of the three mergers I covered in-depth. Xiali needed a rescuer and FAW was motivated by an opportunity to add small cars to its portfolio, by gaining access to Xiali's partnership with Toyota and by the chance to keep itself solidly among China's "big four." Aside from the need to reassemble the assets of MG Rover, Nanjing Auto was also in need of a rescuer as it lacked the funds to continue development of the assets it had bought. Changfeng, faced with declining sales and the prospect of becoming irrelevant due to its limited product mix, needed a larger partner that could not only fund future investment, but whose product mix was complementary to Changfeng's.

The exceptions to this role of the market illustrate that the central government has the power to exert influence when it believes circumstances warrant intervention. SAIC was apparently only a reluctant purchaser of NAC. What it most wanted was the MG Rover assets it did not already own, but the central government made sure SAIC took all of NAC in the process. What GAC most wanted was to gain approval of its proposed Fiat joint venture, but the central government made sure it merged with a regional automaker in need of funds in the process.

As for the reason given that the central government did not want to force mergers for fear that it would endanger social stability, it would seem that this has yet to become a real concern. For example, in the FAW-Xiali case, most of Xiali's layoffs came in the years prior to the merger and were not in any way related to the merger. The layoffs that came after the merger were minimal by comparison, and employment began to *increase* again less than two years later. In the SAIC-NAC case, there was a negotiated increase in investment by SAIC in the Nanjing plant as well as a three-year commitment to triple production in Nanjing, so, by default, layoffs had been excluded from possibility. As for the GAC-Changfeng merger, public announcements about the transaction contained no promises about potential layoffs or cost savings, but as this merger happened fairly recently, it is still too early to tell whether employment at Changfeng has been affected. But even if it has been, GAC's new joint venture factory with Fiat is under construction in the same city as Changfeng (Changsha), so it could conceivably absorb any decrease in Changfeng's employment.

It is also important to note that SAIC's and NAC's introduction of the three-year moratorium on changes to taxes paid or profits retained in Nanjing was a particularly inventive solution to the resistance of local governments against purchases of their local SOEs by companies from other regions. This allowed leaders from both local governments to move beyond immediate impacts to the performance reviews of local leaders in Nanjing. By pushing these concerns into the future, they were able to focus on completing the deal. Perhaps the central government could make use of a similar mechanism to encourage mergers in the future.

Finally, there is the question of why smaller state-owned automakers would allow themselves to be acquired. Why would a local government be willing to give up control of a local automaker to another? As these case studies have demonstrated, the acquirees have each suffered from financial difficulties. While a sample size of three is hardly conclusive evidence that all locally owned automakers nearing insolvency are willing to enter into a merger, this does support the claims of some interviewees. As a former senior LSOE auto executive explained it to me, "while the central government's policy demands consolidation, in actual practice, the market has a big say in whether this happens, but when companies are near bankruptcy, the local government is more willing to consider mergers."

A Chinese automotive journalist who had accompanied me to interview this executive interjected, "Yes, because Hafei's and Changhe's sales had been falling"—as indeed they had been for several years prior to their being sold to Chang'an—"they were more willing to be acquired."

The executive continued, "Yes, local governments, when faced with the choice of bankruptcy or acquisition will naturally choose acquisition, but if a local enterprise makes a lot of money, it has more power to resist the [central] government."

As nearly three decades of policy make clear, the ultimate aim of the central government is to have automakers large and powerful enough to be eventually competitive outside the home market. Yet, as the market share analysis in this chapter has revealed, the problem that China's leaders face is not that the market as a whole is too fragmented, but that production of Chinese-branded cars is too fragmented. The combined Shanghai and Nanjing Auto may be big, but its primary business is still to assemble cars for foreigners.

Notes

1. Zhongguo qiche jishu yanjiu zhongxin, 中国汽车工业年鉴 [China automotive industry yearbook] (Beijing: Zhongguo qiche gongye xiehui, multiple years), 1986, 121. Hereafter, *CAIY*.
2. Ibid., 2009, 447.
3. Mergers: FAW-Tianjin Xiali, Shanghai-Nanjing, Guangzhou-Changfeng, Chang'an-Hafei-Changhe, and Guangzhou-GoNow. New entrants: Chery, Geely, BYD, Lifan, Zotye, Hawtai, and GoNow.
4. Xinhua News Agency, "Chinese SOEs Reborn After Reform," *China.org.cn*, September 13, 2002, www.china.org.cn/english/2002/Sep/42820.htm.
5. *CAIY*, 2002, 53. This Liuzhou Wuling purchase would later become the SAIC-GM-Wuling joint venture after SAIC invited GM to take an equity stake. See SAIC-GM case in Chapter Four.
6. Raymond Li, "Little Red Taxi Is Headed for an Exit," *South China Morning Post*, June 5, 2006.
7. *CAIY*, 2000, 445–449; 2001, 483–487.
8. "Car Firm Slashes Prices of Models," *China Daily*, June 2, 2003.
9. "Tianjin Auto says parent in merger talks with FAW," *Reuters*, May 9, 2002.
10. Ibid. BAIC's merger with Dongfeng never happened, but its JV with Hyundai did. (See Beijing-Jeep case in Chapter Four.)
11. Gong Zhengzheng, "FAW, Toyota Sign Co-Op Deal," *China Daily*, August 30, 2002.
12. Unfortunately for FAW, SAIC would retake the top spot in revenue in 2003 and in vehicle production in 2006.
13. There is also a managerial lesson here. Xiali either failed to recognize that its problem was revenue-related, or it recognized this but was powerless to do

anything about it. Rather than playing offense by acting to boost revenue (e.g., by investing in a revamp of the company's vehicles), Xiali chose to play defense by cutting expenses. By all indications this company was circling the drain before being rescued by FAW.

14. This begs the question of why, among all the automakers in China, Toyota chose Tianjin Xiali, a nearly-bankrupt SOE as its first partner to produce sedans in China. Perhaps it was Toyota's familiarity with Tianjin Xiali having already licensed production of the Daihatsu Charade to the company in the 1980s.

15. Winston Yau, "Car-Maker to Slash Jobs as Merger Sealed," *South China Morning Post*, June 15, 2002.

16. Zhongguo qiche jishu yanjiu zhongxin, *CAIY*, 2002, 2003, 2004, 2005.

17. Eric Harwit, *China's Automobile Industry: Policies, Problems, and Prospects*, Studies on contemporary China (Armonk, NY: M. E. Sharpe, 1995), 93.

18. China Association of Automobile Manufacturers.

19. Mark O'Neill, "Nanjing Auto on Rough Road with Rover," *South China Morning Post*, March 21, 2006.

20. Ibid.

21. Gervase MacGregor and Guy Newey, "Report on the Affairs of Phoenix Venture Holdings, Limited, MG Rover Group Limited and 33 Other Companies" (Department for Business Innovation and Skills, appointed by the Secretary of State for Trade and Industry, United Kingdom, 2009), 749.

22. Ibid., 441ff.

23. Only later was it revealed that Qu Li is the daughter of the former Chief Engineer of NAC. The DTI alleged that Qu Li had been excessively compensated for her work, but the report uncovered no wrongdoing on her part. Jonathan Guthrie, "MG Rover Aide Perplexed by Focus on Sex," *Financial Times, FT.com*, September 24, 2009, www.ft.com/cms/s/0/e47aa14e-a94a-11de-9b7f-00144feabdc0.html; Jason Lewis, "Revealed: Rover Director's Mysterious Lover Qu Li's Links to the Chinese Firm that 'Lifts and Shifts' the British Motor Industry," *Daily Mail Online*, September 26, 2009, www.daily mail.co.uk/news/article-1216411/Revealed-Rover-directors-mysterious-lover-Qu-Lis-links-Chinese-firm-lifts-shifts-British-motor-industry.html.

24. MacGregor and Newey, "Report on the Affairs of Phoenix Venture Holdings, Limited, MG Rover Group Limited and 33 Other Companies," 483.

25. *People's Daily*, May 22, 2005.

26. MacGregor and Newey, "Report on the Affairs of Phoenix Venture Holdings, Limited, MG Rover Group Limited and 33 Other Companies," 504. The U.K. government eventually took on MGRG's pension liabilities.

27. *People's Daily*, July 20, 2005.

28. Mark O'Neill, "SAIC to Fight for Rover Brands," *South China Morning Post*, July 25, 2005.

29. "China's Nanjing Ready to Buy MG Rover," *National Post (Canada)*, July 23, 2005.
30. O'Neill, "Nanjing Auto on Rough Road with Rover."
31. *People's Daily*, June 12, 2006.
32. Photos comparing SAIC's Roewe 750 and NAC's MG7 may be viewed at www.designateddrivers.co.
33. On Chen Liangyu, see: Cheng Li, "Was the Shanghai Gang Shanghaied?— The Fall of Chen Liangyu and the Survival of Jiang Zemin's Faction," *China Leadership Monitor* 2007, no. 20 (February 28, 2007), www.hoover.org/publications/china-leadership-monitor/article/5877.
34. Wang Jing, "我国汽车产业发展过程中政府行为的经济学分析：以上南合并为案例进行分析 [An economic analysis of government behavior in China's auto industry development process: The Shanghai-Nanjing Auto merger]," 沿海企业与科技 *Coastal Enterprises and Science & Technology* 2008, no. 7 (July 2007): 99.
35. "SAIC Invests $1.5 Billion to Boost Own-Brand Car Capacity," *Reuters*, December 27, 2010, www.reuters.com/article/2010/12/27/retire-us-saic-idUKTRE6BQ0IS20101227.
36. James B. Treece, "Mitsubishi to Help China," *Automotive News*, June 3, 1996; "Chinese Company to Make Pajeros," *The Nikkei Weekly*, September 1, 1997.
37. "Mitsubishi Motors May Take Equity Stake in China Carmaker," *The Daily Yomiuri*, December 26, 1996.
38. "Guangzhou Group Nets Changfeng," *China Daily*, May 21, 2009.
39. "北汽还是广汽 长丰汽车的下一步 [BAIC or GAC, Changfeng's next step]," 凤凰财经 *Phoenix Finance*, February 24, 2009, http://finance.ifeng.com/news/industry/20090224/396350.shtml.
40. Ibid.
41. Ding Bin, "长丰重组最快本月定论 广汽为最大绯闻对象 [Changfeng merger to be concluded this month at the earliest; GAC is the most likely (purchaser)]," *Sina Auto* (*from* 第一财经日报), May 18, 2009, http://auto.sina.com.cn/news/2009-05-18/0749492192.shtml.
42. Ren Aimin, "广汽北汽打响长丰'争夺战' [GAC and BAIC struggle to win over Changfeng]," *People's Daily Online*, June 3, 2008, http://auto.people.com.cn/GB/7333405.html.
43. Likewise, GAC's interest in acquiring Brilliance, which is located in northern China, was also resisted by the central government for the same reason. Liang Meng, "独家：广汽长丰重组或最早于23日签约 [Exclusive: GAC-Changfeng merger to be signed perhaps as early as May 23]," *Sina Auto*, May 18, 2009, http://auto.sina.com.cn/news/2009-05-18/1712492526.shtml; "酝酿兼并重组 广汽欲跻身第一集团 [Considering mergers and acquisitions; GAC wants to become the first (auto) group]," *Sina Auto* (*from* 时代周报), May 14, 2009, http://auto.sina.com.cn/news/2009-05-14/1346491631.shtml.

44. Ding Bin, "长丰重组最快本月定论 广汽为最大绯闻对象 [Changfeng merger to be concluded this month at the earliest; GAC is the most likely (purchaser)]."

45. He Jiarong, "北汽集团重组长丰 但长丰却更心仪广汽 [BAIC wants to buy Changfeng, but Changfeng admires GAC most]," 太平洋汽车网 *Pacific Auto Network*, February 24, 2009, www.pcauto.com.cn/news/hyxw/0902/791054.html.

46. "汽车产业调整和振兴规划 [Auto Industry Adjustment and Stimulus Plan]," *The Central People's Government of the PRC*, March 20, 2009, www.gov.cn/zwgk/2009–03/20/content_1264324.htm. Section four, paragraph three of the policy states: "新建汽车生产企业和异地设立分厂，必须在兼并现有汽车生产企业的基础上进行."

47. "Guangzhou Group Nets Changfeng."

48. "Changfeng's 'Volvo S40' Spotted Out," *China Car Times*, July 9, 2009, www.chinacartimes.com/2009/07/09/changfengs-volvo-s40-spotted-out/; "GAC Changfeng to Release a Volvo Look-Alike," *ChinaAutoWeb*, June 11, 2010, http://chinaautoweb.com/2010/06/gac-changfeng-to-release-a-volvo-look-alike/.

49. Ren Aimin, "广汽北汽打响长丰'争夺战' [GAC and BAIC struggle to win over Changfeng]."

50. Yasheng Huang, "Between Two Coordination Failures: Automotive Industrial Policy in China with a Comparison to Korea," *Review of International Political Economy* 9, no. 3 (August 2002): 538–573.

51. Guowuyuan fazhan yanjiu zhongxin, 中国汽车产业发展报告 [China automotive industry development report] (Beijing: Shehui kexue wenxian chubanshe, multiple years), 2010, 29. Xinhua News Agency, January 14, 2011.

Chapter Seven

The Neighbors

Japan's and Korea's auto industries both, in a short period of time, quickly caught up with the advanced world level . . . China's government should learn from the experiences and lessons of other countries.

> —China's Ministry of Science and Technology
> 2009 (Tang Jie, Yang Yanping, and Zhou Wenjie,
> 中国汽车产业自主创新战略 [China auto industry
> indigenous innovation strategy], 2009)

This chapter shifts gears a bit and steps back to compare what we have learned about China's planning for its auto industry with those China's East Asian neighbors, Japan and Korea. At several points in this book, I have mentioned Japan and Korea as contrasting examples, most notably with the introduction of Figure 1.1, which compared the relative importance of auto industries in the United

States, Japan, Korea, and China. But why mention Japan and Korea, and does their comparison with China even make sense?

The three countries do have their regional locations in common, and all three are also considered to be among the later developing economies. Each also has a dynamic auto industry, which is not something to be said for every late-developing country in the world.

Each of these countries launched its respective auto industry at a different time, though all three launched in the more relatively peaceful post–World War II era. Japan's auto industry took off around 1950; Korea's took off around 1962; and China's took off around 1984. Prior to each of these dates, auto production in each of these countries was limited to commercial vehicles and only very small numbers of passenger vehicles. Though the timing of auto development in each of these economies did not occur simultaneously, their frequent comparison as East Asian late developers raises the question of *how* each of these countries managed the development of its auto sector. The following sections compare important aspects of the development of these three countries' auto industries: ownership, key institutions, technology acquisition, foreign involvement, industry support, and industry structure. In this chapter I will compare, not the *current* arrangements of these three countries, but their respective development periods.

This comparison highlights important similarities and differences in several key central government objectives: consolidation, technology acquisition, and Chinese brand development. While all three governments experienced resistance in their attempts to shape the structures of their respective auto industries, the difference lay in the source of that resistance. In Japan and Korea, the greatest resistance came from the private sector, but in China the greatest resistance came from local governments. Though all three countries initially acquired technology from the foreign multinationals, Japan's and Korea's restrictions of foreign brands in their markets allowed their local brands to blossom. China's dominance by foreign brands, on the other hand, has made it difficult for Chinese brands to grow.

Ownership

As China's reforms began in the 1980s, all existing automobile producers were, of course, state owned, but over time a few nominally private automakers were still able to work their way into the top 20, and eventually, the top 10. As we have seen, this was thanks in large part to determined entrepreneurs who were supported by their local governments in various ways. While the central government has only recently begun to appreciate the role of the private automakers, even approving loans to some of the larger private players, the backbone of China's auto industry remains the larger state-owned enterprises along with their foreign JV partners.

In the early, pre-war days of Japan's auto industry (the 1930s), the government first tried to create a national vehicle called the Isuzu, but this effort was a failure.[1] The state then threw its support behind the efforts of two private firms, Toyota and Nissan, to build trucks for the domestic market.[2] From this point forward, production of cars in Japan would remain in private hands, though the state would exert significant influence on the development of the industry.

In the post-war period, the American military administration that oversaw the transition to a civilian government in Japan (known as GHQ or "General Headquarters") broke up the family-dominated *zaibatsu* conglomerates of which Toyota and Nissan were part. As the Cold War began to take shape, however, the Americans reversed policy and began to support a rapid reindustrialization of Japan. Some of the *zaibatsu* reestablished themselves as *keiretsu* industrial groups, each grouped around a large commercial bank. Nissan, as part of the Fuyo *keiretsu*, and Toyota, as part of the Mitsui *keiretsu*, both prospered in the early 1950s as the American military placed orders for vehicles to support the Korean War (1950–1953).

Korea's initial foray into automobiles was similar to that of Japan. In the 1950s Korea's economy was essentially under American control, but that control was gradually ceded back to the Korean government during the decade. In 1961 a military coup installed General Park Chung Hee as the leader of Korea, and Park embarked on a major program of industrialization. In 1962 the government provided seed capital to build a plant that assembled complete knock-down (CKD) kits imported from Nissan of Japan.[3] Within three years, however, the state transferred ownership of the plant to private hands.[4] Similar to Japan, the automakers that would subsequently be formed in Korea would remain in private hands, but the state would take a vital role in development of the industry over the next several decades.

Also similar to Japan, Korea's automakers were part of industrial conglomerates, in this case known as *chaebol*. But in a major difference from Japan's *keiretsu*, the *chaebol* were centered around, not banks, but general trading firms. The banks in Korea would remain state owned.[5] Though the owners of Korea's *chaebol* enjoyed access to the office of Korea's president, the *chaebol* were highly leveraged and remained heavily dependent on bank loans. This ensured that the *chaebol*, though privately owned, would never be completely free from influence of the state.[6]

Key Institutions

The key institutions responsible for China's auto industry have shifted over the years. For much of the 1980s and 1990s, China's central government was both owner and regulator of auto firms. CNAIC was reestablished in 1982, initially as the nominal owner of most of the existing auto factories. Though, as local governments began to establish their own auto firms, the central government only exercised regulatory oversight. Several central government ministries, including the Ministry of Defense and the Ministry of Machine Building, were also owners of auto firms. By the early 2000s, the ministries were required to divest of businesses, and the auto firms owned by the central government were consolidated under the State-owned Assets Supervision and Administration Commission (SASAC).

In the early 1990s, CNAIC was converted into an association and its former regulatory oversight was housed within China's economic planning body, the State Planning Commission. This body would go through several name changes throughout the 1990s, eventually becoming the NDRC that exists today. The regulatory responsibility over the auto industry remained within the Auto Industry Department of the NDRC until 2008, when the Ministry of Industry and Information Technology (MIIT) took over the NDRC's Auto Industry Department.

I found it interesting that most of my interviewees in China answered either "NDRC" or "MIIT" (but usually not both) when I asked them which central government organization is responsible for regulation of the auto industry. When I pressed them further, asking why they did not name the other organization, the answer generally came down to something like this: "NDRC is responsible for macro policy, and MIIT is responsible for micro policy." When I pressed even further, the majority of my interviewees would allow that the NDRC was *dagai* (probably) the ultimate authority over the auto industry. My analysis of policy documentation and case study supports this conclusion. MIIT manages the details, but the NDRC exercises a veto over nearly every decision that affects industry in China. Other ministries, of course, oversee various other details according to their areas of expertise, but, in the end, it is NDRC's responsibility to ensure that the auto industry's actions fit within China's overall Five-Year Plans. Accordingly, all policy made by these other ministries must also be approved by NDRC, even if on an informal basis.[7]

The institutions that oversaw the development of Japan's and Korea's auto industries are much easier to describe than are China's. Without question, the single most influential government organization in Japan's auto industry development was the Ministry of International Trade and Industry (MITI). During the formative years of Japan's auto industry, MITI was responsible for the planning that supported development of the industry, protected it from foreign competition and influenced the industry's structure. According to Chalmers Johnson, MITI "kept Japan's economy on a war footing" throughout the 1950s, and "shifted Japan's industrial structure from light, labor-intensive industries to steel, ships and automobiles."[8] And even though Johnson's *MITI and the Japanese Miracle* seemed to many to hold MITI up as almost completely autonomous from society or other state organizations, some of the details in Johnson's book specific to the auto industry indicate otherwise. I will discuss some of these details below.

In Korea the Ministry of Trade and Industry (MTI) performed a function similar to that of Japan's MITI. Similar to MITI, the MTI made decisions on tariffs and credit policies to support various industries. It also decided which firms were able to enter the industry, and attempted to impose its will on the structure of the industry through mergers and reorganization.[9] But as was the case with MITI, the ability to wield such plans did not always ensure success. Unlike the NDRC or MIIT in China, Japan's MITI and Korea's MTI were both working with auto industries comprised solely of private firms. While they had leverage it was not complete.

Then again, neither was (or is) that of China's central regulators. A key set of institutions in China that wield much influence in the auto industry are the local governments. In both Japan and Korea, the influence of local governments on their respective auto industries is practically nil, but in China, local governments have demonstrated their willingness to work against the central government to establish auto enterprises—both local state owned and private. Furthermore, the local governments in China also provide local auto firms with funding that keeps them afloat even through difficult economic conditions.

Technology Acquisition

For China's automakers, the primary source of new technology has been their foreign JV partners. Until China joined the WTO in 2001, technology transfer was a requirement written into most JV agreements, but China gave up the right to condition approval of foreign investment on technology transfers when they joined. Since 2001 China's automakers have had no less of a desire to acquire foreign technology, but the way they have gone about it has changed.

There are now several ways in which Chinese companies may legitimately acquire technology. Some of the joint ventures have established joint-venture design centers such as the SAIC-GM PATAC venture. In this way, foreign and Chinese engineers work together to design vehicles and components, providing learning opportunities for the Chinese. Some Chinese companies have paid for foreign technology along with its accompanying intellectual property rights (IPR). For example, Chery hired Italian auto design firm Pininfarina to design its A3 model. In some cases, Chinese companies buy foreign companies outright, giving themselves full ownership of all IPR that the foreign company owns. Geely's purchase of Australian transmission manufacturer, DSI, gave Geely full ownership of all of DSI's IPR, past, present, and future. The latest example of technology transfer in China is the "JV brand" concept mentioned in Chapter Four, whereby the foreign partner of a JV transfers the designs of an existing or outdated vehicle model to the JV, which then manufactures the model and sells it under a Chinese brand name. According to the CEO of PSA Peugeot-Citroën, helping their new Chinese partner, Chang'an, to bring a Chinese-branded car to market was "part of the deal" for getting the new JV approved.[10] And finally, though Chinese companies are no longer allowed to demand technology transfer, there is evidence that, by holding out long enough in JV negotiations, Chinese automakers are able to get "voluntary" technology transfers from potential foreign partners under pressure to consummate a deal (see Chapter Four).

Whereas China has relied primarily on foreign investment through the form of joint ventures, the Japanese and Koreans both heavily circumscribed foreign investment. In the 1930s, the two private firms approved by Japan's MITI to assemble vehicles took two different paths to acquire technology. Nissan licensed American technology and hired American engineers to teach their employees.[11] Toyota relied more on "reverse-engineering" of foreign made vehicles and engines.[12] In the early 1950s, MITI approved tie-ups with foreign automakers and part of the requirement always included technical agreements whereby the Japanese could learn from their foreign partners. Unlike Chinese-foreign JV agreements that have tended to last for 20 years or more, MITI restricted Japanese-foreign technical agreements to only 7 years.[13]

Of key importance to the success of the Japanese automakers was not only early technology acquisition from the major global automakers, but also of statistical management techniques from American scholars. The American automakers had employed highly complex statistical techniques for quality control (QC), but kept them in the hands of statistical experts. American experts such as W. Edwards Deming, J. M. Juran, and A. V. Feigenbaum advocated a simplification of these statistical techniques so as to place QC in the hands of line employees.[14] The Japanese automakers welcomed the advice of the foreign experts and implemented their recommendations. The combination of foreign technology obtained through technical agreements and foreign statistical techniques quickly resulted in both high quality and high efficiency among Japanese automakers.

Since the Japanese auto industry got its start about a decade ahead of the Korean auto industry, Korea benefited from a neighbor with recent experience. During the time that Korea was a Japanese colony

(1910–1945), the Japanese had already built a significant auto parts manufacturing industry in Korea to feed the needs of Japan's assemblers. Over the years the Koreans developed expertise in parts manufacture before taking the step up to finished vehicle assembly in the early 1960s.[15] In 1965, following the failed experiment with state ownership of its first automaker, Korea's MTI allowed three private firms to start producing cars. Each of these companies—Asia Auto, Hyundai, and Kia—looked for foreign partners either to license technology or to cooperate in other ways.[16]

In the early 1970s, General Motors took a 50 percent stake in the ailing Shinjin Motors, the company that had been started by the state in 1962 and privatized three years later.[17] After going through bankruptcy and other managerial difficulties in the 1970s, this venture was taken over in 1982 by Daewoo which remained a partner of GM. Throughout the time of its involvement in Korea (until the late 1990s), all of the designs manufactured were transferred from GM to Korea, but the 2000s brought a reversal in which GM began to look to its Korean ventures to design all of its small cars.

As Hyundai gained confidence in the early 1970s, it ended a venture producing the Ford Cortina sedan under license and began to search for a foreign partner who would transfer technology without insisting on managerial control. After negotiating with firms in Europe and North America, Hyundai found Japan's Mitsubishi to be more accommodating to its wishes. Mitsubishi took a small equity stake, transferred technology, and did not move to restrict Hyundai's ability to compete in any other markets.[18] By the end of the decade, Hyundai had licensed over thirty different technologies from automakers in Japan, Europe, and North America.

In all three of these countries, technologies were initially acquired from the more developed markets. In each case, foreign automakers were persuaded to hand over technologies in the hopes of either gaining access to the domestic markets or of using the local automakers as links in their global supply chains. In the cases of Japan and Korea, the pendulum has now swung back in the other direction in which foreign automakers now look to the Japanese and Koreans for design help or collaboration, while selling very few foreign made cars into the Japanese or Korean markets.

Foreign Involvement

Whereas the previous section covered technology acquisition—which, in all three cases, began with transfers from foreign automakers—this section reviews the overall involvement of foreign automakers in these three countries and the roles of these countries' respective governments in restricting or facilitating that involvement.

The critical role of foreign automakers in transferring technology and generating cash for China's SOEs has already been detailed at length in Chapters Three and Four. As has been noted, China's central and local governments began to seek foreign partners not long after China reopened its doors in the late 1970s. While early negotiations brought about differing results in terms of the extent of foreign equity participation in joint ventures, policy eventually settled on a 50 percent limit of foreign ownership, and in general, this has been where negotiations between Chinese and foreign partners begin. The only exception to this 50 percent rule was included in the 2004 auto policy, and it allowed for a share of greater than 50 percent if the joint venture produces vehicles for export. Thus far, the sole exception has been a joint venture among Honda, Guangzhou Auto, and Dongfeng in which Honda of Japan holds 55 percent of the shares.

Japan's Automobile Manufacturing Industry Law passed in 1936 effectively drove both Ford and GM out of Japan by 1939.[19] As noted earlier, the government, through MITI, had already designated two private companies, Toyota and Nissan, as Japan's only producers of sedans, and MITI was laying the groundwork for their success by blocking out foreign capital. After the War, however, the foreign multinationals expressed interest in returning to Japan. At that time, MITI set up rules that limited the size and scope of Japanese-foreign JVs. In the 1950s Japanese and foreign automakers proposed 11 different tie-ups, but only four of these were approved by MITI.[20] Despite the limits, however, from 1953 to 1959, nearly one-third of car production in Japan came from foreign models assembled from kits or made under license with local parts.[21]

Throughout the 1960s and 1970s, the American automakers constantly sought ways to tap the Japanese market. According to Chalmers Johnson, their focus was not as much on selling to Japanese consumers ("tariffs were too high, and American cars were too big and too expensive [for] Japan") as it was on trying to incorporate the Japanese firms into their global supply chains.[22] MITI countered this pressure by attempting to strengthen Toyota and Nissan and forming *keiretsu* around them through mergers with some of the smaller auto firms that had sprung up.[23] Yet in 1969 Chrysler was eventually successful in establishing, over the objections of MITI, a JV with Mitsubishi in which Chrysler held 35 percent. Later, as the Japanese auto industry had begun to produce giants of its own, other foreign automakers gradually began to take stakes in Japanese automakers. In the late 1970s and 1980s, Ford gradually built up a controlling stake in Mazda. GM took a controlling stake in Isuzu in 1971, and then GM and Isuzu both entered a partnership with Suzuki in 1981. By the 1980s, however, Japan's automakers had developed a solid reputation for quality and were rapidly becoming a source of automotive technology rather than a destination.

According to Chalmers Johnson, "Japanese bureaucrats, historically, have been close to paranoid on the subject of the dangers of an invasion of foreign capital. By contrast, the Koreans . . . have given virtuoso performances in how to use foreign . . . capital without at the same time becoming subservient to it."[24] Political scientist Andrew E. Green, notes that Korea never allowed foreign partners of its auto firms to own controlling shares. This restriction "stands in stark contrast to the structure of ownership in the auto industry of virtually every other developing country."[25] This was possible, says Green, because, as part of the *chaebol*, Korea's automakers did not need to rely on foreign funding to build plants.[26] Nevertheless, Korea's automakers did need foreign technology during their period of development, and they were able to acquire it without giving away operational control. During the 1960s and 1970s, all of the Korean automakers signed agreements with one or more foreign automakers that provided them with licenses for production of foreign designs or for technology transfer.[27]

Industry Support

In all three countries we can see gradual shifts in the modes of state support for the auto industry; however, the modes of state support in

China have changed less than they did during the formative years of Japan's and Korea's auto industries. As has already been noted, governments in both Japan and Korea attempted early establishment of state-owned automakers, but in both cases, these efforts were quickly abandoned and the auto industries were left in private hands. This section compares China, Japan, and Korea in terms of state support through funding, policy support, and market protection.

Funding

One of the major differences among the three is in funding. Because China's auto industry remains predominantly state-owned, the Chinese state, both central and local, has been a major source of funding. Central government statistics show that 235 billion yuan was invested by the state in China's auto industry during the Tenth Five-Year Plan (2001–2005), an average of 47 billion yuan per year. During the first three years of the Eleventh Five-Year Plan (2006–2010), spending averaged nearly 80 billion yuan per year.[28] But this includes only the documented investment by the central government. Local governments very likely invested billions of yuan as well.

In the prewar years, Japan's 1936 Automobile Manufacturing Industry Law provided half the capital for the first licensees, Toyota and Nissan, but after the War, the industry never relied heavily on government funding.[29] Kent Calder finds that, post-War, Toyota relied on private sector funding, World Bank loans guaranteed by the state-owned Japan development bank and Ex-Im Bank loans granted to support procurement during the Korean War (1950–1953). When motorcycle manufacturer Honda decided to enter the auto industry in the mid-1960s, the government attempted (unsuccessfully) to *prevent* Honda from getting private sector financial support.[30] Also, the privately owned Industrial Bank of Japan, according to Calder, spearheaded much of the expansion in Japan's auto industry in the 1960s, providing significant support to Nissan, as did the private Mitsui Bank for Toyota.[31]

Korea's experience was different from Japan's. Whereas the Japanese *keiretsu* (during the formative years of the auto industry) revolved around main banks, the Korean *chaebol* revolved around general trading companies, and Korea's banks were owned by the state. Korea's automakers could rely on their *chaebol* for most funding needs, but when it came to expansion, the government, due to its control of the banks, had leverage over funding decisions. Except for a program in the early 1980s in which the MTI provided $120 million in low-interest relief loans to auto parts suppliers, funding was generally obtained by the auto assemblers through their respective *chaebol*.[32]

Policy Support

There is a distinct difference in the industrial policies among these countries. China's policies have throughout the years consisted of comparatively little in the way of concrete support. Instead, they read more as a list of prohibitions. (Chapter Three contains a review of Chinese auto policy over the past three decades.) Though Japan's and Korea's policies do contain the requisite regulations, Korea's early policies in particular offered significant, and very specific, policy support as the country attempted to launch its auto industry.

Though MITI and the auto industry did not always see eye-to-eye, Phyllis Genther describes an industry in which the government and the firms worked together to formulate policies that delayed the effects of market liberalization.[33] In the case of Japan, most of these policies consisted of market protection, but in Korea, there existed a business-government relationship that I think may best be described as "tough love." Many of the MTI's policies seemed to offer both rewards and punishments in an effort to shape an industry with a handful of globally competitive automakers. In the early 1960s MTI provided tax exemptions for imports of auto parts, but then a few years later, MTI established a domestic content schedule requiring 50 percent localization within five years. Companies that were able to meet the target would receive preferential allocation of foreign exchange.[34] In the 1974 Long-Term Development Plan for the auto industry, MTI mapped out a schedule requiring automakers to reach a 90 percent localization rate within 10 years, restricted only three firms to production of small cars, and required them all to submit for approval plans for achieving this goal.[35] Once the automakers had reached international quality standards in local production of a component, that component would then benefit from import bans. Help was made available to the players in Korea's auto industry, but they first had to demonstrate their worthiness.

In the 1980s Korea's focus began to turn toward exports, as had Japan's in the 1970s, and MTI pushed harder for localization of more complex parts such as engines and transmissions.[36] MTI required all three producers of cars to set export targets for different regions in the world and also encouraged them to set export prices below the price of production.[37] Doner describes the business–government relationship as more of a "complex bargaining process" than "state-imposed directives."[38] By the 1980s, MTI's leverage over the automakers began to wane as the companies grew. As Green describes the transition, "the state can foster the creation of a more efficient and technologically sophisticated industry . . . but because the export viability of the auto industry depends on the nature of competition in the international market, the state lacks power to guarantee its long term success."[39] In other words, the state has the power to push domestic automakers to improve their domestic performance, and can protect the market to facilitate their growth, but only international competition in the developed markets can push automakers to lift their quality to international standards. By the 1980s, MTI had supported the auto industry as much as it was able, but the industry had to take it from there if it wanted to compete for shares of the European and North American markets. And exports were critical for Korea because its domestic market is so small compared to those of Japan and China.

Market Protection

One of the most common methods late developers have for supporting the development of new industries is market protection. Without limits on the activities of foreign industrial firms within a country's borders, domestic startups would find it difficult, if not impossible, to compete. All three East Asian countries have made use of market protection to varying degrees.

China's central government exercised its power to limit foreign investment in China from the beginning of the reform era. Even though policy had yet to specify a percentage limit on foreign ownership of a China-based vehicle enterprise, early ad hoc negotiations with both

AMC (for Beijing-Jeep) and Volkswagen (for SAIC-VW) ensured that both joint ventures would not be foreign controlled. Eventually policy settled on an explicit limit of 50 percent ownership with a more recent (2004) exception for JVs producing vehicles for export.

Import limitations came soon after China reopened its doors in the late 1970s. Exports zoomed from 667 vehicles in 1979 to over 19,000 in 1980, so the government implemented import restrictions.[40] Part of the restrictions included a 260 percent import tariff which applied everywhere in China except for Hainan Island. In 1984 Hainan officials took advantage of their exemption to import over 89,000 vehicles, which were then shipped to other areas of China. In response, new policies required that importers of vehicles apply to both CNAIC and the State Planning Commission (precursor to today's NDRC) for permission to import vehicles.[41] And in an effort to spur the joint ventures toward faster localization of production, all imported kits and parts were also made subject to import tariffs.

China's WTO membership in 2001, of course, required China to drastically decrease import tariffs on both parts and assembled vehicles. As has been noted, however, even the *expectation* of a decrease in protection (tariffs were gradually decreased over a five-year period) led to a price war that touched off an explosion in auto sales in China. By comparison the increase in imports as a result of lowered tariffs was tiny. While WTO membership was a positive development for China's consumers, the central government noted that sales of Chinese-branded cars were not experiencing an increase commensurate with those of the industry as a whole. And while China was also forbidden from making overt demands of technology transfer, the latest attempt by the central government to increase the market share of Chinese-branded cars has included pressure for help in developing and selling Chinese-branded vehicles. Foreign automakers who wish to invest in China or apply for an expansion in capacity are now being expected to include their plans for helping their Chinese partners develop Chinese-branded cars that will directly compete with the joint ventures' foreign-branded cars.[42]

Japan and Korea enjoyed an advantage that China did not. Both countries joined the WTO on day one, January 1, 1995. By this time Japan's auto industry was a good 45 years into its launch, and Korea's was over 30 years into its launch. When China joined in 2001, its passenger car industry was still not quite 20 years old. Furthermore, the abilities of the three countries' citizens to afford cars were considerably different. When Japan joined WTO in 1995, its GDP per capita was nearly $20,000, and Korea's was nearly $12,000 at the same time. When China joined in 2001, its GDP per capita was still less than $4,000.[43] When Japan and Korea joined WTO in 1995, their domestic auto firms were already well-entrenched in their home markets, and they had become so competitive overseas that they were subject to serious limitations in other developed markets. When China joined in 2001, its market was (and still is) dominated by foreign brands, and its only export markets were in other developing countries.

Japan essentially kept its home market closed to foreign imports during the critical years that Japanese consumers were determining which aspects of automobiles were most important to them. This gave the Japanese automakers time to introduce innovations in both design and process that satisfied the burgeoning Japanese demand for cars.[44] Small cars were protected throughout the 1960s and 1970s by import tariffs of up to 34 percent. Not until the Japanese companies began to export in significant numbers did MITI move to lower tariffs (to 8 percent in 1972, and to 0 percent in 1979).[45] However, while MITI was lowering import tariffs, it maintained high commodity taxes on vehicles that increased with the size of engines. As most Japanese-made cars came with smaller engines and most foreign cars with larger engines, these taxes further discouraged purchase of foreign cars. Japan also erected nontariff barriers to slow the entrance of foreign imports. For example, Japan's customs inspectors refused to conduct inspections on a sample of cars, insisting on conducting a detailed inspection on every individual car being imported.[46]

When Korea's auto industry was established under the Park regime in the early 1960s, the Auto Industry Protection Law immediately prohibited imports of assembled vehicles, but it did allow tariff-free imports of parts, giving new Korean automakers opportunities to learn how to assemble foreign cars under license.[47] The complete ban on assembled cars would stay in place until 1985, only one year before the Hyundai Excel became a surprise hit in the U.S. market. (In 1987 Korea exported 347,000 cars to the United States.)[48] Despite the lifting of the import ban, nontariff barriers remained. Foreign automakers encountered red-tape with customs inspections, and Korea's govern-ment sponsored an anti–foreign luxury campaign that encouraged purchase of Korean-made goods.[49]

Industry Structure

This section will analyze the different forces that affected the structures of the Chinese, Japanese, and Korean auto industries in their developmental stages. The most significant factor determining the difference in industry structures among the three is the role of China's local governments.

Though industrial planning in all three countries took (or takes) place with the central government, only China has state-owned auto-makers, and most of those are local state-owned enterprises (LSOEs). As Chapter Three noted, the central government's choices of "big three" or "big four" were always the top three or four largest enterprises—an indication that the central government's most valued trait in an auto-maker has always been size—but the sheer *number* of automakers in China has been most influenced by local governments. Since China's economic reforms began in the late 1970s, local governments have been motivated by economic growth, social stability, and, as some of my interviewees opined, the prestige of having their own local auto factories. And while the central government has long made consolida-tion a key component of auto industry policy, as Chapter Six revealed, it has chosen to use its influence selectively, forcing mergers only when mistakes needed correcting or policies needed reinforcing. In general, the many auto firms owned by local governments have continued to exist as long as they can generate a positive cash flow, with only a few reluctantly moving toward merger when dire financial circumstances have dictated.

China's central government has also maintained, since the early 1990s, a catalogue in which all approved vehicles must be listed before a local Public Security Bureau can issue a license for the vehicle. Since the catalogue was launched (today it is issued quarterly on CD by MIIT) it appears to have been effective in creating a barrier to entry as the number of approved auto assemblers peaked at 124 in 1993–1994. But if it has been effective in creating a barrier to *entry*, it has had no effect on *exit* as there were still 117 approved auto assemblers at the end of 2008. Another barrier that has remained in place since the 2004 auto policy (see Chapter Three) is the prohibition of a transfer of certification from a bankrupt automaker to another firm not already in the auto assembly business.

After its failed experiment with the then state-owned Isuzu in the 1930s, Japan's MITI designated only two approved producers of sedans, Toyota and Nissan, though there were a few other *zaibatsu* with commercial vehicle assemblers. In the 1960s, MITI promoted a "three-group" concept that would have limited the number of conventional passenger car producers to only two, again, Toyota and Nissan. It would also have allowed two or three companies to make specialty cars and another two or three to make minicars, but it would only allow any company to produce a single type of car.[50] To support this plan, MITI applied "administrative guidance" to try to merge some of the smaller automakers into either Toyota or Nissan. Through the state-owned Japan Development Bank (JDB), MITI set aside up to 6 billion yen in loans to support large firms in mergers.

Johnson reports that Nissan's takeover of the smaller Prince Auto company was influenced by MITI's provision of an $11.1 billion loan.[51] But Genther's analysis indicates that Prince was also more open to the prospect of merger due to its poor financial condition[52]—a condition not unlike that of Tianjin Xiali, Nanjing Auto, or Changfeng Auto prior to their respective mergers in China (see Chapter Six). In her analysis of several other mergers and tie-ups in the 1960s, most of which failed, Genther concluded that MITI had not been powerful enough, nor provided enough incentives, to bring about the mergers it wanted to see.[53]

MITI was also apparently unsuccessful in keeping out a new entrant in the mid-1960s. Honda had in 1959 become the world's largest motorcycle manufacturer. The company's leader, Honda Soichiro, had wanted, since the early 1950s, to expand into automobiles, against the wishes of MITI, which was trying to merge existing automakers into larger players. When MITI introduced its "three group" concept, Japan's existing automakers were under pressure from MITI to offer verbal support to the plan, but, as the world's largest motorcycle manufacturer, Honda's refusal to go along carried significant weight.[54]

The plan ultimately failed because there was not enough room in the plan to accommodate the number of automakers already in Japan's auto market, and none of them wished to be the one eliminated.

The entrance of Honda into the industry is typically held up as an example of MITI's lack of complete autonomy. However, Wade points out that, in the 1950s and 1960s, MITI had been very successful in restructuring Japan's auto parts industry which ultimately helped to make the assemblers more competitive globally.[55] Yasheng Huang also suggests that, when threatened with mergers, Japan's automakers were suddenly able to quickly achieve minimum efficiency scale (MES). In other words, maybe all the incentive private Japanese automakers needed to increase production and exports was the mere threat of being forced into a merger. Even the startup Honda was able to increase output sixfold from 1965 to 1968.[56]

Nevertheless, Johnson reveals a glaring exception to his assertion that MITI was autonomous through his recounting of MITI's difficulties with Mitsubishi. Because MITI had a network of retired officials working in all of the automakers, they were able to gain support for their plan to consolidate the industry. However, Mitsubishi was the one automaker in which MITI had not been able to place a retired official. When Mitsubishi announced its agreement with Chrysler to form a new joint venture in 1969, MITI did everything within its power to prevent this alliance from happening, but in the end, MITI simply lacked the power to order a private Japanese firm not to ally itself with a foreign automaker.[57]

In the early 1960s, Korea launched its first state-owned automaker, and within three years the state transferred the plant to private owners. By 1973 automobiles were identified as a priority under the country's Heavy and Chemical Industry Plan. In the following year MTI designated only three firms that would be allowed to manufacture passenger cars: Hyundai, Kia, and GM-Korea (Daewoo).[58]

In the wake of the second oil shock of the late 1970s and the 1979 assassination of Park Chung Hee, domestic demand for autos collapsed by over 50 percent. MTI moved to restructure the industry and reorient the industry toward exports, particularly to North America.[59] The first action MTI took was to order Kia to stop producing passenger cars from 1980 until 1987, which it did. Next, MTI wanted to create a single, large automaker by merging the 50:50 joint venture GM-Daewoo into Hyundai. In this case, MTI did not get its way. GM refused to give up its auto venture unless it could own a share equal to Hyundai's in the new venture, but Hyundai insisted on maintaining a majority share. As a result Korea was left with two passenger car manufacturers (until Kia rejoined them in 1987). Though it did not get the merger it wanted, MTI continued to pressure GM to give managerial control to its partner Daewoo, which it finally did in 1982.[60]

In all three East Asian countries, central governments have attempted, with only mixed success, to shape the structures of their respective auto industries, and, in each case, failure of the state to get its way was due to an external force. In Japan and Korea, that external force was the will of privately owned automakers. In China, that external force has been local governments. However, as the fragmentation analysis in Chapter Six demonstrated, China's auto industry actually seems to contain two distinct industries: one, consisting of the top dozen or so automakers, that is intended to become globally competitive, and the other, consisting of the remaining 70 or 80 automakers, that appears to serve as a sort of welfare system. Though this "welfare system" is essentially run by the local governments, the fact that it continues to exist indicates that China's central government is not yet ready to force its demise.

Conclusion

In terms of China's central government objectives, this brief comparison with Japan and Korea illuminates important similarities and differences in how China has attempted to achieve consolidation, technology acquisition, and Chinese brand development.

Though central governments in all three countries have attempted to shape their industries by restricting entry, none seems to have been completely successful. In China several independent automakers were able, with the help of local governments, to establish themselves despite rules forbidding their entry. Likewise, despite its attempts to prevent motorcycle manufacturer Honda from entering the auto industry, Japan's MITI was ultimately powerless to keep it from happening.

In China's case, however, there is also the overarching goal of regime survival that includes the continued rule of a single political party. Because the need for social stability makes China's central government hesitant to close poorly performing businesses, the central government finds itself compromising in order to achieve the contradictory goals of both social stability and a competitive auto industry. Japan and Korea do not suffer from such contradictions. This is not to say that Japan's and Korea's democratically elected ruling parties do not wish to remain in power, but with their auto industries completely in private hands, their governments lack the ability, or indeed the *responsibility*, of utilizing state-owned automakers as tools of political expediency.

The most prominent difference among these three countries is in how their respective central governments managed technology acquisition and brand development. Like China, Japan and Korea also acquired technology from the foreign multinationals, but unlike China, Japan and Korea never allowed foreign brands to gain a foothold in their markets. Furthermore, Japan's and Korea's governments managed to push their automakers to increase quality standards so that they could ultimately export to the developed markets from whence their technology had come. It was this push of their privately owned automakers to export to the developed markets that ultimately elevated Japanese and Korean automakers from *destinations* of auto technology to *sources* of auto technology; both countries are now sources of design for the developed markets.

One might argue that Japan and Korea are ahead of China because they started earlier; however, Japan was already exporting to the United States in the 1970s, and Korea was exporting to the United States in the 1980s—approximately 20 years after launching their respective passenger car industries. Nearly 30 years into the post-Mao relaunch of China's passenger car industry, only one Chinese automaker (Great Wall) has managed to export a few SUVs to Italy and Australia. In all fairness to China, the cars that Japan and Korea were learning how to build in the 1950s and 1960s were far simpler machines than the complex, software-driven vehicles produced today. Perhaps some of the Chinese-branded vehicles being built today would have been superior in quality to the Japanese vehicles of the 1970s or the Korean vehicles of the 1980s. But the reality for China is that its automakers have to compete in the 2010s.

Notes

1. Phyllis A. Genther, *A History of Japan's Government-Business Relationship: The Passenger Car Industry*, Michigan papers in Japanese studies no. 20 (Ann Arbor: Center for Japanese Studies, University of Michigan, 1990), 208.
2. Chalmers Johnson, *MITI and the Japanese Miracle: The Growth of Industrial Policy, 1925–1975* (Stanford, CA: Stanford University Press, 1982), 132.
3. Andrew E. Green, "South Korea's Automobile Industry: Development and Prospects," *Asian Survey* 32, no. 5 (May 1, 1992): 414.
4. Yasheng Huang, "Between Two Coordination Failures: Automotive Industrial Policy in China with a Comparison to Korea," *Review of International Political Economy* 9, no. 3 (August 2002): 560.
5. Kōichi Shimokawa, *The Japanese Automobile Industry: A Business History* (London: Athlone Press, 1994), 16.
6. Yun-han Chu, "The State and the Development of the Automobile Industry in South Korea and Taiwan," in *The Role of the State in Taiwan's Development*, ed. Joel D. Aberbach, David Dollar, and Kenneth Lee Sokoloff (Armonk, NY: M. E. Sharpe, 1994), 141; Green, "South Korea's Automobile Industry," 422.
7. The fact that the NDRC bowed out of Sichuan Tengzhong's proposed purchase of Hummer from GM (see Chapter Five), allowing the Ministry of Commerce to make the decision, appears to stem more from a desire to avoid the unpleasantness of saying "no" than from an abdication of its authority to the Ministry of Commerce. The Ministry of Commerce's claim that they had never even received an application from Tengzhong (which is hard to believe given how hard Tengzhong had lobbied for approval) also seems to stem from a motive similar to that of the NDRC. This is, of course, only my opinion.
8. Johnson, *MITI and the Japanese Miracle*, 240–241.
9. Chu, "The State and the Development of the Automobile Industry in South Korea and Taiwan," 139.
10. John Reed and Patti Waldmeir, "Foreign Groups Told to Make Chinese Cars," *Financial Times*, *FT.com*, March 20, 2011, www.ft.com/cms/s/0/4a5c8d82–5328–11e0–86e6–00144feab49a.html.
11. Michael A. Cusumano, *The Japanese Automobile Industry: Technology and Management at Nissan and Toyota* (Cambridge, MA: Harvard University Press, 1985), 40; Genther, *A History of Japan's Government-Business Relationship*, 81.
12. Cusumano, *The Japanese Automobile Industry*, 62.
13. Ibid., 8.
14. Ibid., 324–325.
15. Meredith Woo-Cumings, *Race to the Swift: State and Finance in Korean Industrialization* (New York: Columbia University Press, 1991), 143–144.

16. Chu, "The State and the Development of the Automobile Industry in South Korea and Taiwan," 147.
17. Green, "South Korea's Automobile Industry," 416.
18. Richard F. Doner, "Limits of State Strength: Toward an Institutionalist View of Economic Development," *World Politics* 44, no. 3 (April 1992): 418.
19. Johnson, *MITI and the Japanese Miracle*, 132.
20. Genther, *A History of Japan's Government-Business Relationship*, 80–82.
21. Cusumano, *The Japanese Automobile Industry*, 7.
22. Johnson, *MITI and the Japanese Miracle*, 286.
23. Ibid.
24. Chalmers Johnson, "Political Institutions and economic performance: the government-business relationship in Japan, South Korea and Taiwan," in *The Political Economy of the New Asian Industrialism*, ed. Frederic C. Deyo (Ithaca, NY: Cornell University Press, 1987), 163.
25. Green, "South Korea's Automobile Industry," 420.
26. Ibid., 423.
27. Chu, "The State and the Development of the Automobile Industry in South Korea and Taiwan," 141.
28. Zhongguo qiche jishu yanjiu zhongxin, 中国汽车工业年鉴 [China automotive industry yearbook] (Beijing: Zhongguo qiche gongye xiehui, multiple years), 2009, 45. Hereafter, *CAIY*.
29. Johnson, *MITI and the Japanese Miracle*, 132; Kent E. Calder, *Strategic Capitalism: Private Business and Public Purpose in Japanese Industrial Finance* (Princeton, NJ: Princeton University Press, 1993), 107.
30. Calder, *Strategic Capitalism*, 110.
31. Ibid., 170.
32. Chu, "The State and the Development of the Automobile Industry in South Korea and Taiwan," 155.
33. Genther, *A History of Japan's Government-Business Relationship*, 207.
34. Chu, "The State and the Development of the Automobile Industry in South Korea and Taiwan," 147.
35. Ibid., 148.
36. Woo-Cumings, *Race to the Swift*, 143.
37. Robert Wade, *Governing the Market: Economic Theory and the Role of Government in East Asian Industrialization* (Princeton, NJ: Princeton University Press, 1990), 310. Wade reports that the Hyundai Pony cost $3,700 to produce, sold for $5,000 in Korea and sold for $2,200 in the U.S. domestic sales were used to subsidize exports.
38. Doner, "Limits of State Strength," 411.
39. Green, "South Korea's Automobile Industry," 412–413.
40. Eric Harwit, *China's Automobile Industry: Policies, Problems, and Prospects (Studies on Contemporary China)* (Armonk, NY: M. E. Sharpe, 1995), 29.
41. Ibid.

42. Reed and Waldmeir, "Foreign Groups Told to Make Chinese Cars"; Michael Dunne, "Launch a New Brand in China—Whether You Like It or Not," *Automotive News China*, April 12, 2011, www.autonewschina.com/en/article .asp?id=6807.
43. GDP per capita figures expressed in 1990 Geary-Khamis dollars as compiled by Angus Maddison.
44. Cusumano, *The Japanese Automobile Industry*, 26.
45. Ibid., 24.
46. Ibid., 25.
47. Chu, "The State and the Development of the Automobile Industry in South Korea and Taiwan," 147; Bruce Cumings, *Korea's Place in the Sun: A Modern History*, 1st ed. (New York: Norton, 1997), 325.
48. Green, "South Korea's Automobile Industry," 411.
49. Chu, "The State and the Development of the Automobile Industry in South Korea and Taiwan," 163.
50. Genther, *A History of Japan's Government-Business Relationship*, 135.
51. Johnson, *MITI and the Japanese Miracle*, 268.
52. Genther, *A History of Japan's Government-Business Relationship*, 148.
53. Ibid., 151.
54. Ibid., 141.
55. Wade, *Governing the Market*, 330.
56. Huang, "Between Two Coordination Failures," 561–562.
57. Johnson, *MITI and the Japanese Miracle*, 286–288.
58. Chu, "The State and the Development of the Automobile Industry in South Korea and Taiwan," 148ff.
59. Green, "South Korea's Automobile Industry," 415.
60. Chu, "The State and the Development of the Automobile Industry in South Korea and Taiwan," 155.

Chapter Eight

In Conclusion

There has been a gradual transition from strict government control and planning to a more ad hoc role . . . The central government only sets policy now, and their guiding direction is economic development.

—Veteran expatriate auto executive
Shanghai, May 2009

This final chapter begins with a summary of the findings of my research and describes the state of China's auto industry. In the final section I assess what I consider to be the critical issues facing China's auto industry today and pose some further questions for research. I also offer a few predictions about what the strengths and weaknesses of the auto industry may mean for private enterprise in general, China's innovative ability and foreign multinationals doing business in China going forward.

243

Summary of Findings

This section is organized according to the four central government objectives for the auto industry identified in the story in Chapter Two: consolidation, technology acquisition, Chinese brand development, and NEV development.

Consolidation

One of the oldest and most consistent of central government objectives for the auto industry has been for this heavily fragmented industry to be consolidated into fewer and larger firms with the necessary scale both to dominate in their home market and to compete in foreign markets. But as the case studies and analysis have demonstrated, while China has taken steps in this direction, the central government has yet to achieve this objective.

China's central government has always maintained a firm hand in industrial and macro-economic planning, and it appears to have possessed all of the tools it needed to bring about the consolidation it wanted in this industry. Through its control of both the purse strings and its power over personnel appointments, the central government has the ability to shape the behavior of both local government officials and SOE leaders. Whether for good or bad, the central government has the power to force mergers among SOEs and to order closure of small, inefficient enterprises. The central government, through its ability to make and enforce policy also erected barriers to entry that should have been able to prevent the establishment of new auto firms. In addition, because the central government holds the power to grant access to China's market by foreign multinationals (MNCs), the central government has the ability to ensure that any foreign presence in China's auto industry works to strengthen China's homegrown industry.

What the foregoing policy analysis and case studies demonstrate, however, is a somewhat more nuanced picture. The central government, though not lacking in either the ability or the desire to shape industry according to its objectives, has elected to make tradeoffs in order to balance contradictory goals. The result is effectively two *different* auto industries. At the top of its auto industry, the central government has set the stage for the emergence of about a dozen increasingly large and competitive auto firms, the largest four of which are massive SOEs that produce more than two million vehicles a year. At the bottom, however, are about 70 to 80 firms that are too small to achieve scale yet whose local governments support their existence by underwriting the cost of their capital.

At the top of the auto industry, the central government, while proclaiming its desire that the market influence the mergers that take place in the industry—and while indeed allowing the market to bring some players together—has also demonstrated that it has the ability to push auto firms together when it wants. As the case studies in Chapter Six demonstrated, there were valid, market-driven reasons that brought the players together in each of the mergers presented, but in some cases, the central government also intervened to hasten mergers when it needed to correct strategic mistakes or enforce a policy provision.

At the bottom of the industry, however, the central government has taken more of a hands-off approach. While it could order closure of the numerous small, inefficient auto assemblers with the wave of a hand, the central government chooses not to do so for fear of creating social instability—a key threat to regime survival. Recall from the market share analysis at the end of Chapter Six that the top five automakers in China have a market share of approximately 70 percent. At the end of 2008 there were 675,000 people employed in auto assembly plants in China.[1] If we figure conservatively that 30 percent of those 675,000 are employed in the firms *not* among the top five, that leaves over 200,000 people who are employed by the smaller firms.[2] If these small firms did not exist, many of these 200,000 people, would be unemployed. (And this figure does not include people employed by the myriad of components manufacturers that supply the smaller firms.) While 200,000 may not seem like a large number in a country of nearly 1.4 billion, I would suggest that China's leaders are not eager to make the job of keeping Chinese citizens employed any more difficult than is necessary. If we were to extend this analysis to other industries that suffer from fragmentation and/or overcapacity, then we would find numbers that begin to add up. *The contradictory goals that the central government must balance in the auto industry affect other industries as well.*

The central government has also had to compromise over its barriers to entry of new firms. While the central government has made clear its desire that no new firms be established, over the past two decades several new independent firms have not only been established, but some have grown large enough to occupy spots among the top-10 largest automakers in China. As the case studies in Chapter Five demonstrated, these new firms, with the full support of *local* governments were able join the industry, often under the radar, thereby presenting the central government with *faits accompli*. The central government, reluctant to add to any local region's stability concerns, ultimately relented to the existence of these firms as, once again, the goal of social stability outweighed that of a consolidated auto industry.

Local governments have had a key role in shaping the auto industry in China. However, far from directly disobeying the central government or ignoring its wishes, local government leaders have simply been acting according to their performance incentives—incentives that the central government has put in place. The key measures by which a local leader may gain promotion to higher office revolve around the most important of central government goals. As long as local leaders can generate local economic growth and maintain local social stability, they improve their chances for promotion. Closing small automakers, no matter how inefficient, would both subtract local GDP and add to the risk of social instability, so local leaders are less inclined to act on the central government's objective of auto industry consolidation. Furthermore, local governments are highly protective of local businesses and will be disinclined to take any action that could reduce local fiscal revenue.[3]

Technology Acquisition

The central government's original strategy for technology acquisition was to bring in foreign multinationals (MNCs) and have them form joint ventures with SOEs which, it was assumed, would simply absorb all they needed to know about the design and manufacture of cars. What the central government did not realize, however, was that neither the SOEs, nor the foreign multinationals, had the proper incentives for such technology transfer.

Due to the short-term, political nature of the positions of SOE leaders, these companies are incentivized to pursue short-term profitability and growth in absolute size, and to avoid taking major risks. This translates into a preference for the least complicated path to short-term profitability and, therefore, a reluctance to undertake long-term research and development. In concrete terms, this means that the leaders of SOEs have been most content to allow their foreign partners to contribute complete vehicle designs, which are then assembled by Chinese workers and sold under foreign brands. This requires no significant transfer of technology.

The MNCs, while motivated to generate a return for their shareholders, are also highly motivated to protect their massive investments in intellectual property. Having invested billions in technology and vehicle designs—intangible assets that belong to their shareholders—the MNCs do not take lightly requests or demands to "share" or give away these assets. As the CEO of a foreign auto components manufacturer told me when I asked him about intellectual property (IP) concerns,

> IP is probably the biggest downside [to operating in China] by far. No matter what [your partner] says, your technology bleeds when you take it over there. You're copied everywhere, [but] you learn to manage the bleed. You don't give them your latest technology, and when you do, you put it in a wholly-owned enterprise, not a JV.[4]

As a result of these conflicting incentives, the initial technology transfers for which the central government had been hoping never took place, or they took place to a far lesser degree than expected. By the mid-1990s the central government came to believe that the JVs were not delivering on their commitments to tech transfer. The result was increasingly specific demands for technology transfer and design expertise. The PATAC design center opened in the late 1990s by General Motors with its partner, Shanghai Auto, represented the deeper level of sharing that the central government had been hoping for, but the central government would soon find its hands tied in terms of its ability to demand technology transfer.

With China's membership in the WTO came an end to its ability to require technology transfer as a condition for approval of foreign investment. And while one may have predicted that this would lead to either an end to the formation of new JVs or charges brought against China by foreign countries accusing it of violating its WTO commitments, neither of these outcomes materialized. Not only did new JVs continue to be formed throughout the first decade of the new century, but no countries formally accused China of violating its tech transfer commitments. The reason for this surprising outcome is that the explosion in auto. ownership in China following its joining the WTO had, by the end of the decade, made China the world's largest market for automobiles. Accordingly, no foreign multinational felt it could afford not to have a significant presence in this market. Many have begun *voluntarily* to hand over technology in order to gain the central government's approval for establishment of a new JV or expansion of an existing one.

And China's central government has also become quite adept at gaining technology concessions while avoiding the appearance of violating its WTO commitments. The latest development has been the concept of "JV brands" in which foreign MNCs contribute complete vehicle designs to their SOE partners to manufacture under Chinese brand names. As the MNCs approach the central government for permission to expand, they are finding that such concessions must be "volunteered" before they are able to obtain approval for expansion.[5]

Despite all of the strategic maneuvering that goes on among the central government, the SOEs and the multinationals, Chinese automakers have still managed to move the needle in a positive direction in terms of technology acquisition. Recall the three hierarchies of technology acquisition presented in Chapter Two. In each case—vehicle assembly, component manufacturing, and intellectual property benefit—China's auto industry has been able collectively to improve its position over the past three decades. Chinese companies have improved from barely being able to assemble CKDs to, in some cases, designing and assembling their own vehicles. In some cases Chinese automakers have made use of technology purchased from abroad, while in others, they have been able to develop their own technologies. The ultimate goal of the central government is to move as far away as possible from use of technology that requires a payment of royalties to foreign patent holders toward the use of technology that keeps all of the money at home, and in this regard, China's auto industry has achieved measured progress.

Nevertheless, after three decades of development, China's auto industry has yet to progress as far as did Japan's and Korea's during their developmental periods. Within 15 to 20 years of launch, both Japan and Korea had begun to export their cars to the developed markets of North America and Western Europe, but China's exports still go primarily to Africa, Latin America, the Middle East, and Russia. However, this may be less of a reflection on China's technical capabilities than on its late start. As Cold War allies of the United States, Japan and Korea were given special trading privileges that China never had. Also, by the time Japan and Korea had joined the WTO their auto industries were fully mature. For China, the timing of WTO membership complicated its ability to gain technology transfer, and this has forced China into adopting more subtle maneuvers so as not to be accused of violating WTO commitments.

Finally, it should be noted that some of China's technology acquisition has taken place as a result of legitimate transfers of intellectual property through purchases of components, designs, and entire companies. Now that car ownership has become affordable for China's middle class, the explosion in sales has resulted in a cash windfall for the larger automakers. This cash, generated primarily from the sales of foreign-branded cars, gives China's automakers the increasing ability to purchase technologies from abroad. Examples include BAIC's purchases of two Saab platforms in 2009 and its participation in the purchase of GM power steering subsidiary, Nexteer. And the larger and more successful of China's private automakers have also been able to acquire foreign automakers and component technologies. Examples of this include Geely's purchase of Australian transmission manufacturer DSI in 2009 and of Volvo in 2010. In this sense, Chinese automakers are making great progress, and whether they buy technology or invent it themselves is becoming less important than the fact that they are able to acquire these technologies and deploy them without having to pay royalties to foreigners for that privilege.

Chinese Brand Development

Among the central government's newest objectives is the development of Chinese brands. This objective grew from the concern that, while sales of cars in China were growing, as much as half the profits of most of the cars sold were flowing overseas to the foreign multinationals. And the central government, though apparently possessing the tools it needed to press SOEs into development of their own brands, has thus far struggled to overcome the SOEs' short-term investment horizons and get them to invest significantly in this area. The SOEs, as noted above, found the assembly and sale of foreign-branded cars to be an easier way to achieve the size and profitability that their leaders are motivated to pursue.

And while the SOEs have all, under pressure from the central government, belatedly and reluctantly begun to develop and sell their own brands, the central government has (also belatedly) begun to recognize that the private automakers have built-in incentives to help it achieve this objective. Because the foreign multinationals have, until now, been steered by the central government into joint ventures with the SOEs, the private automakers, lacking the option to rely on sales of foreign brands, have had no choice but to develop their own brands. The central government has indeed recognized the contribution that the privates make to Chinese brand growth, and has begun to offer support, but that support still falls far short of that offered to SOEs.

Measured in aggregate, Chinese brands have increased as a percentage of all passenger cars sold in China, from 21 percent in 2004 to 31 percent in 2010.[6] However, nearly half of the increase occurred as a result of the stimulus introduced to counteract the global financial crisis in 2009 and 2010. The withdrawal of the stimulus in 2011 has since led to a return to the slower pace of growth for Chinese brands. The recent introduction of "JV brands" appears to be an attempt by the central government to get around SOE reluctance to invest heavily in their own brands without having to directly adjust the SOEs' incentives for behavior. While these JV brands will probably help to increase the market share of "Chinese" brands somewhat, the central government will probably need to take steps to lengthen the SOEs' investment horizons before a substantial increase in market share can be achieved.

The central government has correctly identified the growth of Chinese brands as a key objective to drive the future growth of its auto industry, and the differing approaches toward branding between China and its neighbors, Japan and Korea, has illustrated just how important this objective is. Whereas China invited foreign automakers to partner with SOEs to sell foreign brands to Chinese consumers, Japan and Korea were able to keep foreign brands out of their markets long enough for their consumers to develop preferences for home-grown brands. As mentioned above, this was probably never an option for China as it was not a Cold War ally of the West. Regardless, the unfortunate result is that China finds itself on a long road of organic growth: China's automakers face the uphill battle of convincing the Chinese public, one consumer at a time, of the value of Chinese brands.

New Energy Vehicle Development

This particular objective is the central government's newest and most proactive. While the central government adopted its other objectives in reaction to the perceived conditions of the auto industry, the central government was thinking of the future when it adopted this objective. When the central government began, as far back as the Tenth Five-Year Plan in 2001, to include this objective in policy, not even consumers in foreign markets had begun to demand these energy efficient or zero-emission vehicles. Only Toyota and Honda of Japan had hybrids on the market at that time, and General Motors' 1990s experiment with an electric car had been abandoned years earlier.

Though the central government had at its disposal the tools to pressure automakers into development spending, SOEs lacked the incentives to commit significant funds to this kind of development. And as with the outcomes of Chinese brand development, we find that the most significant development of NEVs in China is occurring in the private sector. But unlike brand development, NEV development appears to be less out of necessity than out of a single private company's assumed competitive advantage in battery development.

The greatest progress achieved to date has come from BYD, a private company based in Shenzhen that got its start as a manufacturer of batteries for mobile phones and laptop computers. Only later did BYD buy a bankrupt automaker in whose cars it could install its battery technology. And as with brand development, the central government has only belatedly begun to recognize the contribution that the private sector is making to this objective, rewarding BYD with preferential access to loans from state-owned banks. In a very recent development, BYD has also become one of the first private automakers to be allowed to form a joint venture with a foreign automaker. In 2010 BYD and Daimler of Germany formed a JV to conduct R&D in new energy vehicles, and the two announced in 2011 that their first jointly developed car would be introduced in 2013.

Since BYD began to make news with its announcement of a plug-in hybrid in 2008, many other automakers have also announced their own NEV projects, and the central government has attempted to encourage this through a limited experiment with consumer subsidies in six select cities. Independent automakers Chery, JAC, Zotye, and Jonway, among others, now have NEVs either in testing or close to production, and all of the major SOEs have announced NEV projects as well. However, there is a reason to doubt the extent of the scope of these projects. In May of 2009, an economist and auto industry expert who had advised China's economic planning organization, the NDRC, on auto industry policy responded pessimistically to my questions about NEVs: "Who [in China] is selling these cars? Who is buying these cars? Nobody! A lot of companies *say* they are building [NEVs], but no one really is. It is all public relations . . . they want to impress the government." An automaker whose goal is simply to impress the government need only give the *impression* that development is taking place. To do that, all a company needs is a single demonstration model to show visiting dignitaries and display at exhibitions.

While the central government's objective of producing NEVs is commendable, both as a strategic move and as an altruistic act that could help to reduce pollution and global warming, there clearly remain questions as to whether Chinese automakers can achieve significant results in the short run. Until there is substantial consumer demand for these vehicles, neither the SOEs nor the privates have real incentives to invest heavily in this area. And the lack of interest among Chinese consumers in NEVs thus far is an indication that the minimal state subsidies on offer still aren't enough to spur sales.

Looking Forward

In this final section I will discuss the implications of this research for the private sector in China, the innovative capacity of China's auto sector, the future of foreign multinationals in China's auto industry and whether automobile ownership in China will continue to grow at such a spectacular pace.

How Safe Is the Private Sector?

As this research has revealed, the largest among the private automakers are on the leading edge in terms of developing Chinese brands and new energy vehicles. And the fact that China's central government has at last recognized the value that private automakers bring to the industry represents a small step away from the trend toward increasing state control over key sectors of the economy. But the central government has only begun to support the larger private automakers out of a pragmatic recognition that some of the privates are driving innovation (limited though it may be) and acting as examples for the SOEs. Yet, if the central government indeed sees the private firms as more innovative than the SOEs, why then does the central government not take steps to privatize the industry and allow the private sector to work its magic?

The fact that China's auto industry contains both state-owned and private firms is an indication that the central government values competition. And the central government's recent acceptance of the existence of the larger private players, along with some minimal funding provided by state-owned banks, attests to the importance of these few firms in the eyes of the central government. However, due to the continued advantages enjoyed by the SOEs, particularly in terms of their superior access to funds and partnerships with foreign automakers, the private sector continues to compete with one arm tied behind its back. *The central government indeed values competition, but only to the extent that it strengthens the SOEs.*

Under state capitalism, a central government full of highly capable and confident technocrats is simply unwilling to leave development of China's economy to chance, especially when the government has established economic growth as one of the key planks supporting the regime's legitimacy.[7] The Party's Central Organization Department can direct corporate policy through appointment of the senior executives of SOEs, but with private businesses, the Party has no such authority.[8] And despite the fact that Jiang Zemin's 2001 theory of "three represents" legitimized co-opting entrepreneurs through Party membership (discussed in Chapter Two), the reaction of the Politburo to the global financial crisis in 2008 and 2009 demonstrated the Party's enduring commitment to state ownership. McGregor reports that, even though "the central bank, the bank regulator and even the banks themselves all counseled caution . . . the Politburo . . . issued an edict from on high for the money pumps to be opened." Fully 85 percent of the new lending intended to counteract the effects of the financial crisis went to SOEs.[9] This is not the behavior of a state interested in further privatization.

Also of great concern to private businesses is the safety of their property. Hope for the private sector increased in 2004 when Article 13 of China's constitution was amended to state that, "citizens' lawful private property is *inviolable*."[10] While this was heralded as a breakthrough for the rights of citizens and private business owners, it follows Article 12, which still reads, "socialist public property is *sacred and inviolable*," which seems to accord public property with somewhat higher status. In addition, China lacks an independent judiciary that can be depended upon to defend the rights of citizens against arbitrary seizure by the state. To the degree that Wang Chuanfu of BYD and Li Shufu of Geely feel comfortable that their businesses would not be seized by the state, the legal grounds on which their comfort rests seem shaky at best.

Does this mean that private business in China is doomed to extinction? Probably not—certainly not in the near term. Despite the government's heavy reliance on state ownership as a means of control, reformers in the central government and the Party have recognized the contributions of the private sector to China's economic growth. This is, of course, no guarantee that the private sector will continue to be looked upon favorably by the central government indefinitely. In industries such as coal and steel, state-owned firms have recently taken over smaller private firms, often with compensation that private business owners claim to be far below the fair market value of their properties.[11]

This still leaves us with the puzzle of why some entrepreneurs insist on competing head-to-head with SOEs in a pillar industry. Some of my interviewees suggested that the combination of the engineering challenge of producing and selling such a complex and high-profile product, along with the tremendous growth potential of China's auto industry, have proved irresistible to entrepreneurs like Li Shufu and Wang Chuanfu. For someone with a passion for building automobiles, it is hard to think of another market in the world with the near-term growth potential of China's. University of California at Berkeley economist, Yingyi Qian also suggests that local governments play a role in helping to assure entrepreneurs that their property rights will be respected.[12] The question is, what is the tradeoff for entrepreneurs? What will be the long-term cost? And how, if at all, do they mitigate these risks?

While a full understanding of the motivations of private entrepreneurs in a state-dominated industry is beyond the scope of this project, it raises interesting and important questions for future study. Perhaps this question could be more thoroughly addressed through a cross-country survey of entrepreneurs designed to understand their motivations, particularly in countries with a history of state domination of certain industries and/or state-confiscation of private assets.

In the meantime, the success of some of the private automakers presents the central government with a dilemma. It wants to push for increased production of Chinese brands, but the incentives it supplies to the SOEs are not adequate to get their leaders completely on-board. The private firms have stepped in to fill the gap, and the central government has (belatedly) learned to appreciate this, but the central government, despite providing minimal help, has not provided the kind of support to the private players that they have to the SOEs. Accordingly, the private players have remained small-scale, and will likely remain so as long as the SOEs continue to receive the bulk of central government support.

There are positive signs that the central government is beginning to open more space for the private firms by allowing them to partner with foreign MNCs. BYD has already formed a partnership with Daimler to develop an electric vehicle, and Great Wall had been rumored to be the top choice of Jaguar–Land Rover as it searched for a Chinese partner (though it now appears Chery may have beaten Great Wall to the punch). But will the JVs provide the same disincentive to innovation for the private firms that they provide to the SOEs? I do not believe they will as the leaders of private firms face a completely different set of overall performance objectives from those of their SOE counterparts. While the conservatism and short-term investment horizons of the

SOEs nudges their leaders away from innovation and toward cash generation through sales of foreign brands, the entrepreneurs running private firms are more highly motivated to take risks. Their partnerships with foreign firms are more likely to add to their innovative efforts than to detract from them. Consequently, MNCs willing to partner with private Chinese automakers need to understand the differences between private and SOE automakers' incentives.

And there also exists the probability, however minimal, that China's central government could decide to privatize the SOEs and create a level playing field on which all enterprises can compete to capture market share. But if recent central government rhetoric is any indication, a wholesale privatization is not in the offing. Wu Bangguo, head of China's National People's Congress (NPC) and number two in the Communist Party hierarchy, surprised many observers during the March 2011 NPC when, during the usual denunciation of things Western (multiple parties, separation of powers, an independent judiciary, etc.), he included a term not normally a part of the litany, *privatization*.[13]

And in the fall of 2010, Shao Ning, vice chairman of SASAC (owner of the central SOEs), released a report stating not only that privatization of the remaining SOEs is not an option, but also explaining in detail why privatization would not be appropriate.[14] He explained that there are only two possible outcomes if SOEs were privatized: either foreigners would buy China's SOEs, or Chinese entrepreneurs would buy them.[15] And while the latter option would be preferable to SASAC, Shao explained that China's entrepreneurs simply are not up to the task yet. "They lack the depth of experience and sources of funding necessary to run major industrial corporations."[16] Of course, entrepreneurs lack access to funding for the simple reason that bank lending still goes primarily to the SOEs. China's central government does not seem interested in making full use of the private sector—at least not in the short term.

Can China Innovate?

Much of what counts for "innovation" in China is merely copying and tweaking of foreign technology. The Chinese concept of "*shanzhai*" (山寨) is used to describe products that are imitations of famous brand-name products. The term "*shanzhai*" means, literally, "mountain village," the idea being that these products are made outside of government supervision. What I found interesting during my travels in China is that the term is not always derisive; often it is merely a term of amusement. One example I saw advertised was a "*shanzhai*" iPhone that looked just like a real Apple iPhone, except that it had both GSM and CDMA systems built in and it could accept two different SIM cards, simultaneously. Such creativity certainly indicates the presence of curiosity-driven, incremental innovation in China, but this type of innovation is taking place largely out of view.[17] The real question is whether China's central government will continue to try to drive innovation from the top down or move to create an environment that encourages and rewards innovation.

And while China's government periodically vows to crack down on theft of intellectual property, occasionally making a show of shutting down the DVD vendors who manage to have copies of first-run Hollywood films before they are even released to DVD in the United States, the government mostly looks the other way. While China has a very modern set of laws and a patent and copyright system for protecting intellectual property, the difficulty often comes with enforcement and commitment. The vice minister of the Ministry of Industry and Information Technology recently told a press conference that *shanzhai* products were beneficial to society: "imitation is also a kind of innovation and a kind of development."[18] If not even China's senior leaders are prepared to confront seriously the violation of intellectual property rights, why should those carrying out such violations ignore the easiest path to profits?

Turning toward the auto industry, unlike Japan and Korea, China's domestic auto brands still fall far short of consumer expectations, even in their home market. Also unlike Japan and Korea, China's exports of autos are only to developing markets. The difference comes down to China's insistence on state ownership and the fact that the SOEs' foreign joint venture partners are basically a double-edged sword. On one hand, they help the SOEs to generate lots of cash, and they contribute technology. On the other hand, the presence of the foreign multinationals makes it easy for the SOEs to remain profitable without having to devote too many resources to their own R&D.

To be fair, the major SOEs are now all either selling, or are in the process of developing, both Chinese brands and new energy vehicles, but as an advisor to the NDRC told me, most of these projects are just for show: "they are trying to impress the government." After explaining to me that much of the flurry of activity I was seeing in development of NEVs was not productive, a (Chinese) former Chief Design Engineer for one of China's major automakers gave me a sociological explanation for what I saw:

> Traditional Chinese [Confucian] culture is one of humility . . . not bragging or exaggerating. A lot of you foreigners still think of China in this way. But the Cultural Revolution instilled in people a tendency to boast of what they do not have, to exaggerate. This is how you should view Chinese industry.

Only a few weeks later, an executive from a foreign auto parts manufacturer located in China explained it another way when I asked about the capabilities of Chinese supply firms. "There is a veneer over everything in China, a veneer we don't have to deal with in, for example, Korea. China projects much more competence than it really has." While self-confidence is certainly an admirable trait for any society seeking to improve its place in the hierarchy of the global division of labor, China's automakers, according to some of the experts I interviewed, may be trying to make up what they lack in competence with confidence. And this may be the very trait that is responsible for tragic accidents such as the fatal July 2011 crash of two of China's much-vaunted bullet trains near Wenzhou, Zhejiang. The eagerness to demonstrate engineering prowess may sometimes outweigh concerns for safety and reliability.

The central government, for its part, seems to understand that more is needed if China is to move up the value-added scale in terms of automobiles. Accordingly, there continues to be a heavy focus on technical and scientific education in China. And the statistics on China's rapid increase in the numbers of patents filed, engineering degrees granted and scientific papers published continue to strike fear in the hearts of readers of foreign newspapers and magazines.[19] Many foreign journalists seem to have accepted that China is rapidly catching up with the West in terms of education and, therefore, this means China will soon "overtake" the West in terms of innovation.

However, this focus on statistics seems to confuse inputs with outputs. Certainly many patents are being filed, engineering degrees granted, and papers published, but how much of this activity is resulting in commercially viable innovation? An analysis of China's innovative capacity is beyond the scope of this book; however, it seems that more analysis is warranted than is given to the topic in the popular media. For example, even though China graduates hundreds of thousands more engineers than does the United States in any given year, what is the quality of engineering education these graduates are receiving? How many of China's engineering graduates truly have a passion for what they study? And does China's system encourage their collaboration with entrepreneurs free to pursue their dreams, or are they more highly incentivized to seek the security of a job in a SOE? Even Chinese educators are becoming more boldly critical about China's educational system which focuses more on rote memorization than on nurturing creativity and imagination.[20] The best engineering skills in the world may be less useful in the hands of engineers who have been taught from a very early age never to challenge authority, and never to ask why.

Another disturbing trend in China that may affect China's ability to innovate is increasing censorship of the Internet. To be certain, China's citizens are better off for not having easy access to pornography, but China's government may be throwing the baby out with the bathwater. What Chinese citizens are also increasingly missing are opportunities to share ideas with people outside of China. While the Chinese state is devoting more and more resources to policing the web, the citizens of more open societies are enjoying an unprecedented level of free and open discussions on uncensored forums and social networking platforms such as Twitter and Facebook. And while most of these discussions are unlikely to lead directly to innovation, the mere cross-pollination of ideas could someday generate the next big idea. Innovation guru Steven Johnson explains the importance of open communication:

> Environments that block or limit those new combinations [of ideas]—by punishing experimentation, by obscuring certain branches of possibility, by making the current state so satisfying

that no one bothers to explore the edges—will, on average, generate and circulate fewer innovations than environments that encourage exploration.[21]

The question is whether China will ever be able to nurture an innovative environment while continuing to crush any possible disagreement with the Party's direction of the country. Can a closed society effectively wall off certain areas of thought while nurturing other areas? Bruce Bueno de Mesquita and George Downs describe the phenomenon of a "sustainable autocracy" in which authoritarian governments attempt to suppress "coordination goods" while continuing to supply economic goods, and perhaps this explains what China is attempting to do.[22] Nevertheless, I would question whether this is a sustainable strategy for the longer-term. If indeed there is a tradeoff between control and creativity, China's leaders may find themselves at a crossroads in the future.

In the meantime, China continues to copy foreign technology while foreigners complain about IP theft. Foreign complaints are typical of the CEO of an American auto components manufacturer I quoted earlier in this chapter: "Your technology bleeds when you take it [to China] . . . You don't give them your latest technology." But if history can be a guide, copying may not be a bad place to start. After all, that is how every other major economic power got its start:

> From the start of the industrial revolution, every country that became economically great began by copying: the Germans copied the British; the Americans copied the British and the Germans, and the Japanese copied everybody.[23]

And even if we assume that all China is ever able to do is copy and tweak foreign technology (an assumption the foreign multinationals would be wise *not* to make), it seems that the Chinese are becoming more skilled at copying and able to do so at a faster pace than ever before. For example, the Japanese, Canadians, and Europeans sold high-speed trains to China whose engineers proceeded to copy and combine the foreign technology to make high-speed trains that the Chinese claim to be their own.[24] The Chinese have done the same with wind turbines, jet fighters, and nuclear technology as well.[25]

And lest we forget, Steve Jobs, arguably the world's greatest innovator in recent times, did not invent the personal computer, the digital music player, the smartphone, or the tablet computer; he built Apple Computer by improving upon the inventions of others. Steve Jobs was one among 300 million Americans, and he didn't even need a college education to achieve innovative greatness. Could there not be at least three or four Steve Jobs among 1.4 billion Chinese? And, if there are, will they be able to work their magic in China, or will they need to emigrate to a place with an environment more nurturing of their creativity?

If China's automakers never truly master the skills of breakthrough innovation, if all they are ever able to do is copy and tweak, will it even matter? And what might this mean for China's foreign joint venture partners?

How Long Will Foreign Automakers Be Welcome?

The early joint ventures in the 1980s only required foreign partners to contribute unspecified "technology," but over the following decades, demands on foreign partners have increased and become more specific. All the evidence now indicates a coordinated push from Beijing for foreign partners to contribute technology that helps their partners build Chinese brands. There is no question that the cost to foreign multi-nationals of being in China has increased. The question foreign multinationals need to be asking themselves now is how long it will be before the benefits of being in China no longer outweigh the costs—or has it already happened?

The previous section asked whether it even matters whether Chinese automakers become innovative. This is an important question for the foreign multinationals to consider. The possibility that most frightens Japanese and European high-speed train manufacturers is not that they will no longer be able to sell their trains to the Chinese; it is that they will no longer be able to sell their trains anywhere else in the world. Why, for example, would the nearly bankrupt State of California want to pay top dollar for Japanese or European train technology when China sells similar technology for less? We may someday ask a similar question regarding automotive technology. Why would consumers in developing markets want to pay top dollar for a Toyota or a Chevrolet when BYD or SAIC sell similar technology for less? And if the governments of the developed world continue to adhere to free trade principles, will the consumers of Europe and North America be faced with similar questions in years to come?

The point here is that, even if the Chinese are never able to overcome their innovation challenges, over time, their ability to acquire and copy foreign technology will gradually shrink the technology gap between Chinese and foreign brands. And this has implications for foreign multinational automakers both inside and outside of China. As Chinese automakers improve in terms of both quality and speed-to-market, foreign automakers must constantly recalculate the costs and benefits of being in China and cooperating with Chinese partners. What are the tradeoffs? Is it possible to both make money and protect intellectual property in China, or will these two objectives become mutually exclusive? Are they already mutually exclusive? If demand for cars in China continues to grow faster than that of other markets, perhaps the absolute number of vehicles sold under foreign brands will continue to increase for the short- to medium-term, but foreign automakers should understand that the ultimate goal is that Chinese brands dominate the Chinese market.

In China, foreign automakers compete, not only against other automakers, but also against the Chinese government, and the Chinese government's goal is simple: the Chinese automakers will ultimately win.

Remaining Challenges

The foregoing assumes that demand for cars in China will continue to grow. The problem with this assumption is that, while China currently only has about 35 cars per thousand people compared to America's 439, no one knows where the ceiling for ownership lies in China.[26] Common sense tells us that it is probably somewhere below that of the United States, but how much less? Even at China's very low levels of vehicle ownership, the streets of China's major cities have already become virtual parking lots. The population density of these ancient cities that grew up around foot traffic and horse-carts simply will not accommodate an American level of personal vehicle ownership.

Furthermore, the pollution in China's major cities has made them practically unlivable. In November 2010, the U.S. embassy in Beijing's automated hourly pollution monitor twitter account (@BeijingAir), at one point, described the readings as "crazy bad," terminology that was later changed to "beyond index."[27] In other words, the environment in Beijing has become so polluted that scientists have yet to invent terminology to adequately describe it. Under such conditions, we should not be surprised that the central government has pushed for development of new energy vehicles.

Or should we? Yes, many Chinese automakers are now developing NEVs, but to whom do they expect to sell them? I would submit that Beijing's aim for NEVs is much greater than that of the Chinese domestic market. If Beijing really were enamored of the potential of this technology to help improve China's environment, they could have been providing subsidies to Toyota and Honda to sell their hybrids in China over the past decade. And Beijing could have been much more supportive of Toyota building the Prius in China rather than allowing it to end production and move it to Thailand.[28] While some Chinese cities are indeed building charging stations for electric vehicles and providing subsidies to buyers of NEVs, the central government's policy is written in favor of Chinese companies gaining a share of the global market for NEVs, and only secondarily in favor of bringing about a reduction in pollution as quickly as possible.

Finally, I would like to reemphasize the fact that China's auto policy has thus far been built around the assumption of maintaining the *status quo* of state ownership. Every step along the way, from demanding tech transfer in the 1980s to demanding that the SOEs conduct their own R&D in the 1990s; from relying on the privates to push the SOEs to tying foreign automakers' expansion plans to their willingness to help develop Chinese brands—every step has been designed to protect state ownership and control. Unless SOE leaders begin to be rewarded for risk-taking rather than profitability, for innovation rather than size, they will continue to reap easy profits from assembling foreign-branded cars while only paying lip-service to development of Chinese technology. Of course, the one bit of good news in all of this for the foreign multinationals is that, as long as China depends so heavily on state ownership, there will always be a place for the foreigners. The Chinese, after all, still need their technology—for now.

Notes

1. Zhongguo qiche jishu yanjiu zhongxin, 中国汽车工业年鉴 [China automotive industry yearbook] (Beijing: Zhongguo qiche gongye xiehui, multiple years), 2009, 470. Hereafter, *CAIY*.

2. Since the top five have a combined 70 percent market share, the rest of the industry occupies the other 30 percent. Thirty percent seems a conservative estimate as I assume the top five are more productive than the smaller producers. Realistically, the bottom of the industry probably employs more than 30 percent of the workers in the auto industry.

3. Kellee S. Tsai, "Off Balance: The Unintended Consequences of Fiscal Federalism in China," *Journal of Chinese Political Science* 9, no. 2 (September 2004): 1–26; Richard Baum and Wooyeal Paik, "Clientelism with Chinese Characteristics: The Political Economy of Local Patronage Networks in Post-Reform China," unpublished manuscript, March 19, 2011, 18.

4. Note that, as a component manufacturer, this company has the option of opening a wholly-owned owned venture in China. Foreign auto assemblers may only operate in China as joint venture partners with a Chinese company.

5. Michael Dunne, "Launch a New Brand in China—Whether You Like It or Not," *Automotive News China*, April 12, 2011, www.autonewschina.com/en/article.asp?id=6807; John Reed and Patti Waldmeir, "Foreign Groups Told to Make Chinese Cars," *Financial Times*, *FT.com*, March 20, 2011, www.ft.com/cms/s/0/4a5c8d82–5328–11e0–86e6–00144feab49a.html.

6. See Table B.4, Appendix B.

7. Ian Bremmer, *The End of the Free Market: Who Wins the War Between States and Corporations?* (New York: Portfolio, 2010).

8. Richard McGregor, *The Party: The Secret World of China's Communist Rulers* (New York: Harper, 2010), 68–69.

9. Ibid., 68.

10. Official English translation of China's Constitution: http://english.peopledaily.com.cn/constitution/constitution.html. Emphasis added.

11. Zhang Boling, "Hebei's Private Steel Mills Join State Family," *Caixin Online*, January 21, 2011, http://english.caing.com/2011–01–21/100219471.html; Gady Epstein, "The Price of Corruption," *Forbes*, October 30, 2009, www.forbes.com/2009/10/30/china-coal-corruption-communist-party-beijing-dispatch.html.

12. Yingyi Qian, "How Reform Worked in China," in *In Search of Prosperity: Analytic Narratives on Economic Growth*, by Dani Rodrik (Princeton, NJ: Princeton University Press, 2003).

13. "吴邦国委员长作全国人大常委会工作报告(实录) [Chairman of Standing Committee Wu Bangguo's NPC Work Report (actual record)]," *China.com.cn*

(official government site for NPC), March 10, 2011, http://lianghui.china.com.cn/2011/2011–03/10/content_22100102_4.htm.

14. Shao Ning, "邵宁　国企改革未来方向 [Shao Ning: Future direction of SOE reform]," *Chinareform.org.cn*, November 8, 2010, www.chinareform.org.cn/Economy/Enterprise/Forward/201011/t20101109_50551.htm.

15. The possibility of dispersed ownership such as that of the American or British systems was not even mentioned. Shao's understanding seems to begin with the assumption that ownership will be concentrated, and that being the case, the state is most suited to hold concentrated ownership.

16. Shao Ning, "邵宁　国企改革未来方向 [Shao Ning: Future direction of SOE reform]."

17. On the difference between "incremental" and "breakthrough" innovation, see: William J. Baumol, Robert E. Litan, and Carl J. Schramm, *Good Capitalism, Bad Capitalism, and the Economics of Growth and Prosperity* (New Haven: Yale University Press, 2007).

18. "工信部：山寨产品非完全侵权　有助社会进步 [MIIT: Shanzhai products do not completely violate property rights, and are conducive to social progress]," *Xinhuanet*, December 1, 2010, http://news.xinhuanet.com/internet/2010–12/01/c_12836371.htm.

19. Patrick Thibodeau, "Five Reasons Why China Will Rule Tech," *ComputerWorld*, July 9, 2010, www.computerworld.com/s/article/9179008/Five_reasons_why_China_will_rule_tech; David Shukman, "China 'to Overtake US on Science,'" *BBC*, March 28, 2011, www.bbc.co.uk/news/science-environment-12885271.

20. Jiang Xueqin, "Beijing's School Kingdoms," *The Diplomat*, March 19, 2011, http://the-diplomat.com/china-power/2011/03/19/beijing%e2%80%99s-school-kingdoms/; "Be Creative, Children," *China Daily*, November 27, 2010, www.chinadaily.com.cn/opinion/2010–11/27/content_11618261.htm.

21. Steven Johnson, *Where Good Ideas Come From: The Natural History of Innovation*, 1st ed. (New York: Riverhead Hardcover, 2010), 41.

22. Bruce Bueno de Mequita and George Downs, "Development and Democracy," *Foreign Affairs* 84, no. 5 (September 2005): 77–86.

23. William Kingston, "An Agenda for Radical Intellectual Property Reform," in *International Public Goods and Transfer of Technology Under a Globalized Intellectual Property Regime*, ed. Keith E. Maskus and Jerome H. Reichman (New York: Cambridge University Press, 2005), 658.

24. Norihiko Shirouzu, "Train Makers Rail Against China's High-Speed Designs," *wsj.com*, November 17, 2010, http://online.wsj.com/article/SB10001424052748704814204575507353221141616.html.

25. Keith Bradsher, "To Conquer Wind Power, China Writes the Rules," *New York Times*, December 14, 2010, www.nytimes.com/2010/12/15/business/global/15chinawind.html; Jeremy Page, "China Clones, Sells Russian Fighter

Jets," *wsj.com*, December 5, 2010, http://online.wsj.com/article/SB1000142 40527487046792045756464726556898844.html; John Gapper, "China Takes a Short-Cut to Power," *Financial Times, FT.com*, December 8, 2010, http://www.ft.com/cms/s/0/d3da8b78–0309–11e0-bb1e-00144feabdc0.html.

26. Norihiko Shirouzu, "Cruising Into China's Booming Car Market," *wsj.com*, April 28, 2010, http://online.wsj.com/article/SB10001424052748703404004575197650571749986.html.

27. Jonathan Watts, "Twitter Gaffe: US Embassy Announces 'Crazy Bad' Beijing Air Pollution," *guardian.co.uk*, November 19, 2010, www.guardian.co.uk/environment/blog/2010/nov/19/crazy-bad-beijing-air-pollution.

28. "Toyota to Produce Prius in Thailand," *Marketplace Morning Report*, October 22, 2010, www.marketplace.org/topics/business/toyota-produce-prius-thailand.

Appendix A

List of Passenger Vehicle Assembly Joint Ventures

This list does not include joint ventures for components, sales, distribution, R&D, finance, or other non-assembly-related purposes.

JV Name	Chinese Partner(s)	Foreign Partner(s)	Formed	Dissolved
Beijing-Jeep	Beijing Auto	AMC/Chrysler	1984	2004[1]
Shanghai-Volkswagen	Shanghai Auto	Volkswagen	1984	–
Guangzhou-PSA	Guangzhou Auto	PSA Peugeot-Citroën	1985	1997
FAW-VW	First Auto Works	Volkswagen	1991	–

(continued)

JV Name	Chinese Partner(s)	Foreign Partner(s)	Formed	Dissolved
(Continued)				
Shenlong Automotive	Dongfeng Auto	PSA Peugeot-Citroën	1992	–
Zhengzhou-Nissan	Dongfeng Auto	Nissan	1993	–
Chongqing Chang'an-Suzuki	Chang'an Auto	Suzuki	1993	–
Jiangxi Changhe-Suzuki	Changhe Auto	Suzuki	1995	–
South East (Fujian) Motor[2]	Fujian Motor Ind. Group	China Motor Corp (Taiwan), Mitsubishi	1995	–
Shanghai-General Motors	Shanghai Auto	General Motors	1997	–
Guangqi-Honda	Guangzhou Auto	Honda	1998	–
Jinbei-General Motors	Jinbei Holdings	General Motors	1999	2004[3]
Hebei Zhongxing Auto (ZXAuto)	Tianye Automobile Group	Taiwan Unite	1999	–
Nanjing-Fiat	Nanjing Auto	Fiat	1999	2007
Tianjin FAW-Toyota	First Auto Works	Toyota	2000	–
Chang'an-Ford	Chang'an Auto	Ford, Mazda	2001	–
Shanghai-GM-Wuling	Shanghai Auto, Liuzhou Wuling	General Motors	2002	–
Beijing-Hyundai	Beijing Auto	Hyundai	2002	–
BMW-Brilliance Automotive	Brilliance China Auto	BMW	2003	–
Dongfeng Yueda-Kia	Dongfeng Auto, Yueda	Kia Motors	2002	–
Dongfeng Auto Ltd.[4]	Dongfeng Auto	Nissan	2003	–
Dongfeng-Honda	Dongfeng Auto	Honda	2003	–
Honda Automobile (China) Co.[5]	Guangzhou Auto, Dongfeng Auto	Honda	2003	–
Guangqi-Toyota	Guangzhou Auto	Toyota	2004	–
Beijing Benz-Daimler-Chrysler[6]	Beijing Auto	Daimler-Chrysler	2004	–

JV Name	Chinese Partner(s)	Foreign Partner(s)	Formed	Dissolved
Guangzhou–Fiat	Guangzhou Auto	Fiat	2009	–
Guangzhou–Mitsubishi	Guangzhou Auto	Mitsubishi	2011[7]	–
Shenzhen-BYD Daimler New Technology Co.[8]	BYD	Daimler	2011	–

Note: During the gap between 2004 and 2009, several joint ventures were attempted, but not completed, this includes JVs between Chery and Fiat, as well as Chery and Chrysler. Meanwhile several *commercial* vehicle joint ventures and parts joint ventures were formed during this period.

1. Merged into Beijing Benz-Daimler-Chrysler in 2004.
2. Mitsubishi joined in 2006. The JV produces both commercial and passenger vehicles and also assembles Chrysler models under license.
3. Merged with Shanghai-GM in 2004.
4. Manufactures both commercial and passenger vehicles.
5. Honda owns 55 percent of the JV which produces vehicles for export.
6. Daimler sold Chrysler in 2007.
7. Not finalized as of June 2011.
8. BYD is the first independent Chinese automaker to form a JV with a major foreign multinational. The JV will initially develop an electric car. Announcements thus far have been unclear as to whether this JV would also manufacture the car.

Appendix B

Additional Data

Data in the following tables support calculations referred to at various points in the text.

Table B.1 Calculation of Market Share of Domestically Produced Passenger Cars, 1995–2009

Units = Thousands of Cars	1995	1996	1997	1998	1999	2000	2001	2002	2003	2004	2005	2006	2007	2008	2009
1. Production, passenger cars (轿车)	326	391	488	507	566	608	704	1,093	2,038	2,312	2,768	3,870	4,798	5,037	7,471
2. Imports, passenger cars	129	58	32	18	20	22	47	70	103	116	77	112	140	155	165
3. Exports, passenger cars	1.4	0.6	1.1	0.7	0.3	0.5	0.8	1.0	2.8	9	31	93	189	241	102
1 + 2 − 3 = Approx. domestic sales (轿车)	454	448	519	524	586	630	750	1,162	2,138	2,419	2,814	3,889	4,749	4,951	7,534
Approx. mkt. share, domestically Produced passenger cars	72%	87%	94%	97%	97%	97%	94%	94%	95%	95%	97%	97%	97%	97%	98%

(Passenger cars produced less exports as a percentage of domestic sales.)
Sources: CAIY, 2009, 46–47; *China Auto Bluebook*, 2010, 252, 256, 259.

Table B.2 Vehicle Imports and Exports, 1995–2009

Units = Thousands of Vehicles	1995	1996	1997	1998	1999	2000	2001	2002	2003	2004	2005	2006	2007	2008	2009
Imports, all vehicles (汽车)	159	76	49	40	35	43	71	128	171	176	161	228	314	410	421
Exports, all vehicles (汽车)	18	15	15	14	10	27	26	22	46	76	164	343	614	681	370

Sources: CAIY, 2009, 326; China Auto Bluebook, 2010, 256, 259.

Table B.3 Domestic Share of Passenger Vehicles

Units = Thousands of Vehicles	2004	2005	2006
Total passenger vehicles*	2,483	3,118	4,302
Chinese branded passenger vehicles	496	741	1,153
Chinese brand market share	20.0%	23.8%	26.8%

*Does not include crossovers.
Source: CAIY, 2007, 4.

Table B.4 Domestic Share of Passenger Cars

Units = Thousands of Cars	2004	2005	2006	2007	2008	2009	2010
Total passenger cars	2,313	2,768	3,870	4,798	5,047	7,471	9,495
Chinese branded passenger cars	484	727	984	1,245	1,308	2,217	2,933
Chinese brand market share	20.9%	26.3%	25.4%	25.9%	25.9%	29.7%	30.9%

Sources: China Auto Bluebook, 2010, 252; Xinhua News Agency, January 14, 2011.

Selected Bibliography

Books and Journal Articles

Aberbach, Joel D., David Dollar, and Kenneth Lee Sokoloff. *The Role of the State in Taiwan's Development*. Armonk, NY: M. E. Sharpe, 1994.

Aervitz, Irina. "The Driving Force Behind the Automotive Sector in China and Russia: The Role of the State in Technology Appropriation." PhD dissertation, Miami University of Ohio, 2007.

Alchian, Armen Albert. *Economic Forces at Work*. Indianapolis, IN: Liberty Press, 1977.

Amsden, Alice H. *Asia's Next Giant: South Korea and Late Industrialization*. New York: Oxford University Press, 1989.

Arnold, Walter. "Bureaucratic Politics, State Capacity, and Taiwan's Automobile Industrial Policy." *Modern China* 15, no. 2 (April 1, 1989): 178–214.

Back, Jong Gook. "Politics of Late Industrialization: The Origins and Processes of Automobile Industry Policies in Mexico and South Korea." PhD dissertation, University of California, Los Angeles, 1990.

Baum, Richard. *Burying Mao: Chinese Politics in the Age of Deng Xiaoping*. Princeton, NJ: Princeton University Press, 1994.

———. *China Watcher: Confessions of a Peking Tom*. Seattle: University of Washington Press, 2010.

Baum, Richard, and Wooyeal Paik. "Clientelism with Chinese Characteristics: The Political Economy of Local Patronage Networks in Post-Reform China." Manuscript, March 19, 2011.

Baumol, William J., Robert E. Litan, and Carl J. Schramm. *Good Capitalism, Bad Capitalism, and the Economics of Growth and Prosperity*. New Haven, CT: Yale University Press, 2007.

Berle, Adolf, and Gardiner Means. *The Modern Corporation and Private Property*. New Brunswick, NJ: Transaction Publishers, 1991.

Bo, Zhiyue. *Chinese Provincial Leaders: Economic Performance and Political Mobility since 1949*. Armonk, NY: M. E. Sharpe, 2002.

Boycko, Maxim, Andrei Shleifer, and Robert W. Vishny. "A Theory of Privatisation." *Economic Journal* 106, no. 435 (March 1996): 309–319.

Bremmer, Ian. *The End of the Free Market: Who Wins the War between States and Corporations?* New York: Portfolio, 2010.

Bueno de Mequita, Bruce, and George Downs. "Development and Democracy." *Foreign Affairs* 84, no. 5 (September 2005): 77–86.

Calder, Kent E. *Strategic Capitalism: Private Business and Public Purpose in Japanese Industrial Finance*. Princeton, NJ: Princeton University Press, 1993.

Carson, Iain, and Vijay V. Vaitheeswaran. *Zoom: The Global Race to Fuel the Car of the Future*. New York: Penguin, 2008.

Chang, Ha-Joon. *Globalization, Economic Development, and the Role of the State*. London: Zed Books, 2002.

Chen Xiaohong 陈小洪, ed. 中国企业国际化战略 = *China Enterprise Internationalization Strategy*. Beijing: People's Publishing House 人民出版社, 2006.

Cheng Li. "Was the Shanghai Gang Shanghaied? The Fall of Chen Liangyu and the Survival of Jiang Zemin's Faction." *China Leadership Monitor* 2007, no. 20 (February 28, 2007). www.hoover.org/publications/china-leadership-monitor/article/5877.

Chu, Yun-han. "The State and the Development of the Automobile Industry in South Korea and Taiwan." In *The Role of the State in Taiwan's Development*, edited by Joel D. Aberbach, David Dollar, and Kenneth Lee Sokoloff. Armonk, NY: M. E. Sharpe, 1994.

Cumings, Bruce. *Korea's Place in the Sun: A Modern History*. New York: W. W. Norton, 1997.

Cusumano, Michael A. *The Japanese Automobile Industry: Technology and Management at Nissan and Toyota*. Cambridge, MA: Harvard University Press, 1985.

Development Research Council of the State Council 国务院发展研究中心. 中国汽车产业发展报告 = *China Automotive Industry Development Report*.

Beijing: Social Sciences Academic Press 社会科学文献出版社, multiple years.

Dewar, Robert. *A Savage Factory: An Eyewitness Account of the Auto Industry's Self-Destruction.* Bloomington, IN: AuthorHouse, 2009.

Dickson, Bruce J. *Wealth into Power: The Communist Party's Embrace of China's Private Sector.* Cambridge, UK: Cambridge University Press, 2008.

Dixit, Avinash. "Power of Incentives in Private versus Public Organizations." *American Economic Review* 87, no. 2 (May 1997): 378–382.

Doner, Richard F. "Limits of State Strength: Toward an Institutionalist View of Economic Development." *World Politics* 44, no. 3 (April 1992): 398–431.

Dunne, Michael J. *American Wheels, Chinese Roads: The Story of General Motors in China.* Singapore: John Wiley & Sons (Asia), 2011.

Edwards, Charles E. *Dynamics of the United States Automobile Industry.* Columbia: University of South Carolina Press, 1965.

Eichengreen, Barry J. *Exorbitant Privilege: The Rise and Fall of the Dollar and the Future of the International Monetary System.* New York: Oxford University Press, 2011.

Evans, Peter B. *Embedded Autonomy: States and Industrial Transformation.* Princeton, NJ: Princeton University Press, 1995.

Fernandez, Juan, and Liu Shengjun. *China CEO: A Case Guide for Business Leaders in China.* Singapore: John Wiley & Sons (Asia), 2007.

Ferri, Giovanni, and Li-Gang Liu. *Honor Thy Creditors Before Thy Shareholders: Are the Profits of Chinese State-Owned Enterprises Real?* Hong Kong Institute for Monetary Research, April 2009.

Fewsmith, Joseph. *China Since Tiananmen: The Politics of Transition.* Cambridge, UK: Cambridge University Press, 2001.

Gallagher, Kelly Sims. *China Shifts Gears: Automakers, Oil, Pollution, and Development.* Cambridge, MA: MIT Press, 2006.

Genther, Phyllis A. *A History of Japan's Government-Business Relationship: The Passenger Car Industry.* Michigan Papers in Japanese Studies, no. 20. Ann Arbor: Center for Japanese Studies, University of Michigan, 1990.

Gerschenkron, Alexander. *Economic Backwardness in Historical Perspective: A Book of Essays.* Cambridge, MA: Belknap Press of Harvard University Press, 1966.

Goldstein, Andrea. "The Political Economy of Industrial Policy in China: The Case of Aircraft Manufacturing." *Journal of Chinese Economic and Business Studies* 4 (November 2006): 259–273.

Gong, Ting. "Corruption and Local Governance: The Double Identity of Chinese Local Governments in Market Reform." *Pacific Review* 19, no. 1 (2006): 85.

Green, Andrew E. "South Korea's Automobile Industry: Development and Prospects." *Asian Survey* 32, no. 5 (May 1, 1992): 411–428.

Gries, Peter Hays. "Narratives to Live By: The Century of Humiliation and Chinese National Identity Today." In *China's Transformations: The Stories Beyond the Headlines*. Lanham, MD: Rowman & Littlefield, 2007.

Halper, Stefan A. *The Beijing Consensus: How China's Authoritarian Model Will Dominate the Twenty-First Century*. New York: Basic Books, 2010.

Hao, Jia, and Zhimin Lin, eds. *Changing Central-Local Relations in China: Reform and State Capacity*. Boulder, CO: Westview Press, 1994.

Hart, Oliver, Andrei Shleifer, and Robert W. Vishny. "The Proper Scope of Government: Theory and an Application to Prisons." *Quarterly Journal of Economics* 112, no. 4 (November 1997): 1127–1161.

Harwit, Eric. *China's Automobile Industry: Policies, Problems, and Prospects*. Studies on Contemporary China. Armonk, NY: M. E. Sharpe, 1995.

———. "The Impact of WTO Membership on the Automobile Industry in China." *China Quarterly* 167, no. 1 (2001): 655–670.

Hessler, Peter. *Country Driving: A Journey Through China from Farm to Factory*. New York: Harper, 2010.

Holstein, William. *Why GM Matters: Inside the Race to Transform an American Icon*. New York: Walker, 2009.

Holz, Carsten. *China's Industrial State-Owned Enterprises between Profitability and Bankruptcy*. Singapore: World Scientific, 2003.

Huang, Yasheng. "Between Two Coordination Failures: Automotive Industrial Policy in China with a Comparison to Korea." *Review of International Political Economy* 9, no. 3 (2002): 538–573.

———. *Capitalism with Chinese Characteristics: Entrepreneurship and the State*. Cambridge, UK: Cambridge University Press, 2008.

———. "Central-Local Relations in China during the Reform Era: The Economic and Institutional Dimensions." *World Development* 24, no. 4 (April 1996): 655–672.

———. "Debating China's Economic Growth: The Beijing Consensus or the Washington Consensus." *Academy of Management Perspectives* 24, no. 2 (May 2010): 31–47.

———. "Rethinking the Beijing Consensus." *Asia Policy* 11 (January 2011): 1–26.

Ingrassia, Paul. *Crash Course: The American Automobile Industry's Road from Glory to Disaster*. New York: Random House, 2010.

Jensen, Lionel M., and Timothy B. Weston. *China's Transformations: The Stories Beyond the Headlines*. Lanham, MD: Rowman & Littlefield, 2007.

Johnson, Chalmers. "The Developmental State: Odyssey of a Concept." In *The Developmental State*, edited by Meredith Woo-Cumings. Cornell Studies in Political Economy. Ithaca, NY: Cornell University Press, 1999.

———. *MITI and the Japanese Miracle: The Growth of Industrial Policy, 1925–1975.* Stanford, CA: Stanford University Press, 1982.

———. "Political Institutions and Economic Performance: The Government-Business Relationship in Japan, South Korea and Taiwan." In *The Political Economy of the New Asian Industrialism*, edited by Frederic C. Deyo. Ithaca, NY: Cornell University Press, 1987.

Johnson, Steven. *Where Good Ideas Come From: The Natural History of Innovation.* New York: Riverhead, 2010.

Katz, Harold. *The Decline in Competition in the Automobile Industry, 1920–1940.* Dissertations in American Economic History. New York: Arno Press, 1977.

Kennedy, Scott. *The Business of Lobbying in China.* Cambridge, MA: Harvard University Press, 2005.

Kim, Yun Tae. "Neoliberalism and the Decline of the Developmental State." *Journal of Contemporary Asia* 29, no. 4 (1999): 441–461.

Kingston, William. "An Agenda for Radical Intellectual Property Reform." In *International Public Goods and Transfer of Technology under a Globalized Intellectual Property Regime*, edited by Keith E. Maskus and Jerome H. Reichman. New York: Cambridge University Press, 2005.

Kornai, János. *The Socialist System: The Political Economy of Communism.* Princeton, NJ: Princeton University Press, 1992.

Kuhn, Thomas S. *The Structure of Scientific Revolutions.* Chicago: University of Chicago Press, 1970.

Lampton, David M. *Same Bed, Different Dreams: Managing U.S.-China Relations, 1989–2000.* Berkeley: University of California Press, 2001.

Li Jiayi 李佳怡. 王传福与比亚迪 = *Wang Chuanfu and BYD*. Hangzhou: Zhejiang People's Publishing House 浙江人民出版社, 2008.

Li, Hongbin, and Li-An Zhou. "Political Turnover and Economic Performance: The Incentive Role of Personnel Control in China." *Journal of Public Economics* 89, no. 9–10 (September 2005): 1743–1762.

Lieberthal, Kenneth. *Governing China: From Revolution Through Reform.* 2nd ed. New York: W. W. Norton, 2004.

Lieberthal, Kenneth, and Michel Oksenberg. *Policy Making in China: Leaders, Structures, and Processes.* Princeton, NJ: Princeton University Press, 1990.

MacGregor, Gervase, and Guy Newey. "Report on the Affairs of Phoenix Venture Holdings, Limited, MG Rover Group Limited and 33 Other

Companies." Department for Business Innovation and Skills, appointed by the Secretary of State for Trade and Industry, United Kingdom, 2009.

Mann, Jim. *Beijing Jeep: The Short, Unhappy Romance of American Business in China.* New York: Simon & Schuster, 1989.

Maxfield, Sylvia, and Ben Ross Schneider, eds. *Business and the State in Developing Countries.* Cornell Studies in Political Economy. Ithaca, NY: Cornell University Press, 1997.

Maynard, Micheline. *The End of Detroit: How the Big Three Lost Their Grip on the American Car Market.* New York: Currency/Doubleday, 2003.

McGregor, James. "China's Drive for 'Indigenenous Innovation': A Web of Industrial Policies." Global Intellectual Property Center, U.S. Chamber of Commerce, APCO Worldwide, July 28, 2010. www.uschamber.com/reports/chinas-drive-indigenous-innovation-web-industrial-policies.

McGregor, Richard. *The Party: The Secret World of China's Communist Rulers.* New York: Harper, 2010.

McNamara, Dennis L. "Industry and National Identity: Globalizing Korean Auto Manufacture." In *Korean Attitudes Toward the United States: Changing Dynamics,* edited by David I. Steinberg, 316–328. Armonk, NY: M. E. Sharpe, 2005.

Megginson, William L. *The Financial Economics of Privatization.* New York: Oxford University Press, 2005.

Naughton, Barry. *The Chinese Economy: Transitions and Growth.* Cambridge, MA: MIT Press, 2007.

———. *Growing out of the Plan: Chinese Economic Reform, 1978–1993.* New York: Cambridge University Press, 1995.

———. "SASAC Rising." *China Leadership Monitor,* no. 14 (Spring 2005). http://media.hoover.org/documents/clm14_bn.pdf.

———. "The State Asset Commission: A Powerful New Government Body." *China Leadership Monitor,* no. 8 (Fall 2003). http://media.hoover.org/documents/clm8_bn.pdf.

———. "The Third Front: Defence Industrialization in the Chinese Interior." *China Quarterly* 115 (1988): 351–386.

Ngo, Tak-Wing. "Rent-Seeking and Economic Governance in the Structural Nexus of Corruption in China." *Crime, Law and Social Change* 49, no. 1 (February 2008): 27–44.

Noble, Gregory W., John Ravenhill, and Richard F. Doner. "Executioner or Disciplinarian: WTO Accession and the Chinese Auto Industry." *Business and Politics* 7, no. 2 (2005).

O'Brien, Kevin J., and Lianjiang Li. "Selective Policy Implementation in Rural China." *Comparative Politics* 31, no. 2 (January 1, 1999): 167–186.

Okimoto, Daniel. *Between MITI and the Market: Japanese Industrial Policy for High Technology*. Stanford, CA: Stanford University Press, 1989.

Öniş, Ziya. "Review Article: The Logic of the Developmental State." *Comparative Politics* 24, no. 1 (October 1991): 109–126.

Organisation for Economic Co-operation and Development. *Corporate Governance, State-Owned Enterprises and Privatisation*. OECD proceedings. Paris: Organisation for Economic Co-operation and Development, 1998.

Polidano, Charles. "Review Article: Don't Discard State Autonomy: Revisiting the East Asian Experience of Development." *Political Studies* 49, no. 3 (2001): 513–527.

Posth, Martin. *1,000 Days in Shanghai: The Story of Volkswagen, the First Chinese-German Car Factory*. Singapore: John Wiley & Sons (Asia), 2008.

Qian, Yingyi. "How Reform Worked in China." In *In Search of Prosperity: Analytic Narratives on Economic Growth*, edited by Dani Rodrik. Princeton, NJ: Princeton University Press, 2003.

Rae, John Bell. *The American Automobile Industry*. Boston, MA: Twayne Publishers, 1984.

Ramo, Joshua Cooper. *The Beijing Consensus: Notes on the New Physics of Chinese Power*. London: Foreign Policy Centre, 2004.

Rattner, Steven. *Overhaul: An Insider's Account of the Obama Administration's Emergency Rescue of the Auto Industry*. Boston: Houghton Mifflin Harcourt, 2010.

Rees, Ray. "The Theory of Principal and Agent, Part I." *Bulletin of Economic Research* 37, no. 1 (January 1, 1985): 3–26.

Rodrik, Dani. *One Economics, Many Recipes: Globalization, Institutions, and Economic Growth*. Princeton, NJ: Princeton University Press, 2007.

Rodrik, Dani, Gene Grossman, and Victor Norman. "Getting Interventions Right: How South Korea and Taiwan Grew Rich." *Economic Policy* 10, no. 20 (April 1995): 55–107.

Shambaugh, David. *China's Communist Party: Atrophy and Adaptation*. Berkeley: University of California Press, 2008.

———. *The Modern Chinese State*. Cambridge, UK: Cambridge University Press, 2000.

Sheshinski, Eytan, and Luis F. Lopez-Calva. "Privatization and Its Benefits: Theory and Evidence." *CESifo Economic Studies* 49, no. 3 (January 1, 2003): 429–459.

Shimokawa, Koichi. *The Japanese Automobile Industry: A Business History*. London: Athlone Press, 1994.

Shirk, Susan L. *The Political Logic of Economic Reform in China*. Berkeley: University of California Press, 1993.

Shleifer, Andrei. "State versus Private Ownership." *Journal of Economic Perspectives* 12, no. 4 (Autumn 1998): 133–150.

Shleifer, Andrei, and Robert W. Vishny. "Politicians and Firms." *Quarterly Journal of Economics* 109, no. 4 (November 1994): 995–1025.

Sit, Victor F. S., and Weidong Liu. "Restructuring and Spatial Change of China's Auto Industry under Institutional Reform and Globalization." *Annals of the Association of American Geographers* 90, no. 4 (December 2000): 653.

Sobel, Robert. *Car Wars: The Untold Story.* New York: Dutton, 1984.

Solinger, Dorothy J. "Despite Decentralization: Disadvantages, Dependence and Ongoing Central Power in the Inland—The Case of Wuhan." *China Quarterly* 145, no. 1 (1996): 1–34.

Standing Committee to Review the Research Program of the Partnership for a New Generation of Vehicles, Board on Energy and Environmental Systems, Transportation Research Board, National Research Council. *Review of the Research Program of the Partnership for a New Generation of Vehicles: Seventh Report.* Washington, DC: National Academies Press, 2001.

Steinfeld, Edward S. *Forging Reform in China: The Fate of State-Owned Industry.* Cambridge, UK: Cambridge University Press, 1998.

Tang, Jie, and Anthony Ward. *The Changing Face of Chinese Management.* Psychology Press, 2003.

Tang Jie 唐杰, Yang Yanping 杨沿平, and Zhou Wenjie 周文杰. 中国汽车产业自主创新战略 = *China Auto Industry Indigenous Innovation Strategy.* Beijing: Science Press 科学出版社, 2009.

Tao, Qingjiu. "The Road to Success: A Resource-Based View of Joint Venture Evolution in China's Auto Industry." PhD dissertation, University of Pittsburgh, 2004.

Thomson, Elspeth, and Jon Sigurdson. *China's Science and Technology Sector and the Forces of Globalisation.* Singapore: World Scientific, 2008.

Thun, Eric. *Changing Lanes in China: Foreign Direct Investment, Local Government, and Auto Sector Development.* New York: Cambridge University Press, 2006.

Tsai, Kellee S. "Off Balance: The Unintended Consequences of Fiscal Federalism in China." *Journal of Chinese Political Science* 9, no. 2 (September 2004): 1–26.

———. *Capitalism without Democracy: The Private Sector in Contemporary China.* Ithaca, NY: Cornell University Press, 2007.

Vickers, John, and George Yarrow. "Economic Perspectives on Privatization." *Journal of Economic Perspectives* 5, no. 2 (Spring 1991): 111–132.

Wade, Robert. *Governing the Market: Economic Theory and the Role of Government in East Asian Industrialization.* Princeton, NJ: Princeton University Press, 1990.

Walter, Carl E., and Fraser J. T. Howie. *Red Capitalism: The Fragile Financial Foundation of China's Extraordinary Rise*. Singapore: John Wiley & Sons (Asia), 2011.

Wang Jing 王静. "我国汽车产业发展过程中政府行为的经济学分析：以上南合并为案例进行分析 = An Economic Analysis of Government Behavior in China's Auto Industry Development Process: The Shanghai-Nanjing Auto Merger." 沿海企业与科技 = *Coastal Enterprises and Science & Technology* 2008, no. 7 (July 2007): 98–102.

Wang Shaoguang. "Central-Local Fiscal Politics in China." In *Changing Central-Local Relations in China: Reform and State Capacity*. Boulder, CO: Westview Press, 1994.

Wang Ziliang 王自亮, ed. 力量—吉利与中国汽车工业 = *Strength: Geely and China's Auto Industry*. Beijing: People's Daily Publishers 人民日报出版社, 2007.

Wang, Hua, and Chris Kimble. "Betting on Chinese Electric Cars? Analyzing BYD's Capacity for Innovation." *International Journal of Automotive Technology and Management* 10, no. 1 (2010): 77–92.

Wank, David L. *Commodifying Communism: Business, Trust, and Politics in a Chinese City. Structural Analysis in the Social Sciences*. Cambridge, UK: Cambridge University Press, 1999.

Williamson, John. "Beijing Consensus versus Washington Consensus?" Interview, November 2, 2010. www.piie.com/publications/interviews/pp20101102williamson.pdf.

———. "Democracy and the 'Washington Consensus.'" *World Development* 21, no. 8 (1993): 1329–1336.

Wilner, Johan. "Privatization: A Sceptical Analysis." In *International Handbook on Privatization*, edited by David Parker and David S. Saal, 60–86. Cheltenham, UK: Edward Elgar, 2003.

Woo-Cumings, Meredith. *The Developmental State*. Cornell Studies in Political Economy. Ithaca, NY: Cornell University Press, 1999.

———. *Race to the Swift: State and Finance in Korean Industrialization*. New York: Columbia University Press, 1991.

Wu Facheng 吴法成. 汽车强国之梦 = *Dream of an Automobile Superpower*. Beijing: Xinhua Publishing House 新华出版社, 2009.

Wu, Jinglian. *Understanding and Interpreting Chinese Economic Reform*. Mason, OH: Thomson/South-Western, 2005.

Yang Biaowu 杨彪武. 奇瑞奇迹 = *Chery Miracle*. Beijing: China Yanshi Press 中国言实出版社, 2008.

Yang, Dali L. *Remaking the Chinese Leviathan: Market Transition and the Politics of Governance in China*. Stanford, CA: Stanford University Press, 2004.

Yeo, Yukyung. "Regulating China's Industrial Economy: A Comparative Case Study of Auto and Telecom Service Sectors." PhD dissertation, University of Maryland, 2007.

Young, Alwyn. "The Razor's Edge: Distortions and Incremental Reform in the People's Republic of China." *Quarterly Journal of Economics* 115, no. 4 (November 1, 2000): 1091–1135.

Zhang Dicheng 章迪诚, ed. 中国国有企业改革编年史, *1978–2005 = Chronicle of China's State-Owned Enterprise Reform.* Beijing: Beijing Workers Press 中国工人出版社, 2006.

Zheng Xianghu 郑祥琥. 比亚迪之父王传福 = *Wang Chuanfu, Father of BYD.* Beijing: Central Compilation and Translation Press 中央编译出版社, 2009.

Zhongguo qiche jishu yanjiu zhongxin. 中国汽车工业年鉴 = *China Automotive Industry Yearbook.* Beijing: Zhongguo qiche gongye xiehui, multiple years.

Zun Liang 樽粮. 奇瑞创造 = *Chery Innovation.* Beijing: China CITIC Press 中信出版社, 2007.

Periodicals

Automotive News
BloombergBusinessweek
Business Times of Singapore
China Daily
Daily Yomiuri
The Economist
Financial Times
Fortune
Global Times
National Post (Canada)
New York Times
Nikkei Weekly
People's Daily (人民日报)
Shanghai Daily (上海日报)
South China Morning Post
Sydney Morning Herald
Wall Street Journal

Websites

Asia Times, atimes.com
Associated Press, ap.com
Autocar, autocar.co.uk
Automotive News China, autonewschina.com
Bloomberg, bloomberg.com
British Broadcasting Corporation, bbc.co.uk
Caixin Online, english.caing.com
Central People's Government of the PRC, gov.cn
China Car Times, chinacartimes.com
China Economic Network (中国经济网), auto.ce.cn
China Internet Information Center, china.org.cn
China Law Blog, chinalawblog.com
China Reform Forum (中国改革论坛网), chinareform.org.cn
ChinaAutoWeb, chinaautoweb.com
Chinability, chinability.com
ChinaBizGov, chinabizgov.blogspot.com
CNBC, cnbc.com
CNN, cnn.com
Computer World, computerworld.com
Daily Mail Online, dailymail.co.uk
The Diplomat, the-diplomat.com
Economic Observer, eeo.com.cn
Finance World (金融界), finance.jrj.com.cn
First Finance (一财网), yicai.com
Forbes, forbes.com
Groningen Growth and Development Centre, ggdc.net
Guardian, guardian.co.uk
International Organization of Motor Vehicle Manufacturers, oica.net
ISI Emerging Markets, securities.com
Jamestown Foundation, jamestown.org
Japan Policy Research Institute, jpri.org
J. D. Power and Associates, jdpower.com
Los Angeles Times, latimes.com
MarketWatch, marketwatch.com
Ministry of Finance, PRC, mof.gov.cn

Ministry of Industry and Information Technology (工业和信息化部), miit.gov.cn

MSNBC, msnbc.com

Nanfang Daily Finance (南方财经), finance.nfdaily.cn

National Development and Reform Commission (国家发展和改革委员会), www.ndrc.gov.cn

The New Yorker, newyorker.com

Pacific Auto Network (太平洋汽车网), pcauto.com.cn

Phoenix Finance (凤凰财经), finance.ifeng.com

Plugincars, plugincars.com

Reuters, reuters.com

Shanghai Daily, shanghaidaily.com

Sina Auto, auto.sina.com

Sina Finance, finance.sina.com.cn

Sohu Auto, auto.sohu.com

State-Owned Assets Supervision and Administration Commission (国有资产监督管理委员会), www.sasac.gov.cn

21st Century Business Herald (21世纪网), 21cbh.com

Unirule, unirule.org

USA Today, usatoday.com

Wall Street Journal, wsj.com

Wangyi Caijing (网易财经), money.163.com

Wangyi Qiche (网易汽车), auto.163.com

Wharton Research Data Services, wrds-web.wharton.upenn.edu

Xinhua (新华), news.xinhuanet.com

About the Author

G. E. Anderson is a specialist in finance and Chinese political economy who has been either living in or frequently traveling to China for nearly two decades. He has previously worked as a teacher, commercial lending analyst, and CFO of a nonprofit organization. Most recently he was Finance Director for Charles Schwab's Tokyo-based joint venture. He holds a BS in Finance from Louisiana Tech, an MBA from Golden Gate University, an MA in Asia-Pacific Studies from the University of San Francisco, and a PhD from the University of California, Los Angeles (UCLA). Anderson's writing has appeared in the *Wall Street Journal*, and he has also been a contributing writer for *Forbes*. He blogs at ChinaBizGov: http://chinabizgov.blogspot.com, and works as a political risk and strategy consultant with his firm, Pacific Rim Advisors. He and his wife currently live in Los Angeles. Follow him on Twitter: @GE_Anderson.

Index

Note: Page numbers followed by n indicate notes.